RED LETTER DAYS

John Searl

Red
Letter
Days

COMPILED AND EDITED BY

Pete Rogers

ILLUSTRATED BY

John Searl

The Crowood Press

First published in 1994 by
The Crowood Press Ltd
Ramsbury, Marlborough
Wiltshire SN8 2HR

© The Crowood Press Ltd 1994

British Library Cataloguing in Publication Data

A catalogue record for this book is available from the British
Library.

ISBN 1 85223 783 X

Picture Credits
Line-drawings by John Searl

Dedication
FOR BERNARD VENABLES

Typeset by Acorn Bookwork, Salisbury, Wiltshire
Printed and bound in Great Britain by BPC Hazell Books Ltd.
A member of The British Printing Company Ltd.

Contents

Foreword

~

F ew men in the long history of angling have achieved the distinction of
becoming a legend in their own lifetime. It is not a distinction that can be
self-manufactured or planned; it arises naturally in the minds of others who
have been touched by the influence of a life's work, and is bestowed without question or second thought. Bernard Venables has long been one of this company, and
now, in his eighty-sixth year, he wears the mantle of living legend with the quiet
modesty and dignity of a truly gentle man. He is deserving of our praise.

How then to honour this special man? He has received tributes aplenty over the
years, both from home and abroad, yet sadly, as is the nature of things, with the
passing of time even the most prestigious of accolades pales and eventually fades.
What better way then, it seemed to me, than to create something tangible – a
book, that medium so beloved of Bernard – to celebrate his unique contribution to
the world of angling, and in a format complementing his own remarkable skills
with pen and palette. In this context, this work is intended to be much more than
just another addition to the ever-lengthening shelf of angling literature. Its
purpose, above all else, is to be a mark of respect and admiration from a few
devotees on behalf of the countless anglers whose enjoyment and understanding of
the sport has been enlarged under the considerable influence of this one man, an
influence that commands our respect now if we care anything for our future . . .

BV's latest book, *The Illustrated Memoirs of a Fisherman* (Merlin Unwin, 1993),
is a magnificent read from cover to cover, beautifully written and superbly illustrated. But I would recommend it as compulsory reading for all modern-day
anglers solely for its opening chapter, 'A Prospect of Angling'. This piece contains
the wisest counsel I have read in a long time, and the threads of its weave suggests
a retrenchment of values and standards we will ignore at our peril.

Some years ago I recall John Bailey writing a touching tribute to Bernard, part
which described him as angling's greatest story-teller. How right he was. And in
considering that simple observation, so the die for this book was cast. It would
have to be, could only be, a volume concerned with stories in the best BV fashion
of descriptive writing. Also, what could be more appropriate for the creator of Mr
Crabtree, the archetypal angling hero, than to reflect his own classic work by
keeping the subject matter on a freshwater theme? From mighty salmon to humble
dace, each would have its tale. The best-known names of the modern angling

scene were soon recruited to help and, allied with the outstanding talent of leading wildlife artist John Searl, the project took shape. As for the title, that chose itself: *Red Letter Days* encapsulates it all.

Much midnight oil has been burnt in bringing this book to print; indeed if ever the expression 'a labour of love' could be applied to a book on angling, then truly this is it. To all who have assisted in its completion, I now offer my sincere gratitude. In particular, thanks go to the principal contributors for their generosity and support, not forgetting Kevin Maddocks of Beekay Publishing for permission to reproduce work from the pen of Rod Hutchinson. Above all, however, I must acknowledge here the invaluable guidance and practical help from my good friend Peter Wheat, and the tireless efforts of John Searl in completing his painstaking artwork to stringent deadlines.

In concluding this foreword to a book primarily devoted to the capture of big fish, it is fitting to consider again the wise words of BV himself, taken from one of his columns in *Angling Times* during the 1950s:

> Fishing, I have often declared to anyone who would listen to me, is worth exactly the pleasure that is had from it. The fishing may be for very big fish, or it may be for quite trifling little things. Either way, as long as the angler enjoys it, the virtue is the same. The main thing is to be fishing.
>
> Of course, we all want to catch a bigger fish than any we have caught before, and when we do the joy is exquisite; but he who invariably catches his half-pound roach through the long contented day, rather than any mightier game, is no less happy for it. You may be a specimen hunter or a browser among the minor fish, just as your taste goes, but anyway you are an angler, and that makes the world a good one.

Peter Rogers
August 1993

Introduction
~
Frank Guttfield

B V. There can be few anglers past or present whose initials have become such a byword for their recognition and contribution to the sport of angling. Indeed, Bernard Venables has achieved so much in the development of angling in the 20th century that it is difficult even to know where to begin. But at the risk of being sentimental, and looking back subjectively, may I pose the question: where would angling be today if BV had not emerged on its scene in the late 1940s? There is no doubt whatsoever in my mind that the sport would be at least ten or twenty years behind, such was the impact of the man in those formative days. To me and other 'wrinklies' of my generation BV was simply a mentor and quiet catalyst, our guiding light in all things fishing.

There is not room here to chronicle accurately the milestone events of those early years in angling formalism, only enough for just a few sketchy notes of how I recall them from my hazy memory.

From about the age of ten (*circa* 1949) I avidly followed the adventures of 'Mr Crabtree Goes Fishing' with the short-trousered Peter in the strip-cartoon pages of the *Daily Mirror*. This column fired the enthusiasm of thousands of youngsters like me, and I suppose it was the equivalent of John Wilson's 'Go Fishing' on television today. It was, in fact, a tiny advertisement next to Mr Crabtree that prompted me to nag my mother to send off for my first fishing 'outfit' – at the grand, all-inclusive price of 4s 6d!

During those early days at the *Mirror*, BV was also the brains (or one of them) behind a unique specimen fish competition that has never been equalled. This mammoth competition was for both individuals and teams, the country being broken down into a matrix of 'weighted' regions in line with the anticipated size of each species. As a direct consequence of this competition, Richard Walker and his team from Hitchin Angling Club emerged as clear winners in the second year of the contest, this also being the year that made angling history for Dick with the capture of his record 44lb common carp. The amazing events of those years during the mid-1950s resulted in the emergence of 'specimen hunters' and 'specimen groups' which developed into the big fish scene as we know it today.

During those exciting days of the *Mirror* Competition, Bernard and his associates had the vision to identify the commercial viability of the first weekly angling newspaper, *Angling Times* being launched during 1953 with spectacular success.

Bernard was its first editorial director, a prolific weekly columnist and, of course, the originator of the long-running '*Mr Cherry and Jim*' strip which I followed avidly in my early teens. Sadly, Bernard acquired a reputation amongst the unapprecia-tive for being a shade too purple in his writings; they said he was too 'arty-crafty'. Fortunately, however, most of his thinking readers did not share this view, and I for one was greatly motivated and encouraged by his writings. His graphic accounts were atmospheric and took the reader with him to the waterside; they gave me an awareness of life in all its riverbank aspects and the realization of that catching a big fish on every outing was not the overriding issue.

It was Bernard and Dick Walker who give me the encouragement to write my first article for *Angling Times*. This was when I was sixteen and still at school, and they made me produce a 500-word account of how I lured a 6lb 14oz brown trout from the Upper Ivel. I didn't really appreciate just how big a fish it was at that time (it was in fact, the largest on a dry fly for twelve years!), and it was Bernard and Dick who were really responsible for my early entry into angling journalism. I must also thank Bernard for including my trout story in the 'Memorable Catches' chapter of his *Angler's Companion* (Allen & Unwin, 1959). (By the time Bernard had given my 500-word account his 'treatment', the story had been transformed into a delightful 2,000-word essay.)

I have only had the pleasure of meeting Bernard briefly on three occasions. The first time was at a *Daily Mirror* prize-giving ceremony at the Savoy Hotel in the early 1950s when I was only just out of short trousers. The next occasion was a year or two later at the NFA Championships presentation on the Severn at Brignorth (I think), and the most recent was some thirty-seven years later at his modest Wiltshire home when I was accompanied by Peter Rogers and my eleven-year-old son, Frederick. Although Bernard had changed just a little in appearance (he was 86!), he still had that quiet, unassuming, gentle manner, that well-groomed, fine beard (not quite as white as my hair), those rosy cheeks, and eyes full of life and sparkle. He looked a bit puzzled when I came in with young Fred – for a moment I think he thought Fred was me as he talked about the young lad who caught the big trout on a white moth! Yes, it was a bit like walking back through time. The lasting memory of those three meetings with Bernard, however, is singularly of a gentleman, slight in build, but truly one of the gentle giants of angling.

In recognition for his contribution to angling in the 20th century, Peter Rogers has done a grand job in selecting some fifty of today's most highly regarded anglers to write about their most memorable catches. Each essay makes exciting reading and the whole is a lasting tribute to BV. The foregoing should have been an introduction to the book; instead it has been an appreciation, and for this I make no apologies.

A Dream Come True
~
Len Arbery

The preparations for the 1989–90 winter's fishing began long before the winter of course. Many trips were made to assess likely venues, and even to weigh up particular swims. There are many good reasons for reconnaissance visits – even accounting for the price of petrol, it is effort and money well spent, for if left until the fishing trip proper such an exercise will be at the expense of time spent fishing, and that is reason enough.

As so often happens, the Christmas holidays coincided with the first of the season's earnest fishing trips to the rivers. There had been some heavy rain just prior to Christmas, but by the time my friends and I arrived on the banks of the Dorset Stour, the water-level had receded and this deluge was but a memory. We found the river still much higher than the summer water-level though, and flowing clear and bright with a temperature of 44°F. All this meant just one thing to our little group – chub!

There were too many of us to fish together, so some went to Throop while Bob

Harrington, Bob Buteux and I fished further upstream. Being a pleasant winter's day and, as said, the Christmas holiday, there were plenty of people on the banks. The one thing we learned from these anglers was that although the conditions looked ideal, the fishing was proving far from easy. When at last we found some unoccupied, decent-looking water, it didn't take long for us to discover that they were right. Nevertheless, we kept at it and ended the day with five chub between us, each one a four-pounder. This is sometimes a feature of winter river fishing – on certain days the few fish that are prepared to feed are all very much the same size. On that particular day, link-ledgered breadflake proved the successful method. On returning to our holiday cottage in the evening, we found that the remainder of the party had a similar tale to tell – few fish caught but a high average size.

For the remaining few days of our holiday I fished on my own, and blanked! However, this in no way deterred me from fulfilling my aim for that winter: a personal-best barbel. The others ribbed me unmercifully each evening, especially as they had caught some very respectable specimens; in fact, Bob Buteux had improved his personal-best river-caught roach to 2lb 9oz. The mickey-taking didn't bother me though as it was all good-natured stuff. Besides, my 'homework' had been done well and I was happy to fish the rest of the winter without a bite, for I was supremely confident I was doing the *right* thing, in the *right* place, at the *right* time.

The following weekend I was back, this time accompanied by my son, Tony. Again the Stour looked perfect for chub, with the added bonus that the temperature had climbed to 46°F.

The main part of each day was spent pursuing chub, with the late afternoon and evening being put aside for further attempts to land a very big barbel. The chub fishing proved very successful, the two days producing ten fish all over 3lb, and a best weight of 5lb 1oz – my first five of the winter. Unfortunately, the barbel once again proved elusive, and although I did have my first barbel bite of the season, I missed it – what a plonker! Tony's results for the weekend were roughly similar, apart from one important difference: he 'nailed' his only barbel bite, and it weighed 9lb 14oz. All the chub were caught on flake, with both barbel bites coming to meat. As normal we touch-ledgered, feeling the line for bites.

I travelled down on my own the next weekend. Apart from the water-level being lower, conditions were similar to those of the previous weekend. I spent the whole time barbel fishing, but no barbel bites were forthcoming. Two (not altogether unwelcome) chub did pick up the meat though, these weighing in at 3lb 1oz and 4lb 4oz.

The following Thursday I went with Tony to witness Roger Newman's monster 7lb 8oz chub from the Hampshire Avon. After leaving Roger and phoning the story to Adrian Curtis at *Angling Times*, we went on to Throop. The water was clear, 44°F, and the chub were going absolutely crazy. We soon lost count of the number we caught and, even though none was particularly big, we weren't complaining.

The next day we anticipated great things, but some subtle change had taken place and we really struggled to get a bite. By late afternoon, we decided a change of venue was required – a very good move, as it turned out.

As dusk approached I found some barbel that were prepared to give small bites. After missing a few, Tony came along and I invited him to sit down and try his luck alongside me. On his first cast Tony experienced the ultimate thrill in river fishing – a good, old-fashioned barbel pull; you know, one of those bites that is almost savage enough to pull your arm from its socket!

Tony whispered through clenched teeth, 'I think it's a little one, Dad.' From the steady bend in the rod I thought it was anything *but* little, but I kept my peace, not wanting to make him unnecessarily nervous. There was nothing spectacular about the fight at all, and yet, on lifting the net, I knew without any shadow of doubt that here was a new personal best for my son. At 11lb 14oz, it was also a family best. Perhaps you can imagine how much more ribbing I had to endure during the long journey home!

Then came the big storms. They didn't prevent me from travelling to Dorset, but they did sometimes prevent me from fishing. On one trip, I tried to get on to the banks of the Avon even though the river was over the fields. A cunning plan was worked out: after gaining access to a field that gradually sloped down to the river, I would wade to the edge and stand up to fish.

Initially, all went to plan. There was I, rod made up in one hand, landing net in the other, making steady but deliberate progress. The water was lapping near the top of my waders but there wasn't much further to go, for I could see plainly the rise in the ground adjacent to the actual river bank from where it would be child's play to fish. What I couldn't see, however, and, I suppose, had forgotten in the excitement of the moment, was the ditch. This is an insignificant feature in normal conditions, but then it was a catastrophic trap for the unwary – meaning me! One second I had everything under control, and the next I was under filthy, freezing water!

My waders immediately filled up and my woolly hat, by then waterlogged and several times heavier than normal, slipped over my eyes. A more efficient blindfold would be difficult to envisage. I couldn't remove the offending garment because the hood of my waterproof suit was keeping it firmly in place, and my hands were full anyway! To this day I don't know how I emerged from that predicament unscathed, and you should have seen the looks on the faces of passers-by as I squelched back to the car!

At every opportunity during this period I made the ritual journey to Dorset. On at least one occasion I didn't even stop, but just turned the car around and went back home. Yes, those storms cost me dearly, especially in lost fishing time.

The next time any serious fishing could be practised was in the third week of February, when Tony and Keith Griffin were my companions. The water at Throop was almost bank-high, clear and 40°F. We could hardly get started quickly enough. Keith began long-trotting a favourite chub swim and was soon amassing an enviable bag of fish. Tony and I wandered off downstream, fishing every likely spot that took our fancy. We reached an area of good-looking water that is difficult to fish effectively because a copse of small trees and bushes grows at the water's edge. Tony took the upper part and I fished from below the copse.

My first cast, using flake for bait, brought a big pull which resulted in an 8lb 8oz barbel. No sooner had this fish been returned when Tony struck into another. Instantly, his almost-new carbon rod disintegrated with a resounding crack! But miraculously the line didn't break and the fish was still attached. It was obvious to me that Tony needed help, so I started to get up from my stool to go to his assistance . . . only to find myself in the river! Whether I momentarily blacked out or just slipped will never be known. What was known was that all my gear fell into the river with me. Though the water was too deep to allow me to touch the bottom, it was a simple job to grasp a tuft of grass on the bank and call to Tony for help. Fortunately, Keith came along just then and between the two of them they soon had me back on terra firma. Because we were fishing together the danger had been minimal, and I just thank my lucky stars it didn't happen when I was alone.

Once again, I squelched back to the car to get changed. As Bob Buteux tirelessly (and tiresomely!) keeps reminding me, I must be much more deliberate and careful now I'm not so steady on my pins. He can talk!

Considerably warmer and certainly drier, I recommended fishing a swim that produces more than its fair share of cagey bites. The fish were at home, and, after scaling down to 2lb line and a size 12 carbon specimen hook, a minute piece of crust produced a bite that pulled the quivertip round several inches. The hooked fish put up minimal resistance and proved to be a pristine roach of 2lb 1oz. The next bite was even bigger and the hooked fish set off for Christchurch Harbour as if its tail was alight! Eventually, a 4lb 6oz chub went into the waiting net, but this performance effectively killed the swim. This alone gave me reason enough to change venues once again in my quest for a giant barbel, though Tony and Keith elected to say put. Perhaps the wiser choice was theirs, for while I went biteless, Tony went on to take a very creditable catch which included a 9lb 4oz barbel *and* a 5lb 8oz chub.

The three of us were all out chubbing very early the next day. This was one of those rare days in winter when the morning was sunny and bright without a hint of overnight frost. Coupled with the rising water temperature, we thought we would 'slay 'em', but it wasn't as easy as all that. By lunchtime we hadn't caught a decent fish between us, but in the afternoon between 1 p.m. and 3 p.m. the chub fed well. Keith and I both included four-pounders in our bag, but it was Tony who topped yet again, with a cracker of 5lb 9oz.

It was even harder the next day. By late afternoon, without a fish between us, Tony and I were ready to leave for home. Keith, however, asked to stay a little longer as, by this time, he was getting a few small bites. Whilst waiting for Keith, Tony and I sat side by side fishing a swim which, though it looked promising for chub, had never before produced so much as a solitary bite. This time, though, my breadflake was taken with a proverbial bang as soon as it hit the bottom, but the answering strike unaccountably failed to connect. I made no mistake on the next cast, yet the feeble resistance gave no indication that anything special had been hooked. My first inkling of a big chub came as Tony lifted the landing net around it and exclaimed, 'Blimey, Dad, how much would you like this one to weigh?' After very careful weighing came the answer . . . exactly 6lb! It was my second heaviest chub at that time.

The final day of the trip again proved difficult, with just a handful of small chub caught, though I did catch a nice roach weighing 1lb 15oz. It was also a similar story the following weekend, with just two chub worth weighing – 3lb 14oz and 4lb 8oz. Tony and Keith, however, showed how it should be done, each of them catching a double-figure barbel. Keith's weighed 10lb 1oz, while Tony's was just one ounce more.

In the early hours of Wednesday 7 March, whilst at work, I began to feel uneasy. It took some time for the penny to drop: my instincts were telling me that I ought to be fishing. Hastily, I arranged a couple of days' holiday before hurrying home for a little sleep. By 10 a.m. my estate car was once again heading south-west, bound for Dorset.

After breakfasting, I arrived on the banks at 1 p.m. to find the venue deserted. Taking advantage of this situation, I prebaited several swims before commencing fishing at the upstream boundary. No bites materialized until I reached a bend in the river, where I missed a positive barbel bite simply because, I suspect, I did not strike quickly enough. My reactions are definitely not what they used to be! Not long after this, two friends arrived, first Richard Graham then Ron Chant. After chatting for a while, during which the missed bite was mentioned, Richard left and Ron started to fish about 400yd downstream of my position. I rebaited my swim with two droppers of hemp and one of diced meat, and then I shared a flask of tea with Ron, thus giving my swim a chance to settle down. I suppose it was the best part of thirty minutes before I returned.

At this point I can do no better than quote from my diary: 'On the first cast, after fifteen minutes, came a savage barbel pull. Hit it okay and immediately knew it was something special, so yelled for Ron.'

Silently, Ron materialized at my side, crouched down and rolled a cigarette. Then he picked up the landing net in readiness, but didn't put it in the water. The last thing he wanted to do was snag my line on the net. The hooked barbel fought with incredible power, but gave none of the savage jerks on the tackle so familiar when playing lesser barbel. In fact, as Ron remarked later: 'The only jerk on the tackle during the whole fight was the one holding the rod!'

Ron flicked away his cigarette end, and still the barbel persisted, but my tackle was sound and the fish was clearly tiring, even though there was still a long way to go. Close to the opposite bank, still deep in the water, the barbel begrudgingly came upstream. Once the fish was well past me I increased the pressure. Now it had to fight the power of the river's current in addition to that of the tackle, and this combination finally broke its resolve. The landing net was dipped and in went the barbel first time, some twenty-five minutes after I had called to Ron. I put my rod down and went to his assistance as he struggled to lift the fish.

And what a fish it was! Both of us had seen and caught many barbel, including double-figure fish, but we had never seen anything as remotely big as this one. I suggested that it was a record, but being more cautious by nature, Ron estimated that it was 13–13½lb. Reading the balance, we confirmed that it was a shade over 14lb! It was just 6oz short of Aylmer Tyron's record and, at that time, the heaviest ever barbel caught in winter, not to mention that it was the joint fourth biggest ever caught in modern times.

I was so excited and thrilled by this event that I abandoned fishing to phone the news through to Tony and my friends Bill Quinlan, Bob Buteux and Kevin Clifford. Their reactions alone could fill a chapter, but I'll keep those precious memories to myself.

Like Clockwork
~
Bruce Ashby

I t was a beautiful warm evening when I pulled into the car-park at my club water on 15 June 1991. I was not the first; in fact, there was already a considerable gathering of the usual carp anglers. It seemed that we had all had the same idea: to arrive early and have a good look around the water before the draw for swims took place at 7.30 p.m. that evening. After exchanging a few words with some of the lads, I made my way down to the lake.

On arriving at the shallow end, I stood for a few minutes before making my way slowly along the bank, passing the many small islands that run down the lake's centre. Fish showed everywhere, but the shallows in particular were seething with carp and the size of some of them certainly got my heart pumping! Continuing along the full length of the bank, I could see carp here and there but not in the numbers that I had observed in the shallows.

Returning to the car-park, I met my good friend Bob Copeland, with whom I was to fish for the next two days. On mentioning what I had seen, he was off like a shot for a look. When Bob returned, I told him that even if my number came up early enough to get a swim in the shallows, I had no intention of taking it as I was of the opinion that once a few 3oz leads made an entry, the carp would soon make a speedy exit! Also, as the next section was the islands, many anglers would fish with tight lines because of the snags, so I didn't think the carp would stay there either. In fact, I felt sure they would move through this area into the open part of the lake, and it was there, with any luck in the draw, that I would lay my trap!

Fortunately, my luck was in because I was about fifth out of the hat and the swim I had set my heart on was still vacant. Bob, who had agreed with my theory, was one of the last out of the hat, but again luck was with us as the swim immediately to my right had not been claimed – he booked it faster than a rat up a drainpipe! We just couldn't get on to the water quickly enough.

By 4 a.m. the next morning we were both installed in our swims. We had discussed our tactics the night before and had decided to bait heavily from the off and fish with back-leads: The idea was that when the carp arrived after their flight from the shallows through the islands and into the clear water, they would find lots of goodies but no lines! At least, that's what we hoped would happen. As the area was weedy, we used markers to pinpoint our spots and baits, and free offerings were soon in position. It would now be up to the carp.

I was in the middle of having a brew up at about 5 a.m. when one of the lads fishing the shallows walked into my camp. He told me that all the fish had left the shallows and that he was looking for another pitch. Things were looking good.

At 6 a.m. another angler fishing in the islands came along to tell me that he was having problems with line bites from fish moving through his swim. When I asked him in which direction they were going, he said: 'Towards you.' And hopefully our bait, I thought!

At 6.45 a.m. Tony Hall, fishing on the opposite bank on the end of the islands, had a take. I was certain that it would be only a matter of time before the fish reached us.

Right out of the blue at 7.15 a.m. I had a take on my right-hand rod. I lifted into a heavy fish, only to experience that feeling of total dejection a few seconds later when the hook pulled free. On inspecting my rig, I found that it had been badly tied and I cursed my stupidity.

The remainder of the morning was uneventful, and by midday the lack of sleep the previous night, coupled with the warm sun, took its toll and I dozed off. It must have been around 2 p.m. when my Optonic burst into life again. I was awake, off the bed-chair and to the rod in an instant. Again it was the right-hand rod, but this time I made no mistake as a heavy fish moved away. I can't say that the fight was spectacular, with the fish moving very slowly and taking some time to come out of the weed, but ten minutes later I could see a very large carp turning deep down in the clear margin, coming ever closer to the safety of the waiting net. Once it was in, one look was enough. I wound in my other rod immediately and went off to find Bob.

'I've got one,' I said.

'Is it a big 'un?' asked Bob.

'Looks like a hippo in the net.'

'What, a thirty?' asked Bob.

'No, I think it's a forty.'

Bob needed no second telling. Winding in both of his rods, he grabbed his camera and we went back to my swim. As we arrived Alan Smith turned up.

'He's got one,' said Bob.

'That's a forty,' said Alan, the instant he saw the fish.

And indeed it was, for when we weighed it a few moments later the scales registered 40lb 10oz of beautiful mirror carp. A dream had come true! At that moment all of the thousands of days and tens of thousands of hours I had spent carp fishing over the previous thirty-four years swept back over me. I had achieved what had been my ambition for so long: I had caught a forty-pounder.

Many photographs were taken by Bob and Alan (for which I will be forever grateful) before the fish was carefully returned to its domain. I asked Bob if I could use his mobile phone to ring my wife, and as luck would have it she was at home. On hearing the news she sounded almost as pleased as I was.

'I suppose you will give it up now?' she asked.

Some hope, I thought.

After many congratulations Alan wandered off and Bob went back to his swim. I recast, but in truth my fishing was over for the day. I just could not concentrate and was still trying to take in what had happened. But the day was not yet over, for an hour or so later it was Bob's turn, with a magnificent mirror of 35lb 6oz.

In the Lap of the Gods
~
John Bailey

If there are two reasons why Crabtree worked so well for anglers of our generation, one of them must be that it was never condescending. Mr Crabtree may well have treated Peter rather severely at times, but the important consideration is that we, the readers, were never talked down to. Treat children as fools, I used to find as a teacher, and you have lost them for good. After all, us forty-year-olds were not fools as children – at least no more foolish than we can be now, given a little encouragement.

The second reason for Crabtree's enduring success must be that it contained so much of importance and so many things that we later proved for ourselves to be true. If you look carefully at the book's pages you will see that the fish reflect their watery environment – a generalized truth but a very real one. What I mean is that each species becomes a personification (fishification, I suppose!) of its setting: the tench, then, bubbles in a sleepy estate lake; the barbel snouts the gravels beneath the lush willows; and the pike patrols the grimly brooding broad. Waterscape and fish easily merge into one another – just as they should in reality.

Had Bernard Venables included a chapter on ferox in his masterpiece, then I know his drawing would have set this mightiest of fish against snow-tipped peaks and forests bending to the gales that whip the leaden lochs into fury. He would also have included bellowing stags on the moors and a bar scene where Crabtree and Peter (sipping a ginger beer, naturally) would be cosy by the fire as the snow, the sleet or the driving rain thrashed against the trembling window-pane.

These are the things that mean ferox to me, just as a woodpigeon's 'coo' is the sound of the tench or the raising of a lily-pad is the sign of the carp. The ferox is the fish of the ice ages, of the vast lochs, of storms, and of untamed forests, moors and mountains. Home to the ferox man is the Highland inn or the lost bothy, while malts, fires and friends huddled against the blasts in their common quest represent the kindest side of ferox fishing.

So, for you poor (and sane) souls who do not know ferox, he is a trout. Not just any trout, but a brown trout, and a brown that has *never* seen a stewpond. This is a brown trout whose ancestors go back thousands of generations to a time when they did something rather different to the typical browns around them: they began to breed apart and develop certain dramatic characteristics. They began to live longer, began to eat fish and began to spurt forward in growth at around five years of age when the normal brown begins to think about dying. Ferox, as a result of all this, grow huge: 7lb is a good ferox, 10lb is exciting, 15lb is quite possible, 20lb is certainly not unheard of, and 30lb is definitely not a dream.

The one-time ferox record was 39lb. Its preserved body was consumed in a disastrous fire and it has been taken from the lists, but why? The Victorians were quite as capable fish biologists as we are today and the fish was thoroughly examined. A well-mended salmon kelt (as had been suggested)? No, the monster was a trout. It was too big, the 'experts' say. That, too, is rubbish. What about the definite, positively authenticated ferox that have been netted in the past couple of years? Their weight? A staggering 37¼lb and 31lb! The ferox is the most beautiful, the most rare and the most complex killer of all our fish. It might just also be the biggest.

Char, you must understand, are the key to ferox. These deep-water fish congregate in huge shoals in ferox lochs; a shoal can number tens, if not hundreds of thousands. The constant wastage of sick and dead members ensures that the ferox always have food – even should a surge into a solid wall of prey fish prove unsuccessful for them.

Now, before you go dashing off, suitably inspired to catch ferox, you must know that you will face many difficulties. Once I wrote:

> To catch a ferox many cogs have to mesh. Firstly, the weather must be right, and this of course is in the lap of the gods. Secondly, you need to find the food shoals, the char. The recorder does that for you. Next you have to choose the right baits. Fourthly, you must troll them at the right speeds. Fifthly, you must troll them at the right depths. Sixthly, you must go over or close to a ferox. Seventh, you must hope

he is hungry – he probably only feeds once or twice a week so you must be lucky. Eighth, you must hope the gear is sound after hours of chafing on rocks and underwater obstructions. Last of all you must pray that the hooks stay in a jaw that is as boney as any stag's antler.'

I could have added: tenth, the ferox is probably one of the rarest fish in the world!

But this book is about red letter days, and not about gloom, doom and pessimism. And, believe me, there have been many glorious successes along the way – even if the first few years were dim and the future looked very stormy. There was that first ten-pounder, caught, surprisingly, on a drifted deadbait in a river that left one of the prime lochs. The bite was ferocious and the fight – well, I suppose there will be enough battle talk in this book for me to leave it to your imagination. Picture a fresh, wild fish in water going like a torrent and you will get the idea. I simply fell on that first big ferox and thanked the Lord!

Things eased a little after that first fish. Ferox had not become anything like commonplace (they never will either), but at least I realized that they were fact, that they were mortal and that they were more than fancy. Best of all, some of my next fish came while I was in the company of friends, and friends are desperately needed when you are out feroxing! I was lucky enough to be present when Peter Rogers, the editor and mastermind of this very book, landed his first good ferox. It was a swelteringly hot day, and the colours, and the drama and the whole action will be etched in my mind forever – as I am sure they will be (and are now) in his.

Then there was the thirteen-pounder, caught with Chris who has had more than his share of big fish – even sharks – but who would probably say that this ferox was his most exciting angling experience to date. Four of us were in the boat when the fish first broke surface. It came out right in front of our noses and I swear the thing's tail knocked my hat back. It was like seeing a UFO or a real-life miracle, and was an extraordinary, cartwheeling sackful of silver.

Never to be forgotten either is the fortnight I spent with Christopher and his spaniel, Maddy, on White Loch during an autumnal period of savage storms. We lived in what is reputed to be the most remote habitation in the British Isles – a small, wind-rattled bothy with the facilities of a chicken run. But who cares? No ferox man does. These were nights of the northern lights and days of storms punctuated by bending rods, screeching reels and the thrashing of big fish in the foam. Looking back now, I realize that half the time we were wet, cold, famished and in fear of our lives, and for the other half we were in absolute ecstasy. For those amazing few days, ferox seemed almost easy – an illusion, of course. Soon the loch wised up to us and the ferox disappeared into the depths. Winter took over and we struggled just as much as we ever had.

There was a big fish lost on the tip of an island on Lough Mask. Then there was a livebait spat out by a huge fish on Loch Arkaig in Scotland – that trout had to be 40in long. There have been sightings of shoals of char thousands strong leaping into the still, dawn air as ferox have funnelled backwards and forwards through them, reaping their breakfast. There have been fish lost in snowstorms and even occasionally landed in sunshine.

Thinking about ferox now, as I write this chapter, I realize that I have forgotten more than I have known, and I have known pathetically little. Bernard is about forty-five years older than me and perhaps that means that I, with any luck at all, have a good few trips north ahead of me. If I could write this piece again in ten, twenty or thirty years time, who knows what I could tell, but at least this is a start. I don't suppose it will inspire in the way of Crabtree, but if it makes just a few more of you think of predators other than pike, who knows? We might just see that true, authenticated 30lb ferox cradled in front of the mountains yet. And what, on God's earth, would Crabtree have made of that?

When Time Stood Still

~

Chris Ball

The forecast looked good for Wednesday and Thursday when I returned home from work. The evening air was warm and still – just right, in fact – and as I sat clutching a glass of port in my 'carp-room', with the yellow rays of the sunset slanting strongly through the windows, my mind began to wander . . . Would those carp at the Army Lake be stirring under the rhododendrons? It was a long shot, but perhaps, just perhaps, they might be back in their old haunts.

Racing away from London, I pushed my car faster and faster as I sped along the M3. It was nearly 3 p.m. when I finally pulled up in the car-park, and the weather was glorious. Could this really be the end of the season? Tackle ready, I set off along the path, but would the carp be there? I darted into the undergrowth and along a rhododendron tunnel that seemed remarkably unchanged since my last visit in September, and bearing no signs of the winter that had just passed.

Stopping at the first available spot, I peered through the branches but saw nothing. A few more paces and I looked again. Surely not, but there before me was a carp. I blinked. Another appeared, and then another! These were small fish admittedly, swimming quite close to the surface, but it was encouraging none the less. I threw out several handfuls of Chum Mixer, and to my delight a fish soon took a number of pieces. This was fine, but what I really wanted was a sight of one of the big, old Leney carp: lean fighting-machines with beautiful scaling, averaging around the 25lb mark.

After fifteen minutes I couldn't believe my luck, for there, swimming only feet from where I lay hidden, appeared one of those fantastic fish with a blue/purple back and a tail the span of two hands. The fish came past me a few moments later, taking a fragment of surface food as though it hadn't a care in the world. By now this piece of bait had, along with the rest, drifted in the light ripple to my left where, of course, I couldn't get a hookbait! But there was still a chance, and I knew at that moment exactly why I will always have a passion for carp.

The trap was laid and it would only be a matter of time before the fish would reappear. My rod and net were in position with the hookbait hanging off the rod tip, hovering just above the water. Other smaller fish joined in the feeding spree, any of which I could have hooked quite easily, but each was half the size of the blue-backed mirror.

The tension mounted, my eyes darting left and right, straining to see the big fish should it approach . . . There! It was taking a piece of Chum just feet from the area where I stood a chance of hooking and landing it. The hookbait kissed the water's surface and up came the fish. A hurried strike, two quick lunges and the rod sprang back, almost throwing me off balance. I swore as I stood there shaking. How could everything go so right one moment and the next go so wrong?

Back at the car I took a much-needed breather to calm my nerves. Rest the swim for twenty minutes, I thought. But would my carp stay put after that racket? Ten minutes later I found out when two fish of about 10–15lb made an appearance. Watching them intently as they took the remaining bait, I very nearly missed a nice one that almost sneaked by unnoticed. As I lowered a hookbait for the second time, up it came straight away and, after a lot of crashing about, it went into the folds of the net. Great stuff. It was not as big as the first but, at 18lb on the scales, I was more than happy. I'd be back tomorrow for sure.

It was 14 March, the last day of the season, and one I traditionally take off from work. But what a change in the weather from the previous day. I even did some work at home before setting off on that final foray. By 2.30 p.m. I was back in position in the rhododendron tunnel, the temperature dropping steadily as the day progressed. After a while I saw two carp, swimming much deeper than those of the previous day. Neither came up for any bait and the situation looked grim. I sat waiting for more than an hour, but other than the occasional small fish nothing looked remotely like coming to the top.

That's it, I decided, I'd try another water for the last few hours of daylight.

JOHN SEARL

Returning to the car I hesitated; I'd just have one final look at the outflow of the lake where I'd managed to catch one or two last summer. It turned out to be the best thing I did that season. When I pushed through the branches, there before me were three big, dark shapes. By then it was past 3.30 p.m. and the daylight was beginning to drain away under the heavy cloud cover. Beneath the rhododendrons it was quite dark.

The loose Chum I threw out was inspected almost immediately by a good fish of around 20lb. Moments later it came back for more. I'd seen enough. Removing myself carefully from the undergrowth, I reached for my rod, bag and net. It was tight inside the bushes, but somehow I managed to get everything organized without arousing the carps' suspicion. I threw out some more Chum and the three fish circled close by just a few inches below the surface. I watched as the Chum drifted away to the left, when suddenly a huge mouth engulfed a piece. What a whopper!

By then I was really excited, for here was an outstanding chance. Once again I lowered the Chum on to the surface under the rod tip, but I couldn't stop it dithering on the water for my hands were shaking so. Draping the line over a small twig at least kept it still. Within thirty seconds I had to take it off the water again as the twenty-pounder was looking at it very hard. The fish was stationary, almost directly below the bait, even though the bait was 2in off the surface. And only then did I realize that the carp might reach out of the water and have a go. I quickly drew the bait higher – just in case!

At this stage I decided to wait for the big fish to come out in to the open. Eventually it did so, and I lowered the Chum right in the monster's path. Up it came, almost in slow motion. At that moment time stood still. A quick strike produced a violent wrench on the rod. I held on like grim death. The big carp thrashed the water to a froth whilst I kept it on a tight line, never letting it get its head down. Somehow, although the actual details were lost in the excitement, I managed to bundle the fish into the net. What a relief! With my heart pounding I slumped down in a heap, taking perhaps a minute to gather my senses. I drew the net upwards, tight around the fish and tried to look at my prize, but it was too dark. Biting the line, I manhandled the whole lot up and over the branches on to dry land.

I remember clearly that the carp was curled up in a U-shape as I put the heavy load gently down on to the soft ground, and only then did it straighten up. There, in the net before me, lay a tremendous fish – a veritable monster. As I sorted out the weigh-sling and keepsack, my eyes never left the fish. My mind was spinning as I contemplated that it must have weighed close to, if not more than 30lb.

A short time later, my sons Duncan and Martyn arrived along with a capable cameraman. Out in the open the carp was a staggering sight in all its winter glory – red and gold with linear scaling, some of the scales measuring 3–4in in length. It was soon up on the scales and a weight of 31lb 8oz was recorded: probably the largest carp ever caught on a floating bait during the winter and certainly the finest looking Leney I'd ever landed. From its nose to the tip of its tail it measured an incredible 36½in. It was a truly magical fish that had grown from a tiny 5in baby when stocked in 1956 to become, thirty-five years later, one of the high spots of my angling career!

The Birthday Present
~
Vic Bellars

A very long time ago I caught a perch, quite a big perch in fact, and one that some might consider very large indeed. I have been lucky enough to have landed a sprinkling of three-pounders over the years, but that fish was rather special. It was special because I was not fishing for the species, special in that it was taken during the closed season and also special because I caught it on my birthday – an unexpected present.

In those days I always went fishing on my birthday, come hell or high water. When it fell on a weekday, many and varied were the excuses for my absence from work: stomach bugs; 'flu; the demise of far-away relatives which necessitated long-distance travelling to the funeral; immediate dental problems; I even asked for the day off once to attend my sow's confinement (I kept large whites at the time, and a farrowing was an important occasion).

My birthday falls in the second week of May, so the only freshwater fish I could legitimately catch were trout or, at that time, eels.

Before the days of 'put and take' fisheries, trout waters were thin on the ground in Norfolk. There were private stretches on some rivers, notably the Nar, the Wensum and the little Babingley; a few trout even lived in the brook at Heacham, as well as in the Glaven and Stiffkey. There was also the odd brown trout in the tiny River Hun, originally stocked by my grandfather, but most had been poached and I hadn't seen one in that little river for years.

The Hun, unknown and never fished except by me as a boy, was as straight as a Roman road. It flowed crystal clear, choked with starwort at the edges, while the sinuous beds of feathery hornwort swayed languorously in the gentle current. After passing through the tiny sluice in the sea wall, the river became lost in the creeks of Thornham Saltmarsh. It was full of flounders (we called them 'butts'), but there were also a few roach, the odd little pike and, towards the end of summer, shoals of smelt which gathered above the sluice.

With no trout left in the Hun to fish for, and without the funds to afford a ticket on the recognized trout streams, I was left with the task of persuading the owners of mill-pools on the Wensum to grant me a day's fishing. These pools often harboured the odd large brownie, as voracious as hungry pike, and, just now and again, one threw caution to the wind and was hooked. These big trout waxed fat on a diet of minnows and dace, and were as cannibalistic as highland ferox. I was upstaged one day by a small boy who was dunking a whole rasher of bacon impaled on a large hook that was tied to some cord sea-fishing line. This monstrous bait, dangled deep in the white water, was snaffled by a big old trout that was immediately and unceremoniously hauled up and over the road bridge parapet. I went round to congratulate the boy on his remarkable feat, but he didn't wait for my coming – clutching the fish to his chest he dashed off up the road, round the corner, and vanished. I have a feeling that that enterprizing lad had no business to be fishing there. But what a fish! It weighed perhaps 6lb, give or take an ounce or two. I caught nothing that day, but began to think seriously about ledgering bacon rashers!

The obvious choice of bait to tempt a mill-pool trout was a livebait. A minnow hardly looked the part and was too attractive to little perch, so a dace would have been just perfect! However, tempting as it was, catching dace in the closed season wasn't an option I was prepared to entertain. I considered large lobworms, but they would also have attracted perch, not to mention eels, so lures it had to be. I had quite a collection: vibro-spoons, Devon minnows – including the recently introduced 'Feathero' variety – and an ancient wagtail or two. At that time, to use contemporary jargon, I was also into baited spoons, and I modified a number of fly spoons of various sizes so that the single hook did not revolve with the blade, baiting the hook with about an inch of lobworm.

Mill-pools attract anglers as a magnet attracts iron filings. They may not hold the largest fish in the river, but they look as though they should, hence their fascination. The continuous murmur of running water is insistent, even soporific, with deep, mysterious eddies sliding past moss-strewn, mellow brick. After rain the

white water in the mill-race erupts from the arches, dissipating at the tail of the pool where the dace dart like silver shadows over the gravel. The eddies hold fish – perch in the deeps and roach – and, if a big trout inhabits the pool, it is likely to rest up nose-to-sill beneath the foaming rapids where only an angler knows how gentle is the current. Pike are present in every pool, and as avoiding them when spinning for trout is impossible, they invariably enliven many an otherwise blank day.

A mill-pool on a bright May morning is pure enchantment. The trees are coming into full leaf – pristine, shimmering and clothed in a cascade of lime-green. Early swallows skim the bubble-clustered surface and your pulse quickens as a fish rises, leaving a fleeting record of its presence in the concentric ripples as they widen and fade. A mill-pool needs to be fished carefully, with circumspection even, and never in a hurry. Such pools are as much for relaxation and contemplation as for fishing, which is only a part of the magic.

I sat down on a patch of grass, just opposite the quickening glide where the pool narrowed into river again. Sipping coffee, I soaked up the atmosphere, and thought of how best to winkle out the old trout that I knew lived in the pool. With the whole day ahead there was little hurry.

A larger rise in the nearer back-eddy sent wavelets slapping against the brickwork and brought me back to reality. Selecting a 2in heavy Devon minnow, I secured this to the well-soaked gut leader. My lovely little split-cane Hardy spinning rod, married to an early Ambidex fixed-spool reel with claw bale arm and loaded with 5lb silk line, was soon searching the lure into the mouth of the road arch. There it was sucked down deep, under the white-water turbulence. I cast again and again, changing lures, but only little pike obliged, as always. Three times the rod was bucking, and three times I returned a dappled-yellow jack. It was time to produce my trump card, the baited spoon . . .

Spinning across the pool produced one enthusiastic little perch and occasional plucks, perhaps from even smaller ones. A search of more promising water was called for.

I cast so I could spin through the eddy, the slowly moving water by the wall rocking as the lure splashed down. I let it sink so that it fluttered enticingly at 2ft, 3ft, 4ft, 5ft and nearly 6ft, then I started to retrieve. Was that a little pull or had I touched bottom? The lure was clean so I cast again. Half-way through the eddy the rod bent sharply, the clutch yielding line in short bursts that sliced through the surface tension. I knew it couldn't be a trout, which would have run fast and powerfully, and the shocks imparted to the rod confirmed this to be so. A better pike perhaps? I played the fish gently, fearing a bite-off. But the fish stayed hooked, fighting slowly, circling and boring ever downward as it thumped the rod tip with heavy, jarring tugs. It was nicely balanced tackle, and the inexorable pressure of a taut line and well-bent rod began to take effect.

The fish – by then forced to the surface – rolled, its spray spattering like raindrops, and for a fleeting second I glimpsed a flash of vermilion and a tiger-barred flank. The rest of the fight, lasting perhaps a few seconds, remains hazy, but somehow, perhaps more by luck than skill, that huge fish was squeezed into the landing net.

I remember laying the net in the grass and kneeling beside a perch that anglers dream of. It was liphooked – just – the blade of the little spoon hanging outside its mouth, and the great hump of shoulder muscle behind its head rising like a mountain from a valley floor.

We looked at each other, I in sheer admiration and not a little awe, the perch no doubt taking a more jaundiced view of events. I hung the fish, still in the net, on the balance. I really couldn't believe my eyes: it weighed over 5lb. Still dazed, I found it surprisingly difficult to subtract the weight of the net, simple enough in normal circumstances, but eventually I got it right. That perch weighed 4lb 7oz. A red letter capture indeed!

In those days any great fish that was caught was usually destined for a glass case. I couldn't afford to have a fish set up and although I wanted to keep that perch desperately, I knew, reluctantly, that I must return it. Quickly, before temptation became irresistible, I was in the pool, the water lapping near the tops of my boots, and the perch was gone.

Right Place, Right Time
~
Mick Bowles

T he weekend of 4–5 July finally arrived, the date set for a British Eel Anglers' Club fish-in on Weirwood Reservoir in Sussex. Having obtained special permission to fish there from the then owner, Colin Simpson, the prospect of tackling this huge 280-acre water was exciting and challenging to say the least.

Our target fish were, of course, eels, but preliminary enquiries into the reservoir's history had been disappointing. Being more than thirty years old, the water's age was right for big eels, as was its position at the headwater of the River Medway. The problem was that at no time during its life as a fishery had one single eel been recorded to rod and line, electro-fishing, netting or fish traps. The omens did not look good. There was, however, one glimmer of hope from two employees of Southern Water who related that during their fifteen years of working at the reservoir they had on two occasions come across eels. Each, they said, bore the dimensions of a motorcycle tyre!

Collecting my friend John Calverley *en route* to the reservoir, any lack of enthusiasm on my part (caused by a disappointing response from members) was soon remedied with talk of potential monsters and the prospect of fishing a new and rather mysterious water that fired the imagination. On arrival though, the daunting task of quite where to start suddenly hit us as we were confronted with an apparently vast sheet of featureless water. Fortunately, experience had taught me that if your water has a dam wall, then you should fish it as these are likely areas for eel patrol-routes.

John headed for the south bank while I, in the company of fellow club member Matt Johnson, set off on the long haul to the northern side. In keeping with BEAC tradition, the weather decided to change. Until that weekend we had experienced a number of weeks of scorching conditions, but now the evening turned humid and the freshening wind blew straight towards me. Even so, the warmth of the breeze was not unpleasant, a bit like that from a warm fan heater.

At that time we were allowed to use four rods, and I therefore decided to fish two with worm and two with small deadbaits (half sardine and roach). Positioning myself some way off the dam wall, I cast back towards it and was encouraged to see lots of small fry leaping out of the water in this general area. Things were looking up. At this stage I had absolutely no idea of the depth of water or bottom layout as we were only permitted to fish from dusk. With the cloud cover thickening and the wind noticeably picking up in strength, the margins soon became quite foamy, and I was interested to see a number of large but very dead roach drifting into my corner of the dam wall. As the night wore on it became apparent that these were spawning victims, as a multitude of fish joined in the frenzied activity in the margins, some with their backs breaking the surface in less than 1ft of water.

Eventually all was quiet, and with the wind dropping I repositioned my baits, fanning them out at different distances from the dam wall. At 1 a.m. and 1.30 a.m. I had dropped runs on sardine baits fished close in, which may well have been line bites from carp moving through the margins. Then, at 3 a.m., I had a steady run on four lobworms baited on a size 2 hook. I connected with the fish, and it took off like a train, fighting strongly for some minutes before coming off. I assumed it was a carp because the water here was only inches deep, but what happened next opened my eyes . . .

Clearly, there were lots of fish close in, so I decided to change my baits for fresh ones and cast out to different areas. Winding in my 'dam wall' bait, I put new worms on the hook, but instead of casting back to the dam I lobbed the bait some 25yd beyond any cruising fish. Might as well catch something for my £8, I mused. To my astonishment, inside of ten minutes line was being taken smoothly off the spool. Moving to the rod I struck, and whatever I'd contacted with charged out to the main body of the reservoir and into the security of deeper water. From the speed of the fish I was convinced that it was either a carp or a trout, and I had to back-wind and apply side-strain to bring it to a halt. Unfortunately, this also had

the effect of making the fish kite round to my left, where it stopped in what I assumed were snags and where nothing would move it. Applying steady pressure, the line suddenly fell slack. I cursed out loud. In anger I wound in furiously, only for the rod to buckle in my hands. Whatever I'd hooked was still on and was now swimming just in front of me. Only then did the fight appear familiar, with almighty 'eely' thumps on the rod tip.

I called to Matt, for if this was an eel it was one hell of a fish. He stood at my side ready with the landing net. Playing the fish as best I could, it came a few yards to the bank and stopped, and no amount of winding or pulling made any difference. A change of tactics was required, so I decided to walk backwards and try to drag the fish out. It broke surface. 'Yes, it is an eel,' Matt cried out. 'It's an absolute monster!' And with that the fish chose to dive into the folds of the waiting net.

Staggering at least 50yd up the bank with the captive prize, and with me in hot pursuit paying out line, Matt finally put the net down. At last we could view the sheer magnificence of this beautiful creature as it lay still in the torchlight. Taking the hook from the top rim of the jaw, a hasty weighing was conducted in the darkness and recorded at 7lb 11oz. Jubilant, we then placed the eel in a carpsack which, for security, was popped into a keepnet. I was taking no chances!

At dawn I rushed over to John Calverley to tell him the good news. Returning together to my swim, we collected the eel gently from the margins and, after the weigh-sling had carefully been neutralized on our three respective sets of scales, it was weighed accurately at 8lb exactly. I was ecstatic – what an eel! Unfortunately, the weather was turning worse and rain was fast approaching, so photographs had to be taken quickly. By then a few trout anglers had appeared at the reservoir, but sadly the significance of my fish seemed lost on them, and the fact that I was going to put it back was an unthinkable heresy in their philosophy. A storm was imminent as I waded into the margins and held the eel for one last look, before gently letting it go. It glided out of my hands and gracefully away towards one of the trout anglers who stood in the water near by, this obviously making him feel uneasy. Quite remarkably, as my eel swam past him to the deeps, he actually raised one leg out of the water!

On reflection, it's difficult to express in words one's feelings on achieving such a personal ambition . . . The first recorded eel from the fishery, a remarkable fight, being in the right place at the right time. All in all, it was a truly wonderful result that made all those fruitless hours of fishing worth while.

A Day to Remember
~
Mick Brown

I 'm not an antisocial person, but when I'm fishing I like to be alone. I don't
want to see anyone and I don't want to talk to anyone. My fishing is a great
escape from reality and as each day goes by I need it more and more.

Much fishing today is like a fairground activity and is not for me. Such high
ideals mean that there are few places where I can fish in peace but, here and
there, I have a few nooks and crannies into which I can quietly disappear and find
solitude. In some cases this may not be strictly legal, and I don't seek to justify my
actions when I say that I do no harm. All I take away with me are the memories
of nature's wonders, like watching a family of mink strip a huge salmon to the
bone in the January snow or an otter playing on a gravel bank in the early
morning mist. Coypu have even popped their heads up to look at me, disappearing
with a 'plop', and recently I saw a bittern drop like a dead weight into a reed
swamp. You don't see these things where others tread and you don't see them
unless you move slowly, sit very, very still and wear clothes that blend in with the

surroundings.

This does not mean that I am distracted from my fishing. Not in the least, for that is the passion that takes me to these places. I love to fish for all species, but more than anything I am driven to catch pike. I no longer try to understand why I do it; it's become a way of life and I cannot imagine doing anything more satisfying. Over the years my piking experiences have taken me to waters of all descriptions: rivers, reservoirs, gravel pits, drains, lochs and broads, one or two of which have become special and which I have come to know intimately.

In a recent wickedly cold January, several nights of sub-zero temperatures saw one of these favourite waters, a medium-sized gravel pit, frozen over. It was never a pit to give up its pike easily and, in actual fact, there were very few pike in the pit, which was not much more than about twelve years old. Because the pike were few, they had the potential to grow very big by feeding on the huge shoals of specimen rudd and tench in the water.

In a way I was glad of the freeze-up. The pike's feeding activity slows right down and this will later work in the pike angler's favour. As soon as the water temperature rises again, pike everywhere go on the rampage. I've seen this pattern re-enacted so many times that I was confident it would happen again. As soon as the ice melted, I would be there to find out!

After two bitterly cold weeks, the frost released its grip. For several days I made the mile-long trek to the remotest part of the pit to check whether the ice had thawed in the area I was interested in. Eventually a few holes appeared, and soon, after the coots and swans had enlarged them, it was fishable at last.

The excitement was unbearable as I headed home to get my tackle ready for the following morning. After thirty years of fishing, one would think that I was past the stage where I stay awake for half the night in anticipation of the fishing to follow. But I'm not and I never want to be!

To an ordinary person the next morning would still have seemed like a bitterly cold day, but to someone who lives for being out of doors it was a superb day. The wind was from the west and a temperature of 43–45°F was promised. There was even talk of the sun showing its presence at mid-morning. After weeks of sub-zero temperatures, this was a piker's dream come true.

I'd chosen to fish an area where I'd found that the rudd shoaled in the cold weather. It was a sheltered spot, spared from the north winds and, even then, still had plenty of heavy bottom weed remaining. That morning my decision was proved correct when I discovered that the pike were really on the move. In the space of a couple of hours I had four runs. One was missed, one was dropped, and the other two yielded a jack and a 21lb specimen. For a water where a single run is a rarity, this in itself was an exceptional day, yet there was even more to come . . .

Naturally, I had to go back the following morning. (Being self-employed has its benefits, even if I don't earn much money!) At 9.10 a.m., after dropping the children off at school, I was negotiating the long track again, laden with a heavy rucksack, rods and net, to drop into the same swim as the previous day.

I can't really think of a more idyllic situation. The swim was still sheltered from the prevailing wind and I got my low chair nicely inside a hole that I'd cut into a tangle of grasses and brambles. I could see the floats beautifully from my comfortable position and, after giving the pike a variety of deadbaits from which to choose, I sat back to take in the pleasure of it all. At moments like this I understand what contentment is all about. The weather was kind and I was in with a chance of a good pike. What's more, I had a big box of sandwiches to devour! Typically, most of them were eaten in the first half-hour.

The resident robin of the swim, no doubt prompted by the rustling of sandwich bags, came down to visit me and settled at my feet. I had started to train the bird quite well. Momentarily, I even got it to settle on my finger and snatch a piece of cheese. I'm sure it thinks I'm its mother! In the distant wood, pheasants and pigeons were very active and behind me, on the edge of the ploughed field, a large group of herons collected as if gathered in conversation. The world was coming back to life again. As usual, the RAF had to spoil it as a low-flying Tornado screamed across the sky, shattering the illusion that I lived in a world of peace and tranquillity.

While enjoying my surroundings, I continually scanned the water and my floats. The home-made orange and white balsa stick floats lay slightly cocked in the gentle ripple as the sun broke through, changing the scene from grey to silver. The disturbance at my feet brought a small red worm to the surface, and this was quickly noticed and devoured by my robin friend.

Rudd activity then began and two crackers suddenly cleared the water near the float that supported the fresh smelt. Rudd don't usually jump in cold water unless there's a big pair of jaws behind them, and I think this was probably the case, for, within minutes, the float stood upright, jabbed violently and then disappeared in a very decisive manner! As I reached for the rod, the line was just pulling tight from the elastic band on the butt. With a properly rigged bait, there is no need to do anything but strike immediately – my Bruce and Walker Waterwolf bent right over and stayed there, as if latched into a weedbed.

Before long I was losing line and could feel the lashing of big fins against it. This was clearly a really heavy fish and the old heart started pounding, with my knees feeling a little wobbly too. I would not describe the fight as spectacular, more a battle that was won by degrees. Inch by inch the fish begrudgingly came to me, veering very little to right or left. At the bank the pike had different ideas, and surged first to the right and then to the left. Although the water was gin clear, I could not see the fish properly as the glare of the sun was by then blinding me.

On introducing the pike to the net, it took off in spectacular fashion and, in a series of power surges, went right out beyond the point where I'd first hooked it! However, that wore the old pike out and I soon had it coming quietly back to me. The netting was interesting to say the least, with the sun really doing its best to make things difficult. All I could see was a huge glistening back coming towards the net. Most of it seemed to go in, but I just couldn't get the rest to follow. In a quick decision, I flicked in the baitrunner and dropped the rod so that I could get two hands on to the net. In a frantic few seconds I managed to shake the rest of the pike's colossal body into the net before I slumped back in the mud in a collapsed heap. I think I must be getting too old for this game!

This is one of those moments when I really savour being alone. I like to absorb what has happened slowly, and sit by the net for a while looking at the fish in the water. For quite a time I gazed down on its green, mottled back. The tiny smelt still hung pathetically from the awesome scissor-jaws that had grabbed it.

When we had both fully recovered, I struggled up the steep bank with the pike and ran a tape measure along its length. No wonder it wouldn't fit into the net that easily – it was 5in longer than the 42in arms! The 32lb Avon scales hit the bottom, so I sacked the fish safely and telephoned my friends at *Angling Times* to see if they would help out with weighing and photographing. Mick Rouse and Dave Phillips arrived with their scales and, although we all expected a lot more, the fish was weighed at 34lb 7oz. A personal best and my eleventh pike over 30lb.

Cold, wet and weary, I made my way home, a very happy man to have caught such a monster, which, as far a I know, was and still is a record for the area.

The Arrogance of Youth
~
Kevin Clifford

T he River Hull is little known outside the immediate area of East Yorkshire. One of its tributaries, the West Beck, was once renowned as a
premier chalk stream, but that was long ago when I was almost a boy.
Today, the ravages of borehole abstraction and the burden of three trout farms
have broken its spirit. These effects are even felt further downstream amongst the
coarse fish populations, and the ever-increasing water supply abstraction has left
the river a sad shadow of its former self, although this wasn't always the case.

My first sight of the River Hull was at Swing Bridge. I was about ten years old
and had come along with my uncle, who was fishing a match. I seem to remember
that very little was caught, or expected, as the river's coarse fish had a reputation
for being extremely difficult to tempt. What impressed me though, even at that
age, was the vast amount of aquatic weed and the sight of huge roach drifting
from under its protective cover.

The river figured little in my early fishing days. Under the tutelage of my uncle, we travelled to venues that taxed our meagre resources to the minimum and where the fish had the reputation of eating the angler's offerings avidly. But the memory of those huge roach gliding across the golden gravel patches remained vivid in my mind over the intervening years.

In my late teens I was offered employment as a laboratory technician, and met a chap called Colin Hyam. Colin was an experienced all-round angler with considerable knowledge of the whereabouts of local big fish. It wasn't long before my new friend had introduced myself, and my regular fishing partner, Malcolm Roberts, to the delights of barbel fishing on the Swale at Helperby and the Ouse at Dunsforth, chub fishing on the Derwent and Rye around Malton, and on the Swale at Thornton Bridge. He showed us the big trout in the mill-pool on the Nafferton Beck, and told us of the big roach and grayling in the Driffield Canal. And, during our night shifts, he spoke of the big chub that lived just above the weir at Hempholme. When he mentioned them it was with a voice tinged with respect, almost as if he was asking permission to fish the preserved waters of some feudal lord. The chub were big, almost beyond belief, and almost uncatchable. The few that had been taken only fell to the well-honed skills of the local match experts, and even then luck and good fortune played a major part.

But the arrogance of youth lured Malcolm and I to believe that we could succeed where so many had failed. It was in the autumn of 1968 that we made our first trip. I had already spent many hours reading old copies of the *Angling Times* for reports of any chub caught from the river, in an attempt to piece together any common factors. Yet so few had been taken – one of 6lb 7oz on trotted maggot went to well-known match angler Sid Norris in 1961, a 5lb 12oz fish fell to Ken Thompson in August 1961 on flake, a six-pounder was caught in 1964 and another of 6lb 5oz fell a year later on floating crust to V. Ellis. A further chub of 6lb 12oz on lobworm went to I. Webb in 1964, and a six-pounder was caught by R. Benwell using maggot in July 1967. These, and a handful of smaller fish, were all that had been reported in over a decade.

Yet the fish were there for all to see. A shoal of about eight chub lived just above the weir at Hempholme. Here the river widened out and a row of old wooden piles down in the middle gathered rafts of floating weed. There was no cover on either bank, yet the chub roamed free in open water, only heading for their thatched sanctuary when disturbed by an incautious approach. At the time we estimated the biggest fish at 8lb. Now I wonder if our inexperienced eyes had played a fancy with our judgement – life's knocks and disappointments tend to stifle the belief in magic. Yet who knows, perhaps a record chub really did swim amongst those emerald fronds, in that sparkling, mysterious world of our youth?

I cannot remember the exact sequence of events during those first few trips, but eventually I managed to catch one. My old fishing notebook tells me that it was taken two days before my birthday, on 26 October, and that it weighed 4lb 9oz. It was the biggest chub I'd caught at that time. What I do remember is that neither Malcolm nor I possessed a camera, and that my excitement sent me scampering off

JOHN SEARL

on my motorcycle on a ninety-minute round-trip to borrow my parents' Brownie 127.

The following early season drifted by in misty mornings, and saw us poaching the tench and rudd in the local civic park lake. A series of trips chasing the barbel on the River Swale followed, and then our thoughts returned to the monsters of Hempholme.

It was a warm, August morning. The clouds drifted gently by, high in an azure sky, as we walked the measured mile from Swing Bridge to the weir. The chub were still there, warming their backs lazily near the surface. They looked just as big as ever. Opposite, the pump-station attendant's wife was hanging out washing, and below the weir George Sissons was busy digging the garden near his cottage.

My first cast sent bait towards the back of the raft of weed, and I settled back amongst the rushes and flag iris. Malcolm had set up almost opposite, fishing from the wall of the lock cutting. A little time passed, perhaps ten minutes, and my rod tip pulled round. A strike met with token resistance as a huge head, with an enormous pair of lips, came towards my outstretched landing net.

A series of self-uttered expletives came from my gibbering mouth. The woman hanging out washing looked up, shocked, and Malcolm was half-way across the bridge. Together, we weighed the monster – it was 6lb 12oz. It certainly wasn't the prettiest chub I'd ever seen, being very dark brown in colour, and at some stage in its life it had lost an eye – but it was, without doubt, the biggest. I don't expect I shall ever hold one bigger.

The Flavour of Success
~
Brian Crawford

I had dreamt many times of moving to north Shropshire, with its undulating green fields and huge, mystery-laden meres. Several times in the 1970s I had made the long trek from Peterborough in Cambridgeshire to Ellesmere, the centre of this lush Shropshire lake district. You have to fish the meres to appreciate their gripping magic; their often great size is awe-inspiring as you soak up the atmosphere, something that is missing from many of today's man-made gravel pits. Created by the action of glacial ice many millions of years ago, who can tell what monsters lurk in their overgrown margins and in their hidden depths?

The National Anguilla Club had enjoyed many successful trips to the area, fishing mainly Whitemere and Blakemere, just outside Ellesmere. At club meetings, conversations would go quiet as the topic of meres was raised. Those who had fished them knew, those who had not could not wait to do so. It was not just the fact that they held some very big eels, as well as most other species, but that a night on the bank, surrounded by ancient trees hundreds of years old, often provided a session that would test even the most experienced of night anglers. The wilds of Shropshire could give any angler a night to remember, particularly at Whitemere. Tales of the 'Whitemere Monster' were written about in the club's magazine. Grown men avoided certain areas of the mere. Most thought the monster was only a badger, but no one had seen it, only heard it.

It was with all this in mind that I eventually moved to Shropshire in August 1984. My feelings were mixed. There was the exciting challenge of many new waters on the one hand, but sadness too at leaving the Fens and other areas that I both loved and enjoyed. I spent little of the rest of 1984 fishing due to problems of settling in, and it was 1985 before I was able to get a good look round and decide on where I would concentrate my main efforts for eels. At the National Association of Specialist Anglers' Conference in April of that year, I had the chance to talk to Dennis Kelly, Chairman of an angling club that controlled Colemere, a large water I fancied. Dennis was very experienced in fishing the meres and suggested that I join his club, but due to its waiting list I was not able to gain membership until the following year – 1986. I then began my campaign to catch my first good-sized Shropshire mere eel, having in the past only been successful with small fish to about 1lb.

Following a number of enquiries, I was delighted to learn that I could fish Colemere during the closed season provided I complied with the relevant by-laws for Severn Trent concerning the size of hook and type of bait. We had a very cold winter in Shropshire during 1985–6, but I was on the bank in February to explore the water in as much detail as possible, walking all the way round it and taking many photographs of potential swims. Colemere is very overgrown for most of its bank, with a bird sanctuary at one end where fishing and boating is prohibited. Fortunately, the boats cannot get near the area as there are many sunken trees. The banks are also well covered with rhododendron bushes, very tall trees and other dense undergrowth, and like many meres they are also host to vast swarms of vicious biting gnats from May onwards, as I was later to find out.

After several circuits of the mere with my wife, I at last decided on the location for my first session in mid-April. Due to the great size of the water and the fact that there were areas with very deep drop-offs, I had a feeling that early trips would be more successful in the shallow, northern end as this would warm up during the day. I therefore selected my swim here. Well, it was hardly a swim, just a narrow gap between two bankside trees with barely enough room to position a brolly-tent and two rods. To the left, about 10yd away, the north bank was a dense mass of trees, several of which had fallen into the water. It would have been impossible to have fished from that area, but from where I was I could at least intercept a patrolling eel with my bait.

The day of 18 April arrived, the first opportunity I could fish. It had been very mild, but rain was forecast for later than evening. Undeterred, my wife and I set off on the 45-minute journey to Colemere, arriving at about 7 p.m. The car was parked up on the side of the little lane and we quickly unloaded the gear. It was

getting very overcast by the time we had deposited everything in the pitch, and we decided the first thing to do was set up the brolly-tent so that it it if it did rain the important things would keep dry. This done, and with my wife making a welcoming first brew. I got on with the serious business of organizing my tackle.

Dusk was settling in its usual damp, spring fashion and with an imminent promise of rain as I cast my first bait into the area near the north bank. My second bait was positioned slightly to my right, to cover any eel moving to the shallows from the deeper water. With everything tightened up and alarms set, I was able to relax for the first time that day. What a wonderful feeling, sitting there sipping a fresh hot brew, looking out over the vastness of the mere as the opposite bank slowly disappeared into the thickening gloom. My first trip in 1986. My first eel-angling session on Colemere. I actually felt that I shouldn't really mind if I blanked – I was so content just being there. The mere was still, without a breath of wind. The coots, mallards and other birds of the mere seemed to be gathered at the far end. I settled back on to my chair feeling on top of the world, and my wife snuggling into her warm sleeping bag in readiness for the long night ahead. At exactly 9 p.m. the Optonic on the left-hand rod began a non-stop bleep, the light-emitting diode flashing so fast it seemed a continuous beam. I could hear line swishing through the rod rings. In a second I was by the rod and, with line still being pulled off the spool, I turned the reel handle to engage the pick-up and slowly lifted the rod. Feeling the pull on the tip, I answered by sweeping the rod upwards and sideways to my left. The rod had hardly moved when it was savagely pulled downwards again as the jagging motion, obviously from an eel – a good eel – transmitted itself through the rod's length. I struck a second time to ensure the barbless hook had set. I could feel a rasping motion as the 18lb braided-steel trace rubbed along the eel's fine teeth, it's head swaying from side to side in its effort to escape.

Unable to retrieve line and not wishing to give any, I sensed the eel starting to kite towards the trunk of a very large tree on my left, half-submerged in the water. 'Come on, come on!' I could hear myself saying, as I slammed the rod hard over to apply maximum side-strain. Thwarted, the eel began to thrust itself in the other direction towards open water. Breathing faster, my arms aching from the constant pressure, I finally felt the resistance from the eel beginning to ease. Suddenly, the eel hit the surface in the by then dark distance and began to thrash the water to a foam. Gradually, slowly, I began to pump it in, raising the rod then winding down. I lowered my landing net into the water. I would have only one chance to net the fish, and it had to be done quickly and neatly as there were dense snags on either side of me. In the dark I could see the eel's head moving nearer and nearer, occasionally spinning in a last desperate effort to break free. I had previously had several excellent eels lost at this crucial time due to traces snapping, hooks opening out or swivels failing, and I prayed nothing would go wrong in the last few moments. Suddenly it was over and the eel was in the net. I could hardly believe it.

Lifting everything on to the bank, I shone my torch into the depths of the mesh. 'It's a four-pounder,' my wife said delightedly. I hadn't noticed her there, nor the fact that it was raining quite heavily, I had been so engrossed in trying to land the fish. Unhooking the eel, I left it in the landing net while I sorted out my scales and weigh-sling. With everything zeroed for the moment of truth, in went the eel, carefully, almost reverently. My wife held the torch; the beam of light on the Avons showed the needle at the 4lb 8oz mark. Brilliant! It was a personal best. However, it was not just the size of the fish that made the moment, it was a whole collection of ingredients: the superb venue, the first session of the year, my wife sharing the moment and, of course, the muscular power of such a good eel. The feeling of elation was still with me next morning.

In the words of the master, Bernard Venables: 'Great triumphs do not come often in angling, and this is a blessing. When they come they have their flavour partly because they are rare. If they were to come often and reliably the flavour would go stale. Failure can make an angler despair, but it gives intensity to these triumphs.' I remembered those words for the rest of the 1986 season as I fished hard at Colemere, but never again did I taste the flavour of the success I enjoyed in that first session.

Over the Moon
~
Bryan Culley

T he rudd fishing at Swithland Reservoir had been very slow that year with just one fish to show, all the usual swims producing only tench. As my son, Jon, and I arrived on the Sunday evening intending to night-fish the west bank, we looked across the reservoir from the dam and saw two anglers settled in our chosen swims. Driving back around the east side, we stopped the car for a better view of the two anglers to see if they were anyone we knew, but as we looked across the water I noticed a fish roll, then another, and then another. Altogether about twenty fish showed in the space of perhaps half an hour. Our chosen swims were now well and truly forgotten as we watched what seemed like every fish in the reservoir rolling, although quite what species they were we couldn't tell. We never did find out who the other anglers were.

Naturally, we decided to concentrate our efforts on the area where the fish were moving, but in this there was just one small snag. That side of the reservoir was out of bounds for night fishing. However, we knew the bailiff had gone home, and so we hoped our small indiscretion would be overlooked.

Our swims were soon baited with 3lb of brown breadcrumbs laced with two pints of maggots and three loaves of mashed bread at a range of about 40yd. On the size 8 hook, four maggots were used with a fingernail-sized piece of breadflake, attached to 4lb line and a Drennan block-end feeder filled with maggots. The baits had only been out about half an hour when we started to experience line bites, and we thought these were tench as by then we had definitely identified some of the fish as such.

Just before midnight, Jon's Betalite bobbin lifted to the butt ring, the strike meeting a solid resistance. I walked round to his swim where he told me he was playing what could only be a tench, as the fish was far too heavy and powerful for a rudd. Some minutes later I netted it for him and in the torchlight discovered it to be a rudd after all. But to call the fish even a big rudd would be an under-statement, as this fish was truly massive. We even thought it could be a possible record. However, after carefully weighing the fish the needle came to rest at 4lb 5oz – the second-largest rudd ever caught. To say that Jon was excited would also be something of an understatement! The rest of the night passed by rather uneventfully, although Jon missed another bite at about 1.30 a.m. and I caught a mere 'tiddler' of 2lb 8oz at 3 a.m.

After photographing the monster it was back to work, where all I could think about was returning to fish the swim again.

The following Thursday I finished work at 11 p.m. and was fishing by 11.45 p.m! The same amount of groundbait and maggots was catapulted into the swim as before, but to my surprise no fish showed on the surface, even though it was a calm, warm night with a half-moon breaking through the scattered clouds. I was beginning to think the rudd had moved on when a fish rolled to my right – or at least what I thought was a fish until a tufted duck popped to the surface like a cork. Then, without warning, at about 12.30 a.m. the bobbin on my right-hand rod lifted a couple of inches and held there. I struck on the off-chance and was plea-santly surprised to find I had connected a good fish which fought hard all the way to the net. As I unfolded the mesh in the torchlight I could see it was yet another huge rudd, which weighed in at exactly 4lb.

After sacking the fish carefully, I recast both rods, but nothing much happened. A fox approached to within 6ft of me and didn't seem in a hurry to leave; as I watched it my left-hand indicator sounded. Turning back to the rod, the bobbin rose slowly towards the butt ring, an unmissable bite, and sure enough I was soon into another good fish. Once it was landed and laid on the ground, I couldn't believe my luck: this rudd also looked a certain four-pounder. However, it was not to be, with the needle of the scales settling at 3lb 14oz.

A friend who was fishing the opposite side of the reservoir came over to photo-graph and witness the catch for me. I was over the moon. Both fish were in pristine condition, with not a split fin or scale out of place. That morning I felt I was the happiest man alive.

Several well-known anglers, including Kevin Clifford, Des Taylor and Bruno Broughton, have either seen or caught rudd from Swithland and none has doubted that all the fish caught were true rudd and not rudd/roach hybrids as is the case in several noted reservoirs, especially those in Northamptonshire. The rudd in Swithland sadly have disappeared now, not having spawned successfully since the reservoir was reflooded after repair work during 1977. The last big one was caught by Andy Lister in September 1990 at 3lb 2oz, and was in poor condition. Ironically, Andy also caught the first 2lb-plus rudd in July 1980. However, Jon's 4lb 5oz fish was the largest, taken in July 1988.

Icing on the Cake
~
John Everard

I t was the second week of the new fishing season and the weather looked more promising. The first week had been quite cold, which had influenced me to abandon my favourite gravel pit for smaller, easier waters where tench were usually plentiful. Unfortunately for me, even these waters proved difficult. However, now that the air had that soft, warm feel to it, I arranged to return to my favourite pit to spend a day with Rolf Wobbeking, my fishing partner at that time. The fact that Rolf had caught a male tench of 7lb 14oz two evenings previously more than persuaded me to have another go. This pit is a large and generally shallow water that holds a very low population of coarse fish. But the fact that the few tench it contains are usually over 6lb makes it extra-special.

I met Rolf at the bankside and we both glanced across the large expanse of water which resembled a mill-pond. The only ripples were caused by the odd coot foraging for weed and a great crested grebe diving for fish to feed its newly hatched brood. Had the water and air temperature been higher, I would have had more confidence, but with the air temperature only just beginning to rise significantly, I was not so sure. By mutual agreement we decided to walk the perimeter of the pit in search of fish in the gin-clear water.

It must have been at least an hour and a half later, during which time not a single fish had been seen, when we reached the spot where Rolf had previously caught the large male tench. Rolf indicated a couple of tench approximately 20yd out, moving slowly through the shallow gully from where he had caught his specimen. There was no doubt in Rolf's mind that he was going to fish this swim again, and who could blame him. But sensing that I was not too happy, he invited me to fish alongside him. This was a kind gesture, but I declined as I did not see any advantage in doing so.

I decided to explore the last 250yd of bank we had not yet scanned before calling it a day. To my surprise, in the very next bay I spotted several tench nosing lethargically over a gravel bar some 18yd from the bank. It was late morning by then, and the sun was beginning to feel very warm on my face as I sat on the bank to watch the tench. It soon became apparent that they were definitely attracted to the gravel bar, even though they were very inactive. This, however, was good enough for me.

I told Rolf that I had spotted the fish, but by this time he was well settled in his swim and had already seen several more tench swimming through his gully. I returned to my swim and soaked some stale bread in my landing net by gently lowering it into the water. Then I mixed brown breadcrumbs with the bread, and added approximately half a pint of maggots and half a small tin of sweetcorn. Taking careful aim, I threw four balls of this mix accurately on to the nearside slope of the gravel bar. Each ball was about the size of a pigeon's egg; I learned many years ago to feed sparsely and often rather than 'fill it in' at the beginning of a session.

My favourite method of fishing for tench is to float fish the margins, this having already accounted for all my specimen tench, including three over 9lb. Unfortunately, on this particular day I would have to light ledger as I calculated this method would be more advantageous at the range. As I threaded the line through the rings of my rod, a pleasant cooling breeze brushed my face. By the time I sat in my chair to complete my end tackle a persistent but very welcome north-west wind was blowing and the water at my feet was choppy. Almost simultaneously, the torpid tench on the gravel bar became active and began to roll over the baited area. My own lethargic mood became hurried too, as I impaled four lively maggots and a small piece of crust on to my size 10 hook and quickly cast into the active area.

It was only a short time before my indicator sailed towards the butt ring. Several minutes later I was staring at the fat, golden flanks of a very welcome male tench weighing 5lb 8oz. A further fifteen minutes later I was into another tench. This time the fight was much stronger as the fish made long, powerful runs through the lush beds of thick Canadian pond weed. Eventually I netted it, Canadian pond

weed and all, and the pointer on my scales settled at 6lb 9oz – my largest male tench to date.

By then fish were obviously very active in my swim, and so I invited Rolf to sit alongside and share it with me. At regular intervals I fed more groundbait on a little-and-often basis. I was getting plenty of line bites which told me that the tench were feeding further down the slope on the edge of the gravel bar. I rebaited with a half-inch piece of lobworm and two maggots, and cast over the deeper section; almost immediately I had a good bite which resulted in a thick-bodied tench of 7lb.

The refreshing north-westerly wind continued and, with the strong intermittent sunlight, made for ideal conditions. Although I was facing the wind, the day was still warm and I found the cool breeze very welcome. To catch three tench in a sitting on this hard water was an achievement in itself, and, when I struck firmly into my fourth of the day, I was beginning to realize that this was now an extra-special occasion by any standard. Large tench in large gravel pits fight in a similar way to carp, and I am always amazed at their sheer speed, especially on the initial run. This particular fish felt very heavy, and as I pulled it into the net, again with a mass of weed, I knew that it was over 8lb. I parted the weed to get a better look at the fish and lifted it into the weighing bag. Rolf performed the ceremony and I was not surprised to hear him say '8lb 11oz'.

As the afternoon wore on, I continued to get indications with most casts. Then I failed to catch two tench that had obviously been fouled (a tench scale was impaled on the hook in each case). Minutes later I was into a very powerful fish which fought for at least ten minutes, making my arm ache. Half-way through the fight, I felt the line go slack before making contact again, and it was then that I realized that I had no control over this fish whatsoever. It is well known that tench will roll around the line awkwardly, but by then I was convinced that the fish was hooked foul. To be honest, I thought I would never get it to the net, but somehow the hook held. Yes, the size 10 was stuck firmly in the tail, but closer inspection revealed the original hook mark *inside the mouth*, where the soft tissue had been torn through, only for the hook to snag a new hold in the caudal fin. This phenomenon happens quite regularly in trout fishing, but I couldn't recall it ever happening to me previously while tench fishing. Rolf did the honours once again, and the needle rested at 9lb 10oz. A great fish!

It was early evening and indications and general activity had almost ceased. The odd fish rolled, but many had moved out of the area and several tench could be seen head-and-tailing some distance from the swim, heading in a north-easterly direction. It was at this time that Dennis Moss, my long-time fishing partner, arrived on the scene. He had guessed from the change in the weather that I would be fishing this special water and had walked its banks looking for me. When I told him of my captures he was not entirely surprised. While we sat talking of the day's event I had a slow but positive lift on my indicator. After a well-timed strike another tench was on. Half-inch segments of large lobworms with a couple of maggots was proving to be a deadly bait, but let's be honest, when tench are *really* feeding you can catch them on most conventional baits. This fish fought as only large fish can, but I was in complete control as I netted yet another specimen. Dennis was amazed at its size, and as Rolf lifted it into the weighing bag he said: 'John, this fish weighs 10lb.'

'9lb 12oz, I reckon,' I said.

'Then you'd better take a look at this.'

The pointer remained steady at 10lb 5oz. Dennis looked at Rolf, then at me, and said: 'You jammy old beggar!' Or something similar, at least. Frankly, I didn't mind at all. It had been *my day*, and this giant among tench was the icing on the cake.

Something Special
~
Neville Fickling

A red letter day; a common expression, but what exactly does it mean? To anglers it is a special day when something notable is caught. To the compiler of a dictionary it is a day marked on a calendar (in red) that is a holiday or a saint's day. The latter definition is therefore not the one for me, but the former most definitely is. Thinking about it further, and with a sense of fun or mischief, I cannot help thinking of the ever-popular Radio 4 panel game 'Just a Minute'. The contestants have to talk on the subject (perhaps a red letter day?) for a minute without hesitation, repetition or deviation. Here I have to attempt this myself, not in a minute, but in 1,500 words. But how to convey the personal significance of my 41lb 6oz pike and my feelings on the occasion? It is a long time since that day, and I have written about it already in my book, *In Pursuit of Predatory Fish* (Beekay Publishers, 1986). The description cannot be rewritten or even elaborated. The facts are as stated. But I can write about how it has affected me since then and what pike fishing means to me now.

But before I begin it is worth while looking at the part Bernard Venables played in all this. Mr Crabtree and Mr Cherry were both characters I read regularly. Both of the softback books were bought for me and I still have them today, though it was *Mr Cherry and Jim* that contained my real inspiration. The books also provided hours of frustration. Where could a young pike angler living in the Fens find all those lovely swims depicted by Venables? What chance had I of finding an undercut bank with tree roots trailing in the water? The river authority had long ago removed all the trees within 30yd of any river I could find! Yet in that book were single cartoons which did more than any words to inspire me. On page 27, Mr Cherry has hooked a very big pike. It breaks surface: 'Look Jim, at least 30lb, a fish of a lifetime.' What an inspirational picture. I am looking at it now and it still gives me a peculiar feeling. Sadly, the next picture has Mr Cherry saying 'Going for the corner under the tree – hope he hasn't got a snag there.' Then we see the pike roll over a branch, and Mr Cherry and Jim looking dejectedly at the broken line.

I was lucky, for my fish of a lifetime would have been hard pressed to find any snag in the River Thurne, being an almost still, reed-lined channel, heavily weeded in some areas and barren in others. The fish was caught from the barren area, so why was it there? Well, Thurne pike roam around a lot, tending to move out of some of the shallow broads in very cold weather, and we had had a heavy snowfall and a very cold spell that had caused the lakes to freeze. Conditions were therefore ideal a couple of weeks later when mild, westerly winds had increased the water temperature, thereby stimulating the pike to feed.

Yes, I was very lucky, having the opportunity to take time off on the right day. I'd done my homework earlier in the year and had found fish in the area. With few other people fishing the section of river I was concentrating on, I was fortunate to have these circumstances in my favour. But, above all, I was lucky to have fate on my side, because fate is about the only thing that can help catch a very big fish. Instead of catching the forty, I might well have caught a twenty-pounder. Of course, I would still have been pleased with such a fish and my good fortune would not have been tempered with the knowledge of what I had missed. We cannot see into the future. We can dream, we can hope, but short of someone else catching a fish from a swim you intended to fish, there is no reason to wonder what might have been.

Yet on that particular day, when I hooked that fish, all could have been so different. The hooks fell out in the net. What if the pike had shed the hooks earlier? Certainly I would never have known it was a forty-pounder, simply because, on hooking it, the fish gave no impression of being that big. Even on the bank, the exact magnitude of the fish was not clear. After all, one does not expect to catch a 40lb pike! Once weighed, photographed and returned, the excitement washed over me. Unfortunately, I am not a romantic person, so perhaps something of the moment was wasted on me. My mind was racing with practical matters, like releasing the news on my own terms. Breathing space was also needed to exploit the river further. In those days I definitely had the 'killer instinct', something one

must have to be successful in modern pike fishing. My recent efforts have been restrained compared with those of the mid-1980s!

How then did the capture of this fish change my own attitudes? Well, to catch a 40lb pike is a rare occurrence, even today when there are more about. Of course, I had always wanted a big pike, 35lb-plus being about right. There was something about catching a fish big enough to be included in Fred Buller's *Domesday Book of Mammoth Pike* (Stanley Paul, 1979). What it did for me was to remove some of the intensity with which I relentlessly pursued pike. After all, what more could there be if very big fish were the target? To catch a bigger pike is not a realistic proposition. Fortunately, my love of pike fishing goes beyond catching the biggest fish, with new targets to strive for constantly. At the time of writing I have caught 228 pike·over 20lb. What is wrong with aiming to catch 250 or even 300? Certainly it is something to try for, even though any sane person will tell you that on a cosmic scale, the number of pike over 20lb anyone has caught is about as important as the number of grains of sand in a sandwich on Hunstanton Beach!

So where am I now? Of course, nothing can ever take that fish away. It is an historical fact. It will always be the first well-authenticated forty-pounder since the Hancock fish. I will never have to 'try' to catch a 40lb pike, though there is a lot to be said for living in hope. Many anglers hope for such a fish. I am in the enviable position (if I feel like it) of being able to hope for another like it. It is a nice situation to be in because you cannot lose! Those who try too hard and then get upset or even obsessed about catching big fish really should stand back and think about where they are going.

My only regret is that things are different now. When I was five I remember walking with my mother alongside a small dyke which was bordered by a vast field of daffodils. The atmosphere of that day can never be recaptured; one cannot go back and relive it. The same applies to those days on the Thurne. Today there are many other anglers fishing there and this is inevitable. Just as I increased the fishing pressure on the area, others who have followed have done the same. I have fished the same spot since, but that something special cannot be re-created. So one moves on, not with regret but thanking God for being so lucky at having been given that one chance of something very special – something even more special than any fish Mr Cherry and Jim caught!

As if by Magic
~
Peter Garvan

I t is inevitable that certain days spent by a favourite venue which result in the capture of something special remain strongly embedded in one's memory. Here is my account of one such day.

The knowledge gained from previous seasons spent at Furnace Pond was beginning to pay dividends, in that a pattern of fish movement had become apparent, and when the weather conditions were right I began to know roughly where the perch shoals would be. I was only prepared to fish from the available boat as the lake, being almost completely surrounded by trees, made long-distance casting from the bank very difficult, and the perch definitely preferred to stay well out from the margins. In the early days the opposite situation had been the case, but as angling pressure had increased, so they had moved out to safer pastures. The boat also made searching them out far easier.

Most of October and the early days of November had been quite calm with little wind, although what there was blew in the wrong direction. Despite several sessions at the lake, either the fish were not feeding or they were proving very difficult to locate. The pike, however, had kept me occupied and were very obliging, especially during October, so my trips had not been a complete loss. I had been studying the long-range weather forecasts and one day noticed that a pronounced area of low pressure had moved in, with accompanying moderate south-westerly winds. These were perfect conditions, so I immediately arranged to take time off work to be at the lake.

I arrived early on the Wednesday morning to be greeted by the sound of leaves rustling in the wind, something that boosted my confidence no end. Picking up the oars of the boat, I walked down to the bottom of the bailiff's garden where the craft was moored and looked out on to the lake. Even in the early morning light a heavy ripple was clearly visible heading towards the dam end, and I couldn't wait to get started. The beauty of the fishing also lay in the easy availability of sufficient livebaits for a day spent seeking perch or pike, as the lake absolutely swarmed with small roach, rudd and (my particular favourite) gudgeon. My perch rods were still set up from the last trip, so I removed the rubber bands quickly and reassembled them in the darkness. As per usual, I intended to fish a free-roving drift rig with greased line on one rod, and a fixed paternoster rig with a small surface float on the other.

In the past I had become aware that the area immediately in front of the bailiff's garden was regarded by the perch as relatively safe because of the lack of bankside disturbance. It was also an excellent spot for catching gudgeon. So it was here, just as it was light enough to see, that I set up my float rod, cast out, and fired a few attractor maggots around the float. Immediately, I caught a small roach and decided to present it on the paternoster rod, which was already set at the exact depth of 9ft. Casting it beside the spot where I was bait fishing, I relaxed in the knowledge that, with a livebait out, my day had really started. For about half an hour I caught bait fish steadily, including a number of perfectly sized gudgeon.

Just as I was preparing myself to load up the boat, the bung on my paternoster rod disappeared. I was soon playing a nice perch which turned out to weigh 2lb 11oz – a good start to the day. I decided to stay put in case a shoal was present, and, sure enough, on the next cast another fish of 2lb 8oz quickly snaffled a gudgeon. Then everything went quiet.

At about 9 a.m. I launched the boat and made my way about a hundred yards up the lake to anchor at a spot where I knew the wind direction would help me drift baits back to the dam, and where the depth steadied at 9–11ft. I fished for an hour or so, but began to sense that I was not far enough up the lake towards the shallows; my earlier captures were obviously confusing me. I moved again to a position approximately half-way up the lake, and as soon as I dropped anchor I felt confident. Resetting the rods for the depth of 7ft, I cast out a gudgeon on the paternoster rod about 25yd to the side of the boat and placed a small roach to drift down with the wind on the roving outfit. Only then did I notice that I had the lake entirely to myself, a factor that contributed immensely to the feeling of

tranquillity as I sipped a cup of steaming coffee.

I began to day-dream, and became mesmerized as I sat watching the bungs bobbing in the waves and the water birds going about their daily chores. Suddenly, the drifted bung was gone and I sprang back to life. I wound down furiously to recover the loop of greased line and felt a good fish lunge as I bent into it. It tore off, pulling out line. I was impressed! Steadily, I gained line, and the heaviness of the lunges reduced until my unseen quarry caught sight of the landing net and shot under the boat, taking me completely by surprise. Fortunately, increased pressure turned the fish back quickly, so the danger of it finding either of the anchor ropes was soon over. As the swirls on the surface became more noticeable, so did an enormous perch, and I was physically shaking with anticipation and shouting for joy as it slipped into the folds of the landing net. Complete pandemonium then followed as I panicked in an effort to find my scales and sling, both hidden somewhere in the boat after my earlier successes that morning. Eventually I found them, together with the large cushion covered in heavy-duty plastic which I used at that time as an unhooking mat.

The hook was perfectly placed in the scissors and fell out with ease. 'Yes!' I exclaimed, as the scales needled past the 4lb mark, finally settling at a weight of 4lb 6oz once I had stopped shaking. I sacked the fish quickly, which was quite unusual for me, but I knew that the action was not over and that moving the boat would certainly disturb any other feeding perch. I felt my actions were fully justified when, as soon as my drift float was recast, it slid from view. At first I was not sure if this was simply the result of a particularly lively bait, but I soon realized that it was a proper take when I wound down into yet another fish. A short fight revealed a perch of 2lb 5oz.

On recasting the float, it disappeared yet again in a matter of seconds. This was getting silly! Unfortunately, I missed the run and only felt the fish slightly when I tightened down to strike. Not surprisingly, the activity then died off for a while . . .

I had just finished another cup of coffee when the paternoster float rattled again, bobbed twice and quickly disappeared from view. Again, on winding down, I felt nothing, even though the bait showed clear signs of a perch attack. I cast a fresh bait further out than previously but still along the same line, and slowly retrieved into an identical position. Immediately, it was taken viciously, but this time my strike met with solid head-shaking resistance and I was forced to back-wind quickly a number of times. It's funny, but although I knew this was a good fish, I didn't panic at all and played the perch calmly into the net, despite it being huge – 4lb 7oz to be exact. I was, by then, *very* impressed!

Sacking this fish, I cast out again and sat back wondering what the devil was happening. Why were the fish feeding so ravenously? Why today? Why me? After another cup of coffee I tidied up the mess in the boat as it looked as if a bomb had hit it. I was still alone and beginning to wonder how I was going to get some decent photographs (the self-timing routine is a particular hatred of mine) when the paternoster float sailed across the surface and disappeared. 'What, again!' I remember exclaiming, as I picked up the rod. A short fight revealed another perch weighing 2lb 14oz. Then, as if by magic, the action ceased.

From time to time I checked that the perch in the sacks were all right, and after a couple of inactive hours decided that photographs were the order of the day. Rowing slowly back to the mooring point, I unloaded the boat and was getting my cameras ready when I heard distant voices. Eventually, two anglers appeared and I asked whether they had ever taken any photographs on an SLR camera. Fortunately, one of them had, so I showed them both how to focus the cameras and checked that they understood. I have to say that although I was very concerned at the time, the outcome of the photographs was much better than I expected. When I look at those photographs today, all the memories of that special day just come flooding back – thanks lads!

The Best-Laid Plans . . .

~

Jim Gibbinson

S o as not to disappoint you later, I shall reveal at the outset that the carp
that forms the climax to my red letter day weighed just 19lb. I have often
claimed that neither merit nor enjoyment can be measured in pounds and
ounces, so despite having caught very many much bigger carp, and occasionally
taken some prodigious catches, I none the less selected this particular capture as
being one of my most memorable. To understand why, you need to know the full
story.

It started, indirectly, on a French trip when I got chatting to a local carp angler
named Stéphane. He told me of a water that held a lot of carp of good average
size. Indeed, the previous November he had taken seven twenties in a day. It held
some big fish too, his heaviest being one of 34lb. Stéphane spoke no English, so I
was forced to resort to my somewhat ragged French.

'Is it hard fished?'

'Only by local zander and bream anglers,' he replied.

It sounded too good to be true!

'Have any English carp anglers been there?' I asked.

'No, they don't know about it.'

Better and yet better still!

I pushed my French to its limits and discovered that it was a very large, shallow lake with a good car access and, as with most French waters, could be fished on the readily obtainable département ticket. Stéphane had made his best catches in the late October/early November period and, as a teacher, I get a half-term holiday then – to fail to take advantage of such a fortuitous coincidence would surely be bucking fate! So within a week of my return to England, Geordie Mike, brother Rick and I had booked our ferry and a gîte about five miles from the lake.

Our first day's recce and the acquisition of permits passed without mishap. It was a lovely looking water too. 'I'm going to enjoy fishing here,' I said.

The others agreed.

We put a few pounds of bait out, 'just to give them a taste', and sat and watched the water for a while. Stéphane had told me that the lake's carp jumped freely, so we thought it a little strange that we saw none, but we put it down to the cold north-easterlies and overnight frosts that had preceded our trip.

So far, so good, but the events that followed took a bizarre, not to say surreal turn.

The following morning, in the half-light of dawn, while we unpacked our gear in our chosen pitches – about 80yd apart on a long beach-like stretch of bank – I noticed Rick talking to a couple of local perch anglers. He looked up and called me over. His residual school French was not up to understanding exactly what they were saying, but he was getting some distinctly negative vibes and wanted a second opinion. I found the local dialect extremely difficult to comprehend, but the underlying message was clear enough. The carp had gone! Gradually, as my ear tuned in, I pieced together the full story which, in summary, was that the previous winter the water had been drained for dam-maintenance and general cleaning.

We thanked our doom-messengers for the information, and collectively wished a plague of carbon-fibre weevils down on Stéphane's rods! I also roundly cursed myself for not writing to the local mayor and double-checking that all was in order. But we consoled ourselves with the thought that we had at least found out at the beginning of the week.

Obviously we had to resort to Plan B.

Unfortunately, we didn't have a Plan B!

So out came the maps. The doom-messengers had suggested another water to us which we found on the map. It was about 20 miles away and, judging from the large amount of blue shading, it was pretty big. A bit further afield was a slightly smaller lake, one that had been mentioned to me a year or two previously by another French angler. So all was not lost.

We packed away our sodden gear . . . oh, I didn't mention the rain did I? Nor the wind. Well, to describe the deluge we suffered as mere 'rain' and the would-be

tornado as 'wind' does not quite do the conditions justice. The weather was such that were I back home in England I would not have gone fishing.

After parking the cars at the nearest of our alternative venues, we set off across country in the general direction of where we assumed the water to be. Eventually, after a considerable trek that made us decide that it was much too far to walk with all our gear, we found it. There was a lane right alongside, with a couple of cars parked there! We could have driven to the wretched place! An hour later we were back with our cars.

We approached the lake from the dam end, and paused to look at the long, serpentine expanse of water before parking and descending the steep bank. A carp jumped not 50yd from where we stood. It was not a big carp, in fact it was a very small carp, but at that stage in the proceedings we were prepared to see it as a good omen.

Tackling up was difficult in the wind, and footholds were precarious as the steep clay bank was slippery. As is the way with clay, it soon formed great, clinging, leaden weights on our boots.

It didn't take me long to realize that I didn't like the place.

Mike's rod-pod blew over, his brolly blew inside out, and the foot-rest of his bed-chair bent as Rick sat on it.

He didn't like the place either.

Rick, having shared Mike's swim, was in possession of an intact bed-chair (he didn't use it) and an undamaged brolly (he didn't put it up), so he was quite happy to stay there.

Mike and I overruled him.

By this stage the wind and rain had reached epic proportions, but our minds were diverted from the weather by the lung-bursting, hernia-inducing climb to the muddy lane where our cars were parked. We disconsolately loaded the saturated, clay-caked gear, and slid and slithered our way down the track that led to the main road.

'Mind that tree,' said Rick.

As advice goes, it was a touch on the obvious side. I acknowledged that I do not share Rick's undoubted advantage of having had advanced police-driver training, but when a near full-grown poplar falls directly across your path, you tend to notice don't you?

We heaved the tree out of the way and set off for our third water.

The new lake was very attractive. An angler was fishing. He was using three rods, the middle of which was on a bite-alarm (rendered rainproof by an inverted plastic half-bottle used umbrella-style). An actual carp angler! He was local, and told us he'd caught a 22-pounder earlier in the day. There was no sign of a sack anywhere, so I asked him if he had returned it. 'Oh yes,' he said, 'I fish just for the sport.' He then explained that he was one of the new-wave French anglers who return their catches.

It was late afternoon by then, but we figured that we may as well put out the rods for an hour or two. Just before dusk, as I talked to our new-found companion, I heard one of his non-bite-alarmed baitrunners clicking away. The subsequent playing lacked subtlety, and I soon netted a low-double mirror for him. On unhooking it, he started to wrap it in a sheet of polythene . . . 'What are you doing?' I asked, fearing the worst.

'Taking it home to photograph it,' he replied.

'I have a camera,' I offered.

'I want to weigh it as well,' he said.

'I can weigh it for you too,' I added, becoming increasingly aware that this poor carp was destined to end up in his freezer.

He then lapsed into semi-silence before pointing out, less than convincingly and not entirely relevantly, that carp can live for six hours when wrapped in polythene. As he departed, I shrugged to Rick and Mike and said resignedly, 'What the hell can we do? He's fully entitled to take the fish away.' But at least we had found some carp.

The following day we squelched our way along the muddy lakeside track towards the area we'd fished the previous evening. Well, almost. In actual fact, Mike's rod-pod straddled the bankstick holes left by the French angler of the previous day! Rick and I decided to pioneer some new swims – like about 30yd either side of Mike's pitch! We blanked. But the sun came out and we got the gear dry. Until late afternoon anyway, when the rain returned and everything got soaked once more!

I was restless. Clearly the water held carp – we even saw a couple jump – but I had a niggling feeling at the back of my mind about another lake, one that Mike and I had fished on a previous trip and which had produced some good fish. It was some 40–50 miles away, further than we really wanted to travel on a daily basis, but I reckoned our best chance of doing a salvage job was to spend the rest of our time there.

Mike agreed readily. He was as anxious as I for a return trip. Rick wasn't totally convinced, but agreed when we assured him he would love the lake when he saw it.

The next day, at dawn, we were in our chosen swims beside the new water. Mike was in the middle, and Rick and I were to his left and right respectively.

In the early afternoon I heard an alarm. It was Rick's. A low-double common came to net. This resulted in smiles all round. 'We've found them,' we thought, 'and they're on the bait.' But we hadn't and they weren't. Not that day anyway. Nor the next. Spirits sank once again. You know that feeling you sometimes get, that your alarms are *never* going to sound again? That's how I felt. I think the others did too.

The next day, when my alarm did sound, it took me by surprise. This was partly because the noise was so unfamiliar that I didn't recognize it, but also because the three of us were at that moment engaged in a throwing-stick (me) and a catapult (them) boilie-firing distance contest. The throwing-stick won, by the way.

The carp, as already stated, weighed 19lb. A beautiful, unmarked common. I laid it on the soft grass, fell on my knees with sheer relief and said, 'Never, but never have I been more pleased to see a carp on the bank.' And that was my one and only opportunity. We had one full day left, which Mike made his own by catching three – up to about 13lb if I remember correctly.

So, three experienced carp anglers spent a week in France for just five modest fish. Was the trip therefore a failure? In pure carp-fishing terms I suppose it was, but against all the odds we laughed a lot, enjoyed each other's company and had a great time. And I suspect I'll remember my nineteen-pounder long after the details of many seemingly more notable fish have become hazy with time. Which, by any standards, makes it a very special fish.

Unfinished Business
~
Stephen Harper

The summer had been extremely wet; not a real summer at all. The skies
had remained overcast for weeks, heavy grey-black storm clouds blotting
out the sun from horizon to horizon. From 16 June almost until the end
of July hardly a day had passed without rain, most of it torrential. The River
Wensum had swollen and burst its banks on numerous occasions, flooding the
valley and the Low Road, and diverting frustrated motorists through the villages.
Meadows had turned into lakes and mill-streams into raging torrents, and fry
invaded the fields that the livestock had recently evacuated. Most sensible anglers
retreated to the still waters where water-levels were very high but at least fishing
was still a practical proposition.

As far as I was concerned, conditions had never been so favourable! After each
flood, as the river fined down and almost returned to within its banks, the barbel
fed with abandon. The meadows were still awash and fishing was often wet,
uncomfortable and awkward, but usually it was also most rewarding.

In such conditions, success had been sweet; a run of large barbel had fallen, culminating in a fish only an ounce short of 12lb. And yet I was elated and miserable at the same time. I had caught that fish but I had no photograph to remind me of it. In some respects angling is a strange pastime that can play havoc with our frail human emotions. What other sport could lift the heart to such heady heights, only to dash it unmercifully back to earth almost in the same instant?

Obviously, the capture of such an impressive fish is all-important and a photograph is secondary, but such an event should have no detractions; mishaps with cameras just should not happen after such effort has been expended in the darkness. Torch, tripod, flash gun, bulb release; all for nothing. It seemed my red letter day had faded to a dull, brownish-pink.

In the past, I had often scorned the all-too-familiar reports in the angling press of giant fish that, for some obscure reason, had managed to elude photography: 'The photographs didn't come out'; 'A dog ran off with my camera'; 'Dropped the camera in the lake'; 'Left my camera at home'. The excuses were legion and none, to me, convincing, until I found myself using one such 'excuse'.

I had caught the fish and weighed it. I had a camera with me, had loaded a new roll of film for just such an eventuality, and prided myself on the fact that I could take a good photograph in the dark using a tripod, flash and bulb release. I had done so on many occasions before. But previously the film in the camera had always wound on. This time it did not.

And so I returned to the river after my 'disastrous' success with a vain hope that I might recapture the huge barbel that had been so camera-shy. We had some unfinished business to attend to. It would have to be a memorable session indeed that could wipe away the irritation of my photographic mishap and replace it with an elation untinged with detractions of any kind, photographic or otherwise.

The weather continued its angry onslaught, saturating the greens and greys of a dull, water-laden landscape. It was heavily overcast, windy and decidedly cool for late July, so I had wrapped up warm against the elements and almost resorted to using the umbrella. The previous day's heavy rain had once again topped up the river, adding to its colour. I flicked out ten large pouches of hemp with a catapult, well upstream so that the seeds would reach the bottom where I wanted them. Barbel, I hoped, were already in the swim, so I decided not to chance scaring them away with a bait-dropper.

Twenty-five to thirty hookbait samples soon followed the hemp. I cast the light link-ledger into the wind, straightened the line and set the rod in its rests. A monkey-climber acted as indicator (along with the rod top) between butt and second rings, the rod pointing directly at the bait.

An early start did me little good as the evening ticked slowly by, growing dark in the overcast conditions. I had to wait for almost three hours, the flask long since empty, before any sign of life showed on the indicators. My optimistic assumption of the barbel's presence had probably been wrong all along.

At around 10 p.m. I put more bait into the swim. This triggered an immediate

JOHN SEARL.

response. A sharp tap on the rod tip had also moved the monkey-climber and I both felt and saw this as the bright green of the isotope jerked across the darkness. No gust of wind or pull of weed could have manufactured such a short, sharp tug. The fish were there, even if they hadn't been until then, and I found myself leaning forward in the low chair, keyed up and expecting action, straining to see and feel the slightest sign of movement.

After fifteen minutes or so of inactivity, I had just begun to relax once again and the bite, when it came, took me by complete surprise. The green glow of the indicator below the rod simply disappeared, it moved so fast. There had been no tell-tale preliminary plucks or knocks. The 'humdinger' had come completely out of the blue. I lunged awkwardly with the rod, but missed it completely. There was no reassuring and comforting contact as my ledger ploughed its way deep into the reeds at my left.

At 11 p.m. my rod tip received another pull, half-hearted this time, and I thought that a chub might have begun to worry the bait or that a fish had merely brushed the line. I was determined not to miss the next 'real' bite and ten minutes later my determination was rewarded. The indicator had moved fast, not as fast as the 'rocket-wrencher' that I had somehow managed to miss earlier, but it was one of those bites that you just know you cannot miss.

In the pitch darkness the fish fought erratically as it charged first upstream and then abruptly downstream. I regained line, bringing the fish much nearer, and after a brief and closely fought duel it was almost directly beneath my rod tip. The fish then shot back upstream at an incredible rate of knots and I knew I would have to let it go.

It was a wonderful battle as I stood alone in the dark, the wind whistling against a taut line, an angry barbel trying its best to snag my line around any and every underwater obstacle – possibly one of the best fights I have encountered with a Wensum barbel. Even as the fish eventually approached my net, it once again charged off, taking me completely by surprise. At 10lb 1oz it was a beautiful fish, with a very distinguishable, tri-pointed tail fin that would be difficult to forget.

After such an impressive battle, I was not surprised that the swim had died. At midnight, with no further indications on rod tip or monkey-climber, not even a tremble, I decided to give it another half an hour and then call it a day. It had been a memorable session in any event. My pitch was tidied, my haversack packed, and it only remained for me to reel in, take down the landing net and bait the swim for the next session. But, with only a few minutes to go, one particular barbel had other ideas . . .

At 12.20 a.m. the unexpected happened: a cracker of a bite! As I struggled to my feet, the solid pressure against the rod tip began to slacken gradually. I reeled in as fast as I could, realizing that the fish was running towards me, upstream. As it passed me, I made contact once again and the fireworks began. This express train continued on its upstream course so fast and for so long that I thought it would never stop.

I experienced a feeling of *déjà vu* as I played this fish, the fight being so similar to that of the 11lb 15oz fish, and it seemed a very long while in the darkness before I began to regain much line. It was obviously another exceptional fish, but I dared not hope for a repeat capture of the '11-15'; it would be too much to hope for.

Repeat captures are usually an angling occurrence that I do not enjoy and do my best to avoid. This instance was an exception. Once in the net, I noticed the large tail and hefty girth, but it was the split dorsal that gave the game away in the dim torchlight. It *was* the '11-15' again . . . this time weighing 3oz less.

Two double-figure barbel in a session, with nothing to detract from their captures, really was a red letter day – especially with photographic evidence this time to remind me forever of such a memorable evening.

A Lesson Learned
~
Shaun Harrison

I
t was 6 September 1987, a date that still brings a warm glow deep inside, and
the end of a long, hard struggle that I wouldn't have changed for anything.

Saturday evening, 6 p.m. After yet another hectic day in the tackle shop I
was finally free to hit the motorway for the umpteenth time that season. Once
again my destination (as it had been four evenings a week for two seasons) was the
middle lake in the grounds of Claydon House. With two feet on the accelerator
the old van ate up the 80-odd miles to the lake, and very soon I was at the lay-by
used as a car-park and sleeping area by myself and countless other catfish anglers
down the years.

There was no time to waste, for I had only half an hour left in which to fish
before I had to be out of the grounds of the house. Past experience had taught me
time and time again that it was well worth casting in for the last five minutes, let
alone half an hour. Often I would roll up, run across the field with a couple of
rods, bait, camera, scales and weigh-sling, and promptly catch a catfish within

seconds of casting out. I know of no easier way of infuriating people! On this occasion, however, the joke was on me. I had a run but promptly missed it. Still, there were always the joys of the Crown Inn to look forward to . . .

With night fishing prohibited at Claydon, no one is allowed to remain in the grounds one hour after sunset and so, at 'last knockings', as they are affectionately known, plans must be made for the evening ahead. Because of the distance, returning home was a little impractical for me and, as always, I travelled to the Crown at Steeple Claydon for a few drinks and a little supper.

This particular week I was in good company, as Martin Brent, Gordon Cross and the two Munns brothers, Alan and Keith, all turned up for a 'quiet' drink – which somehow stretched out a little longer than usual. Eventually, back at the car-park we crawled into our sleeping bags to await the dawn. All too soon the alarm clock signalled that it was time to creep out of the warmth and face the dawn chill. I gathered my gear together whilst listening to the delightful sounds of the early morning smokers, coughing and spluttering themselves back into life. And then I was off, leading the march across the field to my chosen pitch for the day on the House bank, two swims up from the bushes.

When my rucksack, bed and freezer bag were off my back, I went through the usual rituals of setting up. Two carp-and-bream-proof mackerel heads were quickly cast out and soon I was back in the warmth of my sleeping bag in an attempt to finish my interrupted sleep. (Having twice dozed off at the steering wheel on the motorway, I now make sure I get a *proper* kip on the bank.) Some time later I awoke to the sound of rain gently drumming on the roof of my umbrella. A communal breakfast was out of the question that day, so I had to satisfy myself with my own food and drink. Two eggs placed in the kettle whilst I boiled the water for my first cuppa of the day killed two birds with one stone.

Nine o'clock came and, with fish-catching prospects looking rather grim to say the least, I took my cup for a walkabout. The drizzle appeared to be set in for the day and the water temperature was at an all-time low. After consuming several cups of various brews I returned to my pitch to watch the bleak, deserted-looking water for any tell-tale signs of catfish. Soon I had the drinking team from the previous night sitting around my umbrella. Nobody seemed at all confident. Certainly I didn't fancy my chances as I wasn't even getting the usual frustrating pulls and plucks on the bobbins from the abundant carp and bream, my baits having been replaced with smaller, softer morsels now that I'd had enough sleep.

With the kettle constantly on the go, the talk drifted to other activities that had taken place at the venue during these 'scratching' times. They had always been memorable occasions, particularly the games of baseball using a polystyrene ball with Vic Gilling's billiard cue as an argument settler! And then there were the races to the house and back, not to mention the many more obscure diversions. Catfishing at Claydon is very much a waiting game, with most days spent knowing only too well that the chance of a fish will not arrive until that last half-hour allowed on the bank. This seemed to be one of those days, and when the idea of

holding our own Claydon Olympics was suggested, everyone seemed to jump at the chance of a break from watching the motionless indicators.

Event number one was the welly throwing competition. I'm not sure who donated the welly, but we all took it in turns to hurl it as far as we could into the field. All went well until the aforementioned item of footwear split in half, thus bringing the game to an abrupt halt. Next came 'Claydon's Strongest Man', which involved holding a full freezer box out at arm's length. Plenty of mind-over-matter stuff this. And so it went on until we broke off for lunch and settled down to a little more serious fishing for the remainder of the day.

After my boil-in-the-bag meal I set my mind to work. All round the lake nothing stirred, and by mid-afternoon every single spot was occupied. Even the carp anglers were twiddling their thumbs, and to make matters worse the wind was starting to freshen. I wound a bait in, not really sure what to do. Looking at the rig took about three seconds – one Drennan ring plus a 6ft soft-braided hooklink ending in a size 4 hook. Nothing revolutionary, but it had been enough to put twice as many catfish on the bank for me that season than anyone else. I felt that it would be a waste of time offering yet another 2–4in bait, and instead decided to use something small, about the size of my thumbnail. Might as well tempt a carp, if only to brighten the day. Setting up a rig with a small lead on a running paternoster to a size 8 hook, I carefully inserted a piece from the inside of a filleted mackerel. After a gentle lob out into the lake the trap was set.

With the kettle boiling, my pitch was soon full of anglers once more. We were sitting there putting the world to rights (yet again) when for some inexplicable reason I stood up and said: 'I'm going to catch one'. Now I don't normally subscribe to premonitions or other such mumbo-jumbo, but as I was putting my waterproof gear on two sharp bleeps came from the right-hand rod – the one I had retackled. I shot out from the shelter into the rain, my hand poised over the rod. There was another bleep and the bobbin started making its way slowly upwards. I struck hard and then cursed, thinking I had missed it, when suddenly, after winding, the tip pulled over. Whatever had picked up the bait had obviously run straight towards me.

There was no doubt in my mind that this was a catfish as the rod wrenched around with the fish taking line, making for the far bank. Then, with the line steadily ticking off the reel, what was obviously a big fish chugged along the far margin, leaving huge, black mud-clouds as it went. It passed six swims before stopping. Normally I would follow a fish wherever possible to avoid picking up other anglers' line. This time, however, I decided to stand my ground and play it from my pitch. Ostrich-fashion, the fish tried to bury its head in the mud, treating us to the spectacle of an impressive tail waving out of the water. I kept the rod well bent until my opponent got fed up and took off again, leaving me helpless to do anything about stopping its surges of power as the fight dragged on. By then I had eight anglers standing around me waiting for a glimpse of what I had hooked, and I jokingly remarked that it was probably a 'kitten' foul-hooked. At last, the fish was within 30ft of the bank in only 2ft of water, but I simply couldn't raise it enough for a proper look. There were great patches of mud rising to the surface as the fish tried hard to bury itself in the thick silt.

I distinctly remember standing there feeling utterly useless with my 11lb line and fully bent 2lb test-curve rod. Three different conversations were going on behind me, all completely irrelevant to the fishing or the situation I was in, when, suddenly, a great frog-like head broke the water, followed by a long, sinuous body writhing on the surface. There was immediate silence.

This was it. This was the one I had been after. I asked Brian Smalley to take the net. My heart was pounding as I coaxed the fish towards the net inch by inch, hardly daring to look at the tiny hook clearly visible in the corner of its mouth. 'Please don't come out,' I kept muttering to myself. Its head reached the drawcord. 'Nearly mine,' I thought, even though its tail was still hooked firmly in the mud. Eventually, its great jaws were at the spreader block. 'Now, Brian!' Expertly, he plunged the net at the monstrous creature in an attempt to gather the remaining two-thirds of its bulk, but the fish wouldn't fold. He scooped again, managing to get a little more of it in. Finally, at the third attempt, its colossal frame lay captured in the net. Then, without warning, it rose on its tail in the shallow water and was half out again. Brian made a couple of frantic scoops and at long last it was safely engulfed in the bottom of the mesh. There was a big cheer from behind, the first sound to come from the audience since the fish had lifted its head from the water.

Brian carried the beast in the net, gently laying it down on the soft, wet grass. Taking hold of the fish behind the pectorals, I slid it out of the net. It looked magnificent. I tried to keep calm and composed – stiff upper lip and all that – but I don't think I succeeded. With the hook removed and the fish held in the enormous Nash weigh-sling (it didn't look quite so ridiculous with the fish's tail hanging out of its end), the Avon scales bottomed out as the fish was lifted.

The fish was put back into the water for a breather as I started off alone for the larger set of scales. I was on cloud nine as I drifted back to the van. Soon I returned, trying to calm down from a serious state of euphoria. The scales read a fraction under 35lb before a vast audience, and I settled for 34lb 12oz – at that time the largest catfish caught *intentionally* in Britain.

I carried my fish carefully back to the water and released it to fight another day. And fight another day it certainly did, for in the intervening years this fish has been recaptured several times at a heavier weight. A lesson to be learned by all.

One of Those Days
~
Len Head

I
t was just one of those days. As far as I can recall no black cats had crossed my patch, I'd seen no magpies, touched no wood nor had I thrown any salt. So I don't know why it was that on this day lady luck wore a great big smile.

The silly thing was that I almost didn't bother to go. The weatherman had said 'cold with north-easterly winds', usually the kiss of death on the big expanse of exposed water I planned to fish. But something, intuition perhaps, got me out of bed on that bleak February morning at the first bleep of the alarm; something of an achievement in itself these days.

You will have noticed the bit about 'intuition'. Sounds good, doesn't it? Makes you think that here is an angler possessed with great foresight and watercraft. But it's no good, I have to come clean. Intuition really didn't come into the matter; my sharp exit from the warm bed was due not to angling foresight but to the simple fact that the last two pike sessions on this water had yielded thirteen doubles and a couple of twenties. Forget intuition – I wanted more!

As I say, it was one of those days. I even arrived at the lake at first light to find almost perfect conditions: a grey sky, but with the high, full-cover cloud that I love for winter piking. Temperatures were cool, but it was early and the sky promised a rise as the morning progressed. And the wind was not a north-easterly as the forecast had said, but a gentle westerly that put a light ripple on the water.

The rods were ready rigged, held together with elastic bands, and within fifteen minutes I'd got two baits out, one on a sunk-float paternoster, the other on a straight link-ledger rig. Within twenty minutes I had my first take! One of the things I love about piking is the drop-off bite indicator; well, sort of dropping off! The sight of the line pulling free and the polystyrene ball falling, giving an audible 'click' as it hits the back rod rest, gives me almost as big a kick as do the pike themselves.

The pike on the end felt respectable and duly turned out to weight 12lb 6oz. It was a pleasing start that rekindled thoughts of the last session, a nerve-jangling experience when a pike only 2oz lighter was 'taken' as I was playing it. Something had grabbed this pike and had forced me to back-wind some 50yd of line as it ponderously made off with its outsize meal. Obviously, that fish could not actually have been hooked, so I ever so gingerly pumped it back until, 10yd out, the line began to rise in the water as the fish headed for the surface. Alas, just before it got there it let go with an almighty swirl, and I could do no more than gape in awe at the 6ft-long vortex it made as I wound in a very mangled 12lb 4oz pike.

But I digress. After catching the 12lb 6oz fish I recast to the same holding area, and was just putting the rod on the rests when the indicator on the ledger rod dropped and 12in of line slipped quickly out – then stopped. I decided to leave it – perhaps whatever was responsible might come back.

All was quiet for half an hour or so, when a single bleep from an Optonic caught my attention, and I looked up to see the indicator on the paternoster rod fidget, tighten slowly up to the reel and then relax to its former position, thereby causing a further bleep. Pike can be incredibly delicate feeders. Often you can pick up the rod after such an indication and, by putting a little tension in the tip, 'feel' for the presence of a fish at the bait. So I did, and feeling a 'tug-tap' at the business end, wound down hard and pulled into an obviously good fish.

With sunken tree stumps and other dangerous snags all around, there was no time for pussy-footing with this pike. I leaned hard into it, at the same time walking backwards a few steps – a tactic which forces the pike higher in the water – away from the stumps. These big-water fish are in superb condition, but it was February and, in my experience, stillwater pike rarely scrap well at this time. Generally, the fight consists of a heavy, sullen resistance with the occasional heart-stopping run which slams the rod down and rips line from the reel, for no fish accelerates at such incredible speed over short distances as pike – winter or summer.

This particular pike gave me several such demonstrations, skinning my knuckles on one run when the sheer power forced me to let go of the reel handle, this then spinning out of control. Soon, however, the sunk float came into view as the fish

allowed itself to be pumped into the margin. A large flash of mottled green and primrose appeared as the well-bent rod brought the fish slowly to the surface and eventually into the big net.

With the hooks out, I parted the folds of the net in order to get an eyeful of what can only be described as a pike in magnificent condition – not a fin or scale was out of place. On the scales the fish pulled 26lb 8oz, definitely worthy of some photographs, so it went into the sack pending collection of my camera from the car.

In the process of sorting out the swim, I noticed that the indicator on the other rod had dropped once again, and upon investigating I found that some 18in of line had been taken, revealing another short but dropped take. So, having recast the first rod, I decided to retrieve the tackle to inspect the rig and bait, such dropped takes being unusual on this (as yet) unpressured water. A look at the 6in roach told the whole story. It had been descaled on both flanks from a point just forward of the dorsal down to the tail root, revealing that it had been taken and rejected, probably when the steel of the second treble, nicked into the root of the leading dorsal, had been felt. The clues hollered one thing – perch – I'd seen it before.

Being a great perch fan, I needed no persuasion to change to a free-running Dyson paternoster rig to see if I could tempt the culprit again or at least one like it. Perch and wire traces are bad news, but even worse is to be bitten off by a pike through using monofil or Dacron hooklinks. I compromised as best I could, substituting the 20lb wire trace for 10lb, and the two treble hooks for just one size 10, two points debarbed, the other to lip-hook a fresh roach which was recast to the same area.

I had almost tempted a semi-tame chaffinch to take a piece of tuna-fish sandwich from the toe of my boot, when my carefully presented perch bait was snaffled by a pike weighing about 9lb. Not long after recasting, away went the same rod to a really fast take, the line simply hissing from the open spool. I hit it after some 20yd of line had been taken, my brain telling me that this was my perch as such furious takes are rare with the pike.

The rod stopped half-way over my shoulder with a thud as I heaved into the take. This was no perch (or if it was, I wanted it!), and after the fairly predictable sullen scrap, during which I expected the one small treble to pull free at any second, I netted another lump of a pike which turned the scales at 24lb 10oz. It was most certainly one of those days!

By this time it was close to midday, so I wound in the other rod whilst I fetched the camera for a few pictures of the best brace of pike I had caught in many a year. That done, both rods were recast with fresh baits and indicators set to a nicety. These then stayed motionless for the next two-and-a-half hours.

The chaffinch had gobbled up the best part of a whole sandwich, and I was amusing myself (and evidently it) by chucking it bits of rich digestive, when the Optonic connected to the perch rig burst into tune and the line simultaneously pulled out of the indicator clip, this dropping with a satisfying 'bonk' on to the rest. Line was disappearing steadily when I whacked it, this time expecting the heavy resistance of another pike. But no! The fish felt different, by no means heavy, and with a 'thump-jag' fight that betrayed it as a perch long before I saw it.

And that, of course, was exactly what it was, a beautiful, great, prickly specimen, with the hook holding tenuously just inside its top lip. It pulled the needle to 3lb 15oz and put the finishing touch to what, I keep saying, was just one of those days!

Less Than an Hour
~
Dave Howes

F rosts all week meant that things didn't look too good for the coming weekend. I didn't really need the Friday night weatherman to tell me there would be no change. Just one look out of my window was all I needed – clear sky and lots of stars. It was going to be 'rather cold' the next day. Looking on the positive side, it had been cold for at least a fortnight, so at least the fish would be used to the freezing conditions.

Anyway, on Saturday and Sunday I go fishing and *that's it*. I can't change the weather, it just makes things more interesting. But one thing was certain, I wouldn't catch anything sitting indoors. It's a bit like doing the pools really: if you don't play, you will never win. I've caught fish in atrocious conditions and blanked when it's been perfect. There are no rules in fishing, so I told myself that I would catch a netful the following day. This, I suppose, is what you might call psyching yourself up, but I don't know who I was trying to kid; it was going to be hard and I knew it. Still, you never can tell . . .

At seven o'clock on Saturday morning my van really was a sight for sore eyes. Even when new it had never looked cleaner. All nice and white, the only problem being that it should have been blue! I wished the inside looked as clean. After clearing the ice off the windscreen and packing the gear in the back, I was soon bombing down the M3 at 50mph. I had about an hour in which to decide where to go. Straight back to bed would have been any normal person's choice, but even that would have been cold by then, so on I went. I decided to point the van in the general direction of Fordingbridge, on the famous Hampshire Avon. The old van certainly knows its way. I could probably drive blindfold and still get there in one piece, but I wouldn't chance that. I decided to read the newspaper instead! Whoever next owns my van had better be an angler or a least have a very good sense of humour, because it will only ever take him (or her) to a river!

Just as I finished the sports page I noticed that I was at the Cadnam turn-off which would take me through the New Forest. To drive through there in winter is a real treat. What a difference it was to those days in the summer when the place can resemble the Winchester bypass on a Bank Holiday weekend, chock-a-block with caravans, cars pulling speedboats and just about anything else you can think of. That Saturday morning there was just me and a few scrawny old sheep.

Fifteen minutes later the van pulled up at the frost-covered-steel five-bar gate that gave access to the car-park on the stretch of river I'd decided to fish. As I opened the gate, my hand was instantly welded to it. It really was cold. I soon put on a few more layers of clothing: jumpers, bib and brace, moonboots, scarves – the whole works. In conditions like these I was thankful the days of donkey coats and wellington boots were long gone.

I'd chosen this stretch because, contrary to what has been written in magazines and books over the years about fishing the deepest, slowest swims in cold-water conditions with a static bait, I'd found the opposite to be more productive. But then I always was awkward. I like water 2–4ft deep, with the pace just about, or a little quicker than, the speed you can walk. And if the sun sticks it's head out sometime during the course of the day, even better, as I think that the fish feel the warmth of the sun in shallower water. Deep swims don't benefit from the sun and seem to remain cold all day. That's my theory anyhow, and that's why I walked down the normally very muddy path – much easier going that day as it was frozen solid – to the river.

In the gloomy distance I made out two more lunatics – or, rather, anglers – who appeared to be a man and his daughter. They seemed a bit uneasy as I got closer, but relaxed somewhat when I greeted them good morning. Their unease was not surprising really as I appeared through the mist – a 6ft 4in, 17-stone figure dressed in groundbait-covered rags is enough to scare anyone. It turned out that they had made an early start and had already been there an hour or more without a bite. I wished them well and went on my way downstream to the first swim I had in mind. There was no rush; I didn't expect to catch anything until things warmed up a bit. With the river very low and clear, and with less pace than I had hoped for, I

chose a flat-top porcupine-quill float coupled to a 2lb line, a fine-wire 12 hook, a closed-face reel and a 15ft rod. Bait, as always, would be flake – the supreme roach bait. Next came the job I'd been dreading – knocking up some groundbait. Out went my landing net and in went a loaf of dry bread to soak, then the whole lot was tipped into a bucket and mashed up. This is where a potato-masher saves the day as your hands need not get freezing cold. All I needed then was something to get the groundbait into the river without having to touch it and the day would be complete.

For the first couple of hours I simply went through the motions in a number of spots. The swim I really wanted to fish was further downstream. The week before it had yielded a roach of 2lb 10oz, and, as it was a bit out of the way, I hoped that nobody had been there since and that the fish remained undisturbed. I decided to leave it alone until the warmest part of the day. In the meantime, I thought I'd have a few casts in some other swims.

With the mist gone and the sun high in the sky, there were signs of things warming up all around. I moved to my roach swim. Three hours before, the grass under my feet had been as crisp as cornflakes, now it was wet and slippery. It was turning into a near summer's day, and I even considered taking off a few jumpers.

As I arrived at the swim, it was obvious that nobody had been there, and with the sun really shining it looked perfect. The river here was not very wide and about 4ft deep, shallowing up about 35yd downstream and with some tree cover on the far bank. There was a small slack in the middle caused by the dying remains of a summer weed-bed, and this gave slightly pacier water on the near and far sides. I chose to fish the middle. After a few casts I found a snag (a small weed-bed?) about half-way down the swim. Flicking out a piece of wet groundbait and then casting into the cloud, everything seemed to be going well. The old, red-topped float shone like a beacon as it made its way downstream. Every now and then it slid under as the hook caught on the obstruction and I had to ease the tackle over it. The float must have gone under two or three dozen times in the same spot when, as I lifted the rod, I felt a definite nod as a fish took the bait. I missed the only bite I'd had all day. Instead of going straight back out, I decided to rest the swim for a few minutes.

Sitting on my box, I continued the feeding pattern I'd established and drank a cup of tea. I could hardly contain myself; I knew the roach were there and just hoped I hadn't disturbed them. On my first cast, after about fifteen minutes rest, the float reached the snag and slid under. There was no messing about this time as I lifted into a big fish. By holding the rod very low, I prevented the fish from coming to the surface in the shallow water, and from the tell-tale 'thump-thump' it was obviously a big roach. Back-winding, I gave a few yards of line as the fish dropped downstream and over to the far side, out of the swim. Applying very easy pressure, I then drew the fish in front of me and slid the pan net under it. As I lifted it on to the bank I knew I was looking at a 3lb roach, and at 3lb 8drm my judgement was correct. It's hard to explain, but the difference between, say, a fish of 2lb 14oz and a three-pounder seems a lot more than 2oz. This was a really plump fish, and still had more of its bronze summer colour than the blue sheen they get in the winter. I wondered what would have happened if I hadn't rested the swim. What I did know was that where there's one roach, there's usually more . . . But what should I do? Time for another cup of tea!

I was fishing again fifteen minutes later. First trot down, the float went under but produced nothing. On the second trot, placed slightly further out, the float reached the snag, lifted slightly and then disappeared as I was into another good fish. The fight was exactly as the first, with the fish dropping downstream and over to the far bank before I slipped the net under roach number two. It looked bigger than the first, but was not quite in such good condition, being very long and noticeably less plump. A check on two sets of scales showed it to weigh just under 3lb 2oz – I settled for 3lb 1oz 8drm – slightly bigger than the first, but potentially much larger when it filled out.

Well now, two 3lb roach in less than an hour. What can I say? To catch one such fish in a day, no a lifetime, is fantastic – but two! Someone up there must have been looking out for me. I couldn't restrain myself and carried on fishing like a man possessed, but I never had another bite. I decided to walk back upstream to see the man and his daughter, and they were only too pleased when I told them that I had two huge roach that wanted their photographs taken. It turned out that this was the man's first trip to the Avon for many years and that he had come to try to catch a roach. I dare say he was back again very soon!

When it all Comes Right
~
Rod Hutchinson

The alarm clock at my side shrieked its morning welcome. It was 5 a.m. Peering out from over the groundsheet, I could see that the lake was shrouded in mist. Cobwebs hung down from the lip of the brolly, glistening dew hanging limp from the frail tapestries. It was a cold dawn. I filled up the kettle and, while it was slowly boiling, climbed a tree to survey the lake. My view was restricted to only a few yards because of the mist, and no moving fish could be seen. I had a feeling that there would be little feeding that morning.

In one way, I was glad of the mist. It would enable me to bait up my swim whilst preventing any nearby fish being alarmed by my presence. I baited up with approximately 4lb of Chilean hemp, firing it in a direct line out to a distance of 30yd. At this point the lake bed dropped off into a central channel. Any carp feeding between myself and the edge of the channel had to come across that line of bait. I had been carrying out this procedure for the two previous days, but until then only two smallish carp had rewarded my efforts. I was pretty certain that there was a fair amount of that bait still present in the swim.

I rebaited my three rods, casting them at 10yd intervals along the line, and sat back to drink my tea and make breakfast. As I sat beneath the brolly eating my breakfast, dew started dripping from its rim. A lightish breeze had sprung up, chasing the mist across the water. I was thinking how good the bacon tasted when the buzzer sounded to the centre rod and the silver-paper indicator glided towards the butt ring. I try to be calm in such situations, yet I always react in the same way. I leapt to my feet, knocking my tea over in the process. Making a conscious effort to calm myself, I let the line pull really tight across the surface before bending the rod into the fish. During the ensuing fight, my mate, Chris Yates, fishing on the opposite side of the lake, saw the action and set off around the lake to lend a hand. He arrived just in time to net a common carp of approximately 15lb. Now such a fish would be regarded highly on many a lake. Unfortunately, due to the size of fish present in Redmire, such a fish is a disappointment. I returned it without weighing it.

The wind had started to increase in strength, and was probably reaching force 3 or 4 by this time. It carried with it intermittent broken clouds, these masking the sun every few minutes. The time was 6.30 a.m. I rebaited the centre rod and cast it back to its former position. I put the kettle back on while Chris and I discussed what the day held for us. Chris is a great bloke to have along on a fishing trip, always filled with such optimism that it can't help but rub off on you. I tend to be more of a realist than Chris, usually knocking down logically his optimistic forecasts, but this particular morning his optimism definitely lifted me. For reasons I can't explain, it felt right.

I was in the process of handing Chris his cup of tea when once more a buzzer sounded, this time to the nearest, right-hand rod. Once more my pretence of calm deserted me, the tea finishing up down Chris's thigh, accompanied by his high-pitch scream. The line was belting out so fast that I was afraid to put in the pick-up in case I might be broken up. However, all held as the pick-up engaged and I bent the rod gingerly. On feeling the hook, the fish set off on one tremendous run, not stopping until it reached the dam – approximately 60yd from my pitch and about a third of the way down the length of the pool. The fish made several more equally impressive runs, and as I began to worry that my heart would not hold out it was safely netted by Chris. This particular fish was one we had often observed, its immense length giving rise to estimates of 30lb-plus. However, it had little girth to it, but at 27lb 12oz was in no way a disappointment. The fish was a true leather, the intermittent sun highlighting its reddish-brown hue brilliantly.

After putting the fish into a sack we just sat back, mentally exhausted from the unpredictability of the fight. I was elated, yet at the same time felt very tired. Such a fish doesn't come one's way too often. I put the kettle back on while we enthused over aspects of the fight. Chris remarked that it was a pity not to have kept the first double-figure common, and how they'd have made a splendid photo-

graph together. He also insisted that should I catch another fish, and that whatever its size, I should keep it to photograph along with the leather. I replied by saying that two fish in a session was more than one could really ask for, and that three was just plain greedy.

When you embark upon a session at Redmire you hope to catch a fish, at the same time not really expecting to do so. When you do get one, and a good one at that, it seems as if a weight has been lifted off your shoulders. It had all left me decidedly light-headed. I felt as if I were tempting providence as I handed Chris a cup of tea once again. I was! This time the buzzer sounded to the far rod, again all calm deserted me and once more the tea landed in Chris's lap. This fish must have heard Chris talking and for some reason felt the need to oblige. It proved to be another double-figure common that scaled 15lb 8oz. Chris no longer felt the need for a cup of tea and tore round to his swim, hell bent on joining in on this feeding spree.

It would be easy to say that everything that took place that morning was the result of calculated moves. But it wasn't, it just happened. I never expected to take another fish in a million years; I didn't even think about one, I was over the moon with what I'd already caught. Yet for some reason I decided to rebait the swim. Out went another 4lb of hemp in a straight line, the rods again cast out at 10yd intervals along that line. Once cast out, these rods were forgotten about. A glance at the clock showed it to be 7.30 a.m. I was tired and very happy as I settled back on the bed-chair and drifted off into the land of dreams.

Barely had my eyes closed when once more a buzzer erupted. There was no tea to knock over this time, but instead I leapt up with such force that the impact of my head on the brolly rim tore it from its anchorage. On feeling the hook, this fish headed directly for me, surfacing practically at my feet. At this distance I was able to identify the fish – without doubt it was the well-loved and often caught '38', as we in the syndicate called it. The name '38' was one that had stuck, even though the previous two times it had been landed it had tipped the scales around the 40lb mark! However, fate didn't have that fish lined up for me. It turned and headed for the centre of the lake and, as I applied very little pressure to the fish, the line parted. I know it was too much for me to expect to catch that fish on top of what I had already caught, but I was in no state to see reason. I was sick, and in a fit of temper threw my rod away into the bushes. I can take it when I've made a mistake, but in this case I'd done everything right.

I was still lying on the bed-chair feeling sorry for myself when I heard a commotion on the opposite side of the lake. Forcing myself to take notice, I peered out through the bankside cover to see Chris net a nice common. Somehow that event made me pull myself together. There I was feeling sorry for myself, when Chris had been watching me getting stuck into fish all morning. When Chris called out that the fish weighed 23lb, I was not only pleased but even felt relieved that a burden of selfishness had left me. I was back with my feet on the ground.

Able to see reason once more, I fished my discarded rod out from the bushes.

On checking the 10lb breaking-strain line on a balance, it proved to be breaking at around 5lb. Somehow the line had deteriorated overnight. I pulled off and discarded 20yd or so of line before I was confident that the remaining line broke at its stated breaking strain. I soon had the rod fitted up with the appropriate terminal tackle and bait, and cast back to the former central position in the line. As I was attaching the silver paper, the indicator on my near-side rod leapt for the butt ring. This time I was so close to the rods nothing could go wrong. After a short and very fast-moving battle, another double-figure common lay enfolded in the net.

It was at this point that it occurred to me that there were still more fish to be caught. Bubbles kept bursting periodically all along the line of bait. Somehow I felt that even more bait was needed to keep those feeding fish in the swim, so out went another 2lb of hemp along the groundbait line. For ten minutes or so I knelt alongside the rods, expecting a run at any moment. It didn't happen.

Once more I settled back on the bed-chair, trying to convince myself that I'd caught as much as any man could hope for, that it was sheer greed that made me think there was a chance of more fish. Once more I lit the stove and made the tea. Putting it to my lips completed the formula, and the central rod was again in action. The strike brought entirely the same result as before, the fish running directly towards me. Again the fish turned and the line parted. The most sickening aspect of it all was that I am convinced that it was the same fish as before – '38'. No great fit of temper resulted from this incident; I merely jumped up and down on the rod!

With everything off my chest and all thoughts of fish off my mind, I climbed back into my sleeping bag. A glance at the clock showed that it was 8.45 a.m., but I couldn't sleep as my mind was too full of the events that had taken place. Surely a fried-egg sandwich would pull me round? Just as the fat was getting nice and hot and the egg nice and crispy, a buzzer sounded. I tried to ignore it, but it wouldn't go away! As I approached the rod, I noticed Chris look out from his pitch opposite. He, too, had heard the buzzer. In went the pick-up, and I let the line tighten right to the reel before I pulled the rod round. What happened next I have never seen before or since. The carp leapt from the water like a salmon shaking sea-lice from its back. I swear it came a full 3ft clear of the water. It was a magnificent spectacle. Unfortunately, the energy expended in performing this feat left the carp very little in reserve with which to fight, and after less than five minutes it was in the net. And what a gorgeous, beautifully marked fish it proved to be – a mirror carp with scales like gold sovereigns that pulled the scale down to 26lb 8oz. As quick as the fight had been, Chris had somehow managed to get round the lake in time to net it for me.

At that moment, all the blank hours, all the hundreds of miles I'd travelled to get to the pool and the financial hardship I'd suffered through taking time off work seemed worthwhile. Such compensation was more than I could have wished for. I didn't feel the need to catch other fish – in fact, it didn't even occur to me to rebait the rod and cast it out. I just wanted to relax and bathe in my elation for a while.

The long hours spent sleeping on the bank and living on tinned or fried food eventually take their toll of the human body. An irresistible urge came over me to answer nature's call. About 15yd away from my swim, behind a high mass of brambles and nettles, the syndicate members had built a toilet. I was soon installed in it, oblivious to everything but the job in hand, so to speak. I was aroused from this semi-hypnotic state by a funny sort of repetitive, hammering sound. It seemed ages before it occurred to me what it might be. Leaping out of the toilet, I caught sight of the silver-paper indicator hammering hell out of the remaining forgotten rod which I'd left out. The line was tearing off the spool at such a rate it had jumped over the buzzer-head antenna. With my usual calm and grace I rushed for the rod. Unfortunately, I had forgotten that my trousers were still round my ankles and ended up in the pile of brambles and nettles. However, that fish meant to have the bait, and despite the time it took me to extract myself painfully from the undergrowth and redistribute my attire, the line was still belting out. On feeling the hook, the fish surfaced by the dam wall, 60yd up the pool to my right.

That fish gave me the most enthralling fight of all. On the long line it kited into a bay further up on the right-hand side of the lake, and out of my sight. In doing so it also took the line through a bush on the corner of the bay. There was nothing else I could do but wade in to try to remove the line from the bush and get a more direct pull on the fish.

So, for the second time that morning, down went my trousers, off went my shoes and socks, and in I marched. Somehow I managed to remove the line from the bush, and with constant pressure forced the fish to move out into the centre of the pool. At this point my feet came across an underwater snag – a long length of trailing tree root. If I had gone back to my position on the bank, that snag could have been a problem, so I decided to play the fish out from where I stood, keeping my foot hard down on the tree root to prevent any mishaps. I conveyed my thoughts to Chris, who threw the landing net out to me. Eventually I netted the fish, and it was a very happy man indeed who waded his way back to the bank, prize in hand. Setting foot back on terra firma, I was shocked to find my legs covered in leeches – I felt like Humphrey Bogart in *The African Queen*!

The carp turned out to be a mint-conditioned, shining common carp weighing 22lb 4oz. If I were a card player, I think I could say that I had a very good hand that morning. Three twenties, a leather, a mirror and a common, with a trio of doubles to back them up. Sometimes fate looks kindly on us all.

Trial by Camera
~
Bob James

E very angler knows just how fickle roach can be, especially big roach. Those of you who have watched television programmes compiled from film out-takes and video disasters will be aware of the pending calamities that seem to await anyone who dares to put himself or herself in front of a camera. Combine the two, and you have the potential for a major catastrophe, believe me. This, however, was my brief: I was to catch a bag of roach, preferably including one of over 2lb. I had five days in which to do it; the venue was for me to choose, but the camera would follow me and my every move.

The Hampshire Avon at Longford Castle was my choice. Bernard Venables once said of the Avon: 'The roach are splendid, many days' catches having more over a pound than under, and it is not unusual for them to be over two pounds.' The Castle water fitted the bill perfectly: home of big roach, very beautiful and within walking distance of my home. I felt confident that here I would satisfy my brief.

Having both seen and caught some large roach from around Iron Bridge at the bottom of the fishery, this was to be my starting point. Chris Yates and I had tea and toast for our pre-dawn breakfast at my house, and then set off up river at first light, parting company at the bridge – my trial had begun.

The run of the river at Iron Bridge is steady, shallow and very clear. I settled for feeder fishing, feeling that a float might well spook these shy fish in the conditions, but I need not have concerned myself for I neither caught nor spooked anything for two days! It was time for a move – maybe the roach were in the deeper water up by the island? I moved and, as I walked upstream, I could feel the dreaded pangs of pressure already starting to build up inside me as doubt nibbled away at my confidence. Perhaps we should have filmed it on the Thames at Richmond; then nobody would have expected anything more than a few dace and gudgeon, with maybe a couple of 'goer' roach, I found myself thinking.

Fortunately, with the new swim things began to improve: the weather became more settled and so did I as at last I found the fish I was seeking. By day's end I had taken a good net of roach, over thirty fish in all, on both the float and the feeder; they were not difficult, they were also not big. Had I been fishing for pleasure this bag of fish would have been most welcome – the roach might have got a bit bigger as the story was told and retold in the pub, and then a few excuses about why I had not caught any really big ones could have been added for good measure. But a film about excuses might not make for very interesting viewing . . . I had just two days left in which to 'do the business'.

It was Edward Ensom (Faddist) who wrote: 'The roach fisherman must be prepared to serve a reasonable apprenticeship before achieving an all-round competency. There is no short cut. Persistence, thoroughness, patience and common-sense application are the essential keys.' Well now, my apprenticeship had been served – it had started on the Thames at Richmond thirty-five years before – and until the start of this week I felt that I was competent. I had also certainly been persistent and thorough, and my patience was holding up well. I decided that the problem must therefore lie in the common-sense department. I checked things out: the weather could not be better, I was sitting on a prime roach water, I was using baits and tactics which had caught me more big roach than I wish to admit, and I had tried all the areas that had produced in the past.

Something *must* be different. What could it be? What could have changed since I was last there? This is not a stretch that we can normally fish but had been given over solely for the purpose of making this film. The end of the season match is the only time we are normally allowed on the Castle water. Something clicked – end of season only – that was it! I had not taken into account the seasonal movements of the fish! It was early November, a full four months before the end of the season, and no time to be fishing steady water; the roach shoals would still be in what remained of the ranunculus beds.

Before the next day had dawned, I was in position immediately below the Castle bridge where the river was restricted and the flow increased as it was forced

between the bridge piers. By the time it was light my rods were ready, everything in its place and confidence high – so high in fact that I had made up a huge amount of groundbait.

Soon there was enough light to see the great fronds of weed swaying in the current, and I could just make out a long channel a third of the way across the river which ran from the bridge 35yd downstream. I cast two feeder rods – one to the middle of the run and the other at the tail. As I waited for some response, I threw in a steady stream of groundbait at the head of the swim, right against the first arch of the bridge. My attention was drawn to the scene of the castle opposite me. The building was surrounded by rolling mist and had taken on a dreamlike appearance. Some may have said it appeared sinister, but to my senses it was perfectly peaceful – not haunted but happy. The urge to throw something across the river so as to hear the noise ricochet off the Castle wall and confirm that this was not a dream welled up inside me; then suddenly there was no need. My upstream rod yanked round, the welcome splash of my first roach broke the eerie silence and I moved from one dream world into another as the spell was broken.

The day eased itself lazily into life as if in no hurry, autumn being in no rush to yield to winter. I have lived in the Avon Valley for ten years now, but still I marvel at the variety and density of its wildlife, much of it enjoying the fruits and berries that hung heavy from the trees and bushes that day. The adults of the population, tatty and almost worn out from a summer of rearing young, were busy trying to regain their strength and condition in preparation for the long, cold months ahead. Their young, full-grown, noisy and boisterous in the way of youth, were blissfully unaware of what lay ahead of them. Our world is a beautiful place at such times as this, and never more so than when fish are on feed.

As is often the case, my biggest fish came at last light, my seventeenth good roach on a classic day. As I weighed it I became aware that Hugh was not filming me! He was away fishing, the camera behind me standing idle and unattended. 'What, are you on strike, Miles?' I bellowed.

'Oh, now that's a cracking roach, what does it weigh? It must be over two,' were Hugh's words as he appeared through the gloom of the gathering mist.

'It's 2lb 5oz, but why aren't you filming me?' I asked.

'The light's gone, plus I spent most of the day getting shots of all those birds and ducks which have shared your swim with you. Absolutely glorious,' said Hugh.

To say that I was lost for words would not be true, I just chose not to use those that came to mind!

After a couple of glasses of claret in the campervan, Hugh announced that he knew I would do better the next day. His confidence was touching and yet he could be right, for all my fish had come from the top end of the swim – the motherload _might_ just be under or above the bridge . . .

The still mild weather remained with us overnight and, as we stood on the Castle bridge the next morning, the air was sweet with the smell of damp fallen leaves. However, two things were different: I had developed a heavy cold and we could hear the sound of fish rolling. It was still too misty to see them, but as it got light a warm zephyr pushed away the veil to reveal roach turning through the surface above the bridge. A carrier rejoins the river upstream on the west bank, and this was the reason the roach were here. After a dry summer with low water-levels, there was plenty of dying weed which would bring the already low oxygen levels lower still. This carrier, however, contained water that had flowed across acres of water meadows; it would be sweet, full of oxygen, carrying plenty of food and hence attractive to the fish. By lunchtime my net contained seven 2lb roach.

After lunch at the Radnor Arms, Chris and Hugh took the boat out and moored right across my swim! 'Okay, cast right next to the boat, it will look great,' said Hugh. This I did.

'Right, do it again please,' he called. I couldn't; a roach had taken my bait on the drop! Hugh filmed it all the way to the net, where it turned out to weigh 2lb 12oz.

We called it a 'wrap' just before the light faded; my grand total was thirteen roach, with ten of them over 2lb and most of these over 2½lb. Hugh had his film and I had written myself into roach-fishing history. My sense of achievement was incredible, and we all shared a sense of deep relief. Time for a glass of port maybe? 'I'll buy you enough port to float a punt in,' exclaimed Hugh.

So, was this my red letter day? No, it was to be the next day . . .

I stayed in bed until lunchtime whilst my mind relived every roach, every bite and every moment of that incredible experience. We did not answer the telephone and I had breakfast in bed served to me by a delicious blonde (my wife). My cold had gone too, or perhaps I just forgot I ever had it!

Season's End
~
Martin James

D uring the winter of the 1982–3 season I decided to spend as much time
as possible on the River Wensum in Norfolk in search of big roach and
chub, the latter in particular. I first got to know the river back in the
1950s during holidays spent on the Norfolk Broads, and what a lovely place it was
in those far-off days. It was during this period that I met a couple of interesting
and great characters. One, George Gallant, who was disabled with a hunchback,
hired out boats at Martham and sold canned food from a small, green shed. On
wet, cold nights he would let me sleep in the shed – far better than my old pup
tent. It was he who arranged for me to go fowling with another character, Billy
'the Gun' Drum.

Now Billy was also a roach angler, and on some days the guns were put away in
favour of the cane rods and centre-pin reels. Often we fished the Wensum, but
Geldeston Lock on the Waveney was our favourite spot for roach, with many
weighing over 2lb. As a result, these two Norfolk rivers became such a part of my

life that forty years on I'm still fishing them with cane rods and centre-pin reels.

In 1976 I was diagnosed as having multiple sclerosis, and this hit me very hard indeed. My specialist advised me to stop wildfowling and angling, the two sports that I loved and couldn't imagine life without. Over the next few years I had to struggle to survive. Quite how I did I shall never know. Thankfully, I had a team of consultants, doctors, nurses, health workers and friends who helped in many ways, most notably when I was depressed. The long days of winter were always the worst.

Come the early 1980s I was becoming more mobile, being able to operate a wheelchair, manage a few paces with a zimmer frame and even managing to drive a car. Life was once again worth living. Slowly I returned to the sports that I loved and had dearly missed. I hoped that I could catch some quality fish, particularly chub, which had always been a favourite of mine (if it's possible to have such a thing) from the time I caught an 8in specimen during a camping holiday with the Cubs in 1947.

During the autumn and winter of 1982–3 I spent all my time in Norfolk and Cambridge, wildfowling on the black earth of the Fens and angling on the Wensum, relishing every minute of the days spent outdoors. Sunday 14 March 1983 is one day I shall never forget. It was the last day of the coarse fishing season and I had decided to try to catch some big roach. If I was to succeed in my efforts though, I had to get some good advice and, thankfully, this was given freely by Basil Todd of the Dereham Rod and Gun Shop – a most helpful person. On 13 March I phoned Basil for his thoughts on where to fish and he suggested the Swanton Morley fishery, which cost just 50p a day. Arrangements were made to meet the following morning at 7.30 a.m. so that he could show me over the water.

The next day the weather was cold, with a strong north-westerly wind, the sky a leaden grey colour and looking full of snow. Wisbech was dark and quiet when my companion, Arthur Sayers, and I left at around 6 a.m. for the 50-mile journey to Swanton Morley. Arriving at the same time as Basil, and after the usual greetings, we made our way to the river. I found it a struggle to use the zimmer frame over the rough ground, but finally we made it. Arthur and Basil carried my tackle, which was a great help.

Eventually, I elected to fish a straight stretch below a bend where the water ran about 4ft deep. About 5yd below my chosen swim was a slight bay, but for some reason I chose to ignore this spot. The wind whistled through the Norfolk reeds and a skein of Canada geese flew overhead. Shivering, I pulled the scarf tighter around my neck for extra warmth.

All thoughts of chub were far from my mind as I wanted big roach, and I tackled up with a light quivertip rod, paternoster rig and size 22 hook baited with a single bronze maggot. The mainline had a 1½lb breaking strain and the hook-length a pound, as recommended by another local expert, Terry Brown, for roach on this stretch of the Wensum. In the next four hours I had six bites, missing three, and being broken on three. These fish, I suspected, were chub.

At 12.30 p.m the bailiff came along for a chat and mentioned chub. My theory was confirmed. With this news I tackled up another quivertip rod on 4lb line, a link ledger carrying three swan shot and a number 8 hook. Bait was a large piece of breadflake, which I cast across and downstream about 15yd. Within minutes I had a 3lb chub in the net.

Having rebaited, I cast to the same spot, again with flake, but this time covered in Cheddar cheesepaste. Every so often a strong gust of wind would shake the rod, making bite detection difficult, but after about ten minutes I had a couple of gentle indications and then the tip pulled round about two inches. I struck and was into a really good fish which put up an excellent fight, thumping hard all the way to the net. It was a super chub in excellent condition, and I trembled as the scales were produced. The fish weighed 5lb 7oz. What a way to end the season, I thought, as I flopped into my chair and, turning to Arthur, said: 'I think I will sleep the rest of the day.' And then, as an afterthought, I added: 'I think if I'd caught a six-pounder I would have done a streak across the field,' although I soon discounted the idea as unlikely. Thinking about the pictures we would take of the fish, I shared my cheese sandwiches and lukewarm tea with the bailiff. I was in a good mood; I'd caught another five.

After a rest I decided to have another go and baited again with breadflake smeared with cheesepaste. Moments later, the tip pulled round and my answering strike saw the rod savagely pulled down to the surface. Line whined from the clutch and for some minutes it was an even battle. Finally, the fish swirled on the surface and soon I was easing it over the landing net. The adrenalin was pumping through my body as I realized that I might have managed a brace of 5lb chub in a single session. Out came the scales and weigh-bag and in went the fish. The scales bumped down to 7lb 10oz and the bag's weight was checked and deducted at 1lb 8oz, which meant my chub weighed 6lb 2oz. Witnesses were rounded up, both fish were weighed a couple more times and then some pictures were taken. After all this, the chub were returned to the river, hopefully to grow into seven-pounders.

I pinched myself to make sure that I was not dreaming, but the ice-cold wind on the back of my neck told me otherwise. The bailiff said that with my luck I could probably catch one of the Wensum trout. I baited with a big lobworm and cast well down the river, and inside ten minutes I had a 4lb trout on the bank!

Morning Glory

~

Simon Lush

The sun appeared slowly over the Downs, signalling the start of another hot day as I sat looking over a flat, calm lake from the Stables swim. I had first fished here back in July 1983, catching my biggest ever tench of 7lb 10oz, which improved on the best fish from my native Yorkshire by nearly two pounds! Over the following seasons I spent as much time as possible on the lake, and enjoyed tench fishing of a quite unbelievable standard, catching numerous 8lb-plus fish and many more six- and seven-pounders. Plenty of friendships were also forged with fellow tenching enthusiasts who had come to fish here from all over the country. In fact, I enjoyed every minute spent at Johnson's, even when the lake became moody. And if the tench wouldn't play, you could always adjourn to the pub to try to work things out. This week, in particular, had been a bit like that.

It was the last day of the traditional opening-week pilgrimage to this amazing complex, the previous seven days having been very frustrating indeed. Directly in front of me was a deep gully which ran parallel to the bank and the end of a long gravel bar, the latter about 40yd long and covered in sunken bushes. To my right was a massive weedbed which completely covered one corner of the lake – an obvious spawning site where the tench tend to congregate early in the season. My baits were positioned on a small gravel patch that was surrounded by dense weed, on the slope at the end of this bar. Some tench had frequented this area for most of the week and they were driving me mad. They were clearly not feeding very hard, as often happens just prior to spawning when their behaviour becomes very erratic. But two big fish of 8lb 13oz and 8lb 7oz had made mistakes, so I was fairly content even though my main ambition still remained: to catch one over 9lb. It was this elusive creature that kept me coming back year after year.

In fact, several of my friends had caught nine-pounders that week. Jimmy Bigden, Chris Turnbull and Dave Cable had all taken fish to 9lb 8oz, but pride of place went to the diminutive James Harewood, who caught an absolute monster of 9lb 12oz on opening day. They were all taking great pleasure in reminding me of my failure to join their 'nines club', and had even thrown me off their exclusive table in the local hostelry! The lake was obviously peaking in terms of big fish, and I would never, it seemed, have a better chance than this.

I had recast my baits at first light using ultra-spice-flavoured boilies on long, 3ft hooklengths. The 'confidence-style' approach seemed to be working very well at the time, with short rigs producing lots of twitches and dropped takes. As I watched, a big, black, dorsal fin cut through the surface over my baited area and I was really on edge. But by 5 a.m. no bites had materialized and all was very quiet. I decided to have a quick walk round to the Gap swim, and there found Jimmy Bigden with a huge grin on his face. I peered over the bank to see a sack lying in the margins and then looked back at Jimmy: '9lb 1oz mate,' he said with a smile. I congratulated him and we chatted for a while over a cup of tea.

As I walked back to my swim, I went over it all in my mind. The lake was producing big fish everywhere and I had just one day left! I noticed a few bubbles coming to the surface behind the bar, just before the indicator smacked against the rod. The Mitchell 410 started to spin, and I simply picked up the rod and leaned into the fish as the rod bent round. At first the fish tried to go back along the bar, but I hung on. The strain on the tackle was appalling, but the fish finally gave way and dropped into the gully where it stayed for a few minutes, cruising up and down in front of me.

'Bloody hell, this feels good,' I thought to myself – and then my nerves started playing up. I edged down the bank, picked up the net and the fish went straight in. Taking one look at this tench I knew that I had finally done it. A nine at last! At times like these, I fall to pieces. I started shouting and giggling, just as I did when I caught my first fish from the local river as a boy.

That tench meant the world to me. It only just made the mark, with half an ounce to spare, which surprised me as it looked a bit bigger. I ran back to the Gap, grinning like a Cheshire cat. Jimmy looked up, and my face must have said it all,

'How big?' he enquired.

'9lb ½oz,' I replied.

He leapt up and grabbed me by the hand. 'Well done mate,' he said, knowing how badly I had wanted that fish. I even woke James Harewood to tell him! He just smiled and muttered something about low nines. I then stopped off to see Steve Hollibone in the next swim before I returned to mine, by which time I had managed to calm down a bit.

I looked at the sack lying in the crystal-clear water and smiled to myself. The sun was well up and it was already very warm. I was a happy man indeed.

I recast and catapulted twenty or so free offerings around the hookbait. Ten minutes later, just as Steve appeared with a very welcome cup of tea, the same rod was in action again. After tearing up the weedbed for a couple of minutes, then just hanging heavy in the gully, the fish simply gave up. Steve netted it, took one look in the net and pronounced: 'You've got another nine.' I stared in disbelief. It looked every bit as big as the last one, but the scales stopped at 8lb 11oz. Still, what a brace!

Dave Cable shouted from the Pub swim, enquiring how big the fish was. 'Not quite as big as the other one,' I said, 'It's 8lb 11oz.'

'What *other* one?' he queried.

'The nine I've just had,' I replied.

There was a slight pause, and then 'Ohhh Nooh!' in his appalling imitation of a Yorkshire accent.

There then followed three hours with no activity whatsoever. Just as I was thinking that it was all over for the day, at 9.45 a.m. the same rod took off again. This fish really did get its head down, making repeated efforts to get behind the bushes. It then decided it was getting nowhere in that direction, and so ripped the weedbed to bits instead. It really was annoyed, but soon headed deep into the gully, sending big vortexes to the surface as it fought.

When the fish finally showed itself, 3ft or so down, it looked absolutely massive and very, very long. Steve had run round to me and was ready with the net. The fish rolled over on the surface and we both saw clearly the huge pelvic fins of a male fish. It went into the net first time and I just gaped at it. My best male up until that moment had weighed 6lb 4oz, but this one was *big*. The scales read 7lb 2oz, and it looked every bit of it. Indeed, like all male tench, it looked bigger than it actually was, being very narrow across the back.

'How big?' enquired Cable.

'7lb 2oz,' I replied.

'Oh, a small one then!' he smirked.

'Yeah, but it *is* a male!'

There followed a pause, then 'Ohhh Noooh.'

I cast again on to the same spot and sat back in a daze. This session was fast turning into a dream! Phil Jones arrived to say that he had caught a double-figure carp from another lake, asking if I would photograph it for him. I said that I would, but not just yet. As I relayed the events of that morning to him, the indicator hit the rod again.

Immediately, I knew that this was another biggie. It was very powerful, but more sullen compared to the energetic male. It came through the weed fairly easily, but then sulked deep in the gully out of sight. For the fourth time that morning my nerves got the better of me. Phil grabbed the net, and when the tench finally surfaced he calmly lifted it from the water, looking at me in disbelief. 'I've just caught a carp that didn't look that big!' he said. That really got me worried. On taking a good look at the fish I realized that it was bigger than my nine. But how much bigger? It was certainly carrying more spawn. Phil said: 'I think it's a double.' I had another look, but it didn't seem long enough, although it was certainly a nine. The scales stopped at 9lb 5oz.

I was dumbfounded. What a morning! After all that time spent after a 9lb tench, to get two in the space of a few hours was unbelievable. I sent Phil off to get Chris Turnbull, who duly arrived and summed things up by calling me a 'jammy beggar'. Despite the constant heckling that goes on between us, we're great friends really, and I know that he was pleased for me.

That lunchtime I put £20 behind the bar and sat, on my own, at the 'brace of nines' table! I talked myself into staying for another day, just in case there was more to come.

At 6.30 p.m. another fish of 8lb 15oz to me and at 10.30 p.m. one of 9lb 4oz to Jimmy, put the seal on a truly remarkable day. The next morning was a complete blank. It was all over. Tony King, who moved into the swim after me, had only one fish in an entire week – and a four-pounder at that!

I packed up, said my goodbyes to everyone on the lake and then hit the M25. On the journey home I thought long and hard about what had happened the previous day, and about the fact that not so very long ago I would never have believed it possible. Who knows what the future may hold?

A New Dawn
~
Tim Marks

Sywell Reservoir, near Northampton, needs little introduction in tench-fishing circles, being 70 beautiful acres of deep, weedy, rush-lined water packed with big tench. Famous since the late 1960s, when some of the country's top anglers frequented its banks, it developed a reputation as a prolific tench fishery, with nets of fish to over 6lb being commonplace. Indeed, many modern techniques – feeder fishing in particular – were developed there during this era.

However, as with most tench fisheries the good times were short-lived. After a handful of years at the top, Sywell slipped into obscurity in the early 1970s as the tench stock aged and the fish declined in numbers. It was not until the hot summer of 1976 that a rebirth took place as the few remaining tench in the reservoir at last spawned successfully and commenced a new chapter in the Sywell story.

The offspring grew fast in the rich water, and by 1982 bags of small tench weighing 3–4lb were being caught by the few anglers who visited the water. My angling companion then, as now, Jim Ridgway, was a little older than me and had fished Sywell extensively during its heyday. He had fond memories of 'The Res', as he calls it. Keeping a keen watch on the progress of these new fish, he returned there again during 1983 when his catches consisted of fish to nearly 6lb – and in perfect condition due to the lack of fishing pressure. A visit in 1984 again produced bumper catches, with fish pushing 7lb, and still few other anglers had cottoned on. All this time I had steadfastly refused to accompany him as I was already catching 6lb-plus fish from another water and saw no reason to move on.

However, things changed in June 1985 when a frosty start to the season put paid to our catches on a shallow lake in Wales, and so I reluctantly agreed to the four-hour drive to Sywell. All the way there I was convinced that the secret must have got out and that we would find a sea of bivvies on our arrival. How wrong can you be! Not only was the water virtually empty, it was also much more beautiful than I had imagined.

We staggered with all our gear down to the bottom of the west arm – a hell of a walk and even worse with the second load – and collared two swims close to the boundary. Night fishing has always been banned at Sywell, but at this time anglers were allowed to stay on the water at night, hence the 'session-fishing' approach. Having asked the chap in the next swim to watch our gear, we set off for Northampton in search of a grocer's shop and square meal before we tackled up.

On our return, we set up traditional (for the time) Sywell gear consisting of Avon-type rods, 5lb line and ledger or feeder tackle. With a bucketful of cereal beyond the marginal weed and our baited rigs in place, we were ready. As the evening drew in, so tench began to roll in front of us. Things were certainly looking up. The first bite came at 9 p.m. and Jim soon netted a lovely fish of 6lb 15oz. This was the biggest tench I had ever seen and I was beginning to enjoy Sywell. My first chance came at 9.40 p.m., the result being a new personal best – up 2oz at 6lb 13oz. By then I had decided that Sywell was definitely the place for me!

The next couple of days further cemented my feelings for the water as a succession of big tench came to the net. The climax was a brace of sevens taken on the Thursday morning. It is often said that when you are striving to achieve a target, all pressure is removed once you finally realize that ambition and from then on it becomes easy. So it proved, and I finished the session with a total of five sevens up to 7lb 13oz. All had fallen to either maggots, casters or worms, and they had fought like tigers on the light tackle. Sywell tench are particularly short, stocky fish anyway, and so when they reach these sort of weights they really scrap. Jim had an astounding bag on the last day, with eighteen fish totalling some 118lb. His catch included seven sevens!

That was it for the 1985 season, as the distance involved made a return trip impossible that summer. However, in 1987 we arrived at Sywell once again halfway through the opening week of the season. This time an abortive start at neighbouring Hollowell was to blame. After four days and only two small fish between

us, we found the lure of Sywell too much to resist. But things had changed since our last visit; the pressure on the water had become very severe and swims were at a premium. In addition, the influx of new faces had resulted in the mass introduction of boilies and the beginnings of a switch in the feeding habits of the tench. Both of these negative factors were balanced by the major incentive that the fish were peaking regularly at over 8lb. Indeed, another friend, Stuart Sharp, spent the first week of the season that summer on Sywell and was rewarded with sixty or so fish, including three eights to 8lb 12oz.

After a couple of depressingly wet and unsuccessful days Jim left for Wales, but I decided to stay on for one last night. I was living in Scotland at the time, and so this was my one and only chance of a big tench that summer. A move was in order, but where to? A friend vacated a good swim on the far side of the west arm, and after plenty of soul-searching I somehow found the motivation to move in there. My gear was pared down to an absolute minimum and then Stuart was conned into giving me a hand on another long trek. What else are friends for?

Once installed in my new swim, I found a new lease of life and things began to brighten up. Tench were still showing in the general area, so I had a chance of some fish. After depositing 200 seafood-blend boilies into the swim (I'm nothing if not pragmatic!), I turned in for the night. I had one day left to rescue an otherwise disastrous week and wondered if Sywell could do it for me.

My heavy slumbers were cut short by a steady take at 3 a.m. which yielded a good male fish of 5lb 9oz. Things started to go berserk at 6 a.m., and over the next few hours I landed another ten fish. Life became very hectic as groups of tench found the feed – on two occasions I had two fish on the bank at the same time. All my subsequent fish were larger than the first, and once again seven exceeded 7lb. I even outdid Jim's catch of two years previous, as the largest went to 8lb 1oz! The long trip back to Stirling passed in a self-satisfied daze.

The catch could have been even greater had I not run low on bait after banking about eight fish. Indeed, I caught the last two fish on baits cadged from Stuart, who was snoring away in the next swim. I also had to wake him twice to borrow sacks as the fish came in thick and fast. Interestingly, he had only one take to my twelve (I missed one) and the chap on the other side of me only had two, although they both produced eights. My neighbour said he was specimen hunting!

Since 1987, Sywell has continued to produce ever-bigger tench, and 9lb fish are now fairly common captures. However, the heavy angling pressure has resulted in a marked deterioration in the condition of many of the fish. Much of this can be blamed on anglers who use very heavy tackle in an attempt to drag fish unceremoniously from the sometimes extensive summer weed growth. So-called 'parrot-mouthed' fish are unfortunately quite common now. For this reason neither Jim nor I have returned for any summer fishing since 1987.

However, a welcome new dimension to Sywell tenching appeared during the winter of 1991-2. A few hardy souls stayed on the water right through this winter and were rewarded with regular captures of big tench. Always a good autumn water, as several local friends had proved, the catching of these fish in the depths of December came as a revelation. Jim and I decided to venture back in February 1992 for a couple of day-trips, and after some careful experimentation with rigs and baits managed to land a handful of fish. It was challenging fishing as the tench were in tight groups, and their preferences for both bait flavour and presentation appeared to vary greatly from one day to the next. The average weight was high as large numbers were caught, and we subsequently learnt of an incredible winter-caught nine-pounder. My largest fish was a handsome 8lb 5oz, one I am sure will stand as my best-ever winter tench for many years to come.

Like many tench waters, success runs in cycles and this time round Sywell has reached even greater heights. I count myself fortunate enough to have been on the scene when the water was still on the way up. By being in the right place at the right time I had the opportunity for some superlative tench fishing with traditional baits and methods, and a chance to really let the fish fight. (The latter years have seen a switch to boilies and scaled-down carp tackle, which in my view restricts the sporting aspect of tench fishing, particularly in weedy water.)

Having fished at Sywell over the last eight years, both summer and winter, I have been able to follow the rapid progression of baits, rigs and methods. In this respect, the water has been a marvellous proving ground for new techniques, many of which I still use today. There have been countless good days, but without doubt Sywell in 1985 remains the most memorable and rewarding tench fishing that I have ever experienced.

That Certain Feeling

~

Graham Marsden

It was a morning when every angler worth his salt, barring weddings or funerals, was behind a rod. Conditions had been the same for weeks which, no matter where they are, are usually productive. This particular morning, mist rolled slowly over the meadows and covered the surface of the estate mere like a damp blanket. Looking misleadingly weak behind the greyness, the sun fought for supremacy, a battle it had won most often of late. The dry algae around the edge of the mere lay witness to the hot summer that was now well into September and showing no sign of turning to autumn. It was already warm, even close, and would be shirt-sleeve weather later in the day.

My only regret was that I hadn't arrived earlier, for though I knew the fish would not visit my chosen swim until the gentlemanly hour of around 10 a.m., I would have liked to have had time to savour the atmosphere and wallow in eager anticipation of what was to come. Yes, I knew, just *knew*, that I was going to make a good catch. And not simply because the conditions were right, or because I had made two good catches earlier that week in the same swim and in the same conditions. I had much stronger evidence than that. I could *feel* it. It was tangible. I have never been so certain of something so uncertain in all my life. I would have bet a week's wages on it, a gold clock, all the tea in China and all the other clichés in the book.

The mere is typical of many in Cheshire and Shropshire, covering an area of about 25 acres. More than half the margins are encroached by beautiful shrubs, which in spring glow with pink, blue and lilac, If you are lucky these shrubs are still in flower when the season opens, making a gorgeous backdrop to photographs of great, bronze bream held in the grateful hands of proud captors.

The remainder of the mere's surround is open meadow, with the odd silver birch and occasional willow that droops its wooden fingers into the water. Typical of the mere, again, is its lack of depth for some distance out, as it gradually shelves to an average of 7–10ft. It is rather like an elongated saucer, and with few additional features. Apart from one, that is . . .

Years ago, long before my time and before the 'saucer' flooded to mould the mere into what it is today, a stream ran through the land, about 50yd from one bank. Today you can only see the stream where it runs in and out of the mere but careful plumbing has given me a picture of it in my mind's eye every bit as good as a photograph. The groove it gouged is still there, eroded by time and less distinct than it must have been all those years ago. It is distinct enough, however. If you drift from the margin in a punt and look over the side at the pale bottom, scattered with fronds of bright green algae and broken swan mussels, the water darkens suddenly as you pass from the 3ft depth to the 8–9ft of the old stream.

This is not a great change in depth, but it is sufficient. Nor is it a sheer drop-off, but it is sudden enough to be meaningful. Better still, the ledge lies some 50yd or so from the margins – distant enough to suit the big bream's natural inclination to feed well out from the bank. And even better still, the old stream terminates in a deeper hole, a spot where we, who had fished the water for many years, knew the bream lived during the non-feeding daylight hours.

My swim was near the end of the stream, a few short yards before the ledge tapered away to the deeper hole. It was a scene that Bernard Venables would have sketched to illustrate a big-bream angler's dream swim.

I set up my 13ft match rod with a 3lb mainline and a 2½lb hooklengh to a size 14 spade-end hook. The float was a 9in-bodied insert waggler, set to fish the bait laid about a foot off the bottom. One rod was sufficient, for if this day was to be anything like the two days I had fished earlier in the week, then one rod was all I would be able to cope with. I assembled the landing net and loaded it into the punt along with my rod, six pints of casters, my chair, and all the remaining bits and pieces I would need for the day. Finally, I added water and a half-pint of crushed casters to just a pound each of white and brown groundbait, and then mixed the lot thoroughly. This was my 'noticeable' bait that the bream could not help but see when they arrived at my swim. A peculiar notion, I know, but I felt better for it.

The mist was dissolving rapidly by this time, for I could just make out the outlines of the trees on the far bank. Using one oar, I paddled the punt quietly towards the swim, scanning the water's surface to my left where the shelf began as I looked for rolling bream. That would be the first place they would show after leaving the deeper water where they invariably fed through the night. No one had fished the usual night swims since the previous weekend, and this was a good thing for me as the bream would not be full of bait. I realized that I was holding my breath as I paddled out, and made an effort to breathe normally. If everything was going to plan there wouldn't be any bream in the swim yet, and if there were they certainly wouldn't hear me breathing! Instincts are difficult to suppress though, even if they are largely redundant in this modern age.

I slid between the algae-encrusted plastic bottles that floated my anchor ropes on the surface and tied each end of the punt to them. I was positioned over 3ft of water an easy float cast from the shelf. I would have preferred to have been a little further away from the bream, but the distance was dictated by how far I could catapult loose feed if a facing wind blew up. In these calm conditions everything was easy, but it was still important to plan for all contingencies. In any case, I was hidden from the bream by the shelf. I threw in the groundbait, spreading a little down the shelf but with the bulk of it at the bottom where it levelled out. Then I fired in almost a full pint of casters, hooked three on to the 14 hook, cast in, poured a cup of coffee from my flask and sat back to wait for events to unfold.

The first bream to show did so with a splash, slapping the surface with its tail as it completed the roll. I had been watching the surface 50yd away – between glances at the float – and had been taken completely by surprise as this bream rolled no more than 10yd away. Then another one swirled just below the surface, causing a vortex that would have been seen as a calm spot if the water had been rippled. For the next few minutes I could have been at Wimbledon, as my head swung from side to side, watching the bream prime to my left and keeping a wary eye on the float in front of me.

The first movement on my float was caused by a bream. It was not a bite but was caused by a bream that rolled right alongside it, the float wobbling in the wake of its movement. Before the float had time to settle, it lifted slightly then sank away as another bream accepted the cocktail of hook and caster. I struck into it and held, then back-wound as the bream made the usual initial effort to run against pressure. I held again, allowing the bream to kite around in a big arc close to the surface. Round it came, over the shelf and into the shallower water. I could then play it with all the time I wanted, causing no disturbance to the baited swim.

I had a set of scales already zeroed to a wet weigh-sling. The bream weighed 7lb. 10oz and turned out to be the smallest I caught that day – the only one *less than* 8lb.

I netted a few more fish in the next hour or so, but was beginning to miss more bites than I was hitting – shelled casters were commonplace. I was firing in casters constantly, and the bream were showing at the surface very little as they stayed below to claim their share of the spoils. Many baits were being taken on the drop. As a result, I changed the 14 hook for a 16 and used a double-caster bait instead of three, and was back in business for another hour or two before the fish became totally preoccupied with the loose feed. I finally settled for a size 18 hook and single caster, changing the hooklength to 2lb. It took me longer to land each fish, but on the credit side I was making most bites count.

Six hours later, at about 4 p.m., I ran out of bait and the fish were still feeding. I had counted twenty-eight bream, twenty-seven of which were over 8lb. Several had weighed over 9lb, and I had caught the biggest bream ever from the water at that time: the first double at 10lb 2oz.

As I tied the punt to the silver birch, feeling tired and hungry (I'd had no time to eat), I knew that whatever else happened in my angling career I would never forget this day, the third and best in a week that belonged in a dream rather than reality. Since then I have caught many double-figure bream from this mere and other waters, and have made some big catches. But never have I experienced anything like this. The light float tackle, the number of big fish, and the water's first double had all added up to a very special red letter day.

On the Quiet Side
~
Mark McKeown

I t was midsummer 1991, and the question for me was this: where were the bream? As I jumped into the car on that pleasant June evening I thought only of the location of these bream, and whether I would find seventy of them, seven of them or even one of them. That's all you need to catch. Bream that are deeper than most are also long, and are almost a different species to those thin, pallid, slimy things most anglers encounter. These bream are humpbacked almost to deformity, but where would they be? Like everyone else who tries to answer this question successfully, I get it wrong nearly every time. It's about 25 per cent calculation and 75 per cent guesswork.

Two weeks of the season had gone, and the words 'bream' and 'caught' hadn't been mentioned in the same breath, not even as a question. The syndicate was new and not every member was known to the other. Perhaps no one risked bringing up the topic of bream in conversation as it would force the hand of the inquisitor, push him into a corner where he would have to own up to some capture that might, in his imagination, flood the water with the wrong type of bivvy-dweller. A horrible thought, but one I'm glad to say has subsequently proved unfounded.

Before I even saw the water I chose the relatively quiet side of the lake, one that can frequently be barren of bream. But I knew I would get a pitch and it had also produced a near fourteen for me the previous July. And I was late. I hadn't time for a full lake reconnoitre but my confidence was middling to high; the bream, a bream, must be somewhere. The sun was dropping quickly as I stumbled, festooned with tackle, along the briar-infested path. As I passed each gap in the foliage, my neck craned to view the lake, and I slowed appreciably at every swim – there was movement on the calm lake surface. Not just the coots, but dimples appeared, little rings emanating simultaneously that were too big for fry or insects.

I stopped at the first suitable swim to view the situation, my tackle being heavy and the straps tight. At 60–80 yd out fish were either lying, priming, moving slowly or something like that. Staring at the water resolutely, I made a quick resumé of the situation by naked eye; my binoculars were in the car and I probably wouldn't be any the wiser looking through them in such fading light. I had to choose a swim and started to make some hopeful assumptions about the cause of those ripples. If they were caused by bream there might be a dozen or more, and priming bream often become feeding bream once the sun has dropped. Carp? I'd never seen them in this part of the lake before, and besides, they break the surface in a much less delicate way. Roach? Highly possible. The previous year there had been a huge breeding explosion that resulted in isolated but large shoals of small roach. I had witnessed similar movements from roach before, though I would probably expect almost non-stop activity from a shoal of these 4–5 in 'pests'. As I pondered all this I thought I saw a dorsal and tail fin break the surface, or was it two little roach? Just one humped back would have given it away. But I had something to go on – the fragment of hope that causes every angler to get the groundbait out fast and the tackle made up quickly. I chose a swim as close to the fish as practicable and continued to stare into the water.

It started to rain very lightly and I reluctantly put up the umbrella. I sat on top of the tackle that, save the rods, could be described as vintage but very functional. Between each of those mundane tackle-assembling tasks I gazed fixedly at the water. A tench rolled close in and to the left of the swim. I baited the swim by catapult, thirty balls laced, as they say, with all sorts of goodies. The bait landed within 10–15 yd of the 'dimple-zone'. I was aware that this could put the fish, if they were bream, out of range, but I was mindful of a successful catch the previous season that followed a period of bombarding priming fish with groundbait. The alternative was to fish just hookbaits, hoping that the fish would naturally up-end and feed, but I had no confidence in this method.

Eventually, I sat back fishing. One rod, the softer one, had half a lobworm and two grains of corn as bait, the other had an open-end feeder with flake and maggot on the hook. If roach were the originators of the activity, I thought I

JOHN SEARL .

would catch one before the light finally disappeared. But I didn't, and an hour passed during which nothing happened. The surface movement had ceased.

By this time it was dark, damp and mild, with a gentle westerly breeze blowing into my face. I absorbed the atmosphere while mosquitoes, those creatures *par excellence* of the wet, warm night, attempted to absorb my blood. They kept me alert on this oasis of a lake situated in the increasingly dirty and suburban Thames Valley sprawl. Grass snakes, terns and that avian anachronism, the nightingale, gave an exotic tint to the lake, counterbalancing the drone of traffic, the threat of car theft, the thoughtlessness of some anglers and all the other banes of modern life. The nightingale's song floated across the lake, sounding like a song-thrush at one moment, chirruping like a grasshopper or a warbler the next, and then descending into a harsh echo before reaching a fluting crescendo. It sounded like a lost bird from a rain-forest. Then there were two, the other delineating its territory from the island on the adjacent lake. I was both transfixed and yet boiling hot, my body heat attracting a hundred more mosquitoes whose buzzing and biting infuriated me. A third nightingale then joined in, although by this time the first had lost his vigour. All the while, the more I swatted, the more mosquitoes I alerted to the deliciousness of my blood.

The Optonic bleeped. Except for wind-blown debris, of which there was none, only a fish could have caused that. It was a single bleep, something unlikely to have been caused by a margin-swimming tench. I continued to stare at the water. A flat patch disturbed the continuity of the small waves close to the baited area. This was no roach. More time passed. I climbed into my sleeping bag, as much to escape the lethal insects' probosces as to drift off to sleep.

The Optonic bleeped again. By this time I was getting tired, but I still managed to sit bolt upright in response to the alarm. No bites developed and it was getting hard to prime myself after each bleep. I knew that fish must be bumping into the line somewhere, possibly over my baited area, but I needed to relieve my fatigue. The bleeping stopped and sleeping started. For two hours I lay untroubled, but for the events that followed I shall quote my diary from that morning verbatim:

> At 4 a.m. exactly, my left-hand Optonic bleeped twice. I sat up. The indicator proceeded upwards steadily. Almost immediately I struck, the rod bent but not furiously. I maintained strong contact by winding but couldn't wriggle from my sleeping bag. I didn't panic but consistently gained line in between trying to unzip the bag. The fish just sauntered up and down, I knew it was a bream. I moved upwards caterpillar-like and stepped bare-socked into my galoshes. I could carefully monitor the fish's up and down plodding and gain line. Sixty yards to retrieve takes some time. On two occasions I conceded some line, there were no obstacles to capture. I soon had it in the net. It was huge, obviously bigger than my previous best. I quickly took out the 8 hook (corn and worm) and weighed the fish. 16-9.

One could eulogize *ad nauseam* about a fish like this. I had, like all my contemporaries, been brought up with the fixed notion that 10lb was a big bream and 13lb a near record. For the last ten years we've had to revise these thoughts as we have watched our bream fatten year by year. My first was 4lb in 1978. How big would they grow? Well, so far, 16lb 9oz.

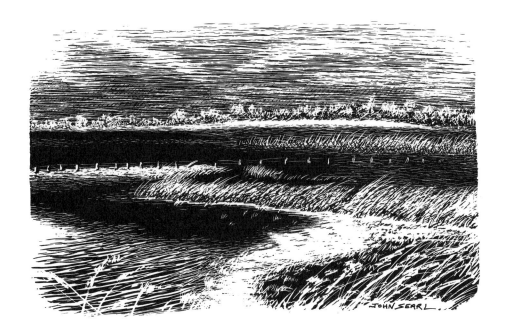

Absolute Euphoria
~
Tony Miles

A bitterly cold, bleak February morning, with an icy wind to make the ears tingle and a clearing river frozen over in all but the faster flows, is hardly the setting I would ever predict for a red letter day with chub. Such, however, were the conditions that greeted me at dawn in 1991 as I surveyed the Upper Ouse from the road bridge, my breath hanging in great clouds and involuntary shivers running down my spine.

Lying snow crunched crisply underfoot as I slowly made my way upstream, peering into every glide and eddy, and studying every raft, as only anglers can. By the time I had reached my destination – a lovely crease swim at the base of a weir-pool – a definite plan had formed in my mind. Four of the swims I had passed would be baited with mashed bread, rebaited every hour or so, and then fished no sooner than six hours after starting. This was in deference to a theory I was testing at that time that progressive baiting entices bigger-than-average chub selectively. The mashed bread was flavoured strawberry, both as an experiment and just for the fun of it. Those preparations over, I settled into my weir run-out for a few relaxing hours in the winter wonderland.

The first daylight hours of a crisp winter morning, where a freezing mist effectively deadens distant harsh sounds of civilization, is one of my favourite times to be at the riverside. No alien sounds disturb the murmuring melody of the stream, save the cheery chattering of birds, an occasional ominous crack from the marginal ice and, now and again, that special 'plop' from a rising fish that makes every angler's heart beat just that little bit faster.

That morning my crust baits searched the long crease for several hours with no response, save the ambitious forays of infant dace. In truth, it mattered not, for it was just good to be there. For the thousandth time, I wondered at the intricate lacework of the frost-embellished cobwebs, and mentally re-enacted the drama that must have unfolded at the spot where the fresh tracks of a vixen ended in a pitiful pile of goose feathers. As I patiently fished my way down the glide, I had an interested spectator in the form of a chubby, cheeky robin which darted between my feet as breadcrumbs fell to the floor each time I rebaited. Eventually, I placed a pile of crumbs on a snow-encrusted grassy tussock and watched in amusement as the robin busily filled its little belly. This bird, at least, appreciated my strawberry-laced feed, but then Great Ouse robins always have been discerning.

Come midday, there was a detectable change in the weather. A milder air stream was becoming very noticeable, as was the fact that ice floes were breaking away all along the river. My first real bite, at 2 p.m., had resulted in the loss of a heavy fish only seconds after the strike, but this was not to be repeated. Thus it was, at about an hour before dusk, that I moved silently into the first of my carefully prebaited pitches. This was a swim the like of which has graced the pages of many a treatise on chubbing: a steady, near-bank glide disappearing under the sheltering arms of a gnarled old willow. The mat of flotsam around the trailing fronds, welded together by a raft of ice, would give any chub present shelter from heavenly intruders. I wondered if the fish were at home.

The first cast into a prepared pitch is always a moment for enhanced anticipation, and my pulse raced as the first strawberry-laced crust offering fluttered its slow descent in the steady flow. Soon, the quivertip eased back into a normal slight tension as the bait settled. Unmoving, I sat expectantly, eyes glued to the quivertip, as much a predator as the heron stalking silently in the margins a hundred yards downstream.

So keyed up was I that I remember the quivertip shaking from the influence of my trembling fingers, and I made a conscious effort to relax my grip on the rod butt and let the rest take the rod's weight. For perhaps thirty seconds the tip was still, before it came alive with a sudden urgency. Some unseen power was drawing it towards the dark, mysterious depths, a power that surged dramatically downstream as it felt the hook. That chub fought long and hard, a fitting struggle for one of its size, but it was overcome eventually by a power greater than its own; 11ft of carbon fibre had done its work well. That February chub was majestic in

every detail. Perfect in every fin and scale, thick of shoulder and deep of chest, it was a chub fit only to grace the landing net of a true believer. And it weighed 5lb 3oz.

At that moment my day was complete. I would have a photograph of my prize and then wend my way home. (I had decided to curtail my fishing time that day as I had been in increasing discomfort the longer I fished, as a result of a heavy fall on the ice the previous evening which had resulted in severe bruising to my back. I bounce nowhere near as high as I used to!) Carefully consigning the magnificent chub to a carp sack, I took a leisurely stroll back to the van to collect my tripod and cable-release mechanism.

It was as I was returning to my swim in the gathering dusk that the rain started, a fine deluge of cold drizzle and sleet. Back at my tackle, the rain had become a steady downpour and I was in a dilemma. I never use an umbrella for winter chubbing, and I could not therefore use an expensive camera without exposing it to needless damage. After contemplating the options for a couple of minutes, I made my decision. The rain was possibly a fleeting thing, and despite the now excruciating pain from my back I would fish on for a short while in the hope that the rain would stop and I could get my precious photographs.

Shortly after, another crust offering was invading the sanctuary under those willow branches, and this time there was no pause for reflection. Barely had the bait settled when the quivertip again plunged round to the attentions of a second hungry resident, and once more I was up on my feet, doing battle with a worthy adversary. It was nearly dark when I was down again on my knees, admiring the classic lines of another pristine Ouse chub, a fish that took the scales to 4lb 7oz. I had been delighted with the five-pounder, but such a brace was indeed a bonus. When the rain eased, I would have a photograph of the pair. A second carp sack was put to use.

Not expecting for a moment any further action on that black February evening, I lazily dropped another bait into the same spot, and this time the crust never even settled. Before I was aware of what had happened, the rod had taken on a mysterious life of its own and, for a third time, I found myself in plunging confrontation with a big chub. This was the stuff of which dreams are made, and when my torch beam illuminated a scale reading of 4lb 8oz it began to dawn on me that something rather magical was occurring.

Although the rain had stopped by this stage, my third and last carp sack was brought into commission, and I made yet another cast into that dark, exciting glide. Although my back was agonisingly painful, I knew I could not pack up – at least not yet. Something was driving me on, something I could not resist.

Ten long minutes passed by slowly. All was still and silent, the moonlight was flooding the valley and the old willows threw long, ghostly shadows on to the bleak landscape. My wet fingers tingled and I realized that, with the passing of the rain, a good frost was forming. A disembodied Betalight hovered in mid-air, the line was crooked loosely around the index finger of my right hand, and I let my mind wander back over the wonderful events of the last hour.

I love to feel the first pulse of life when a bite registers as a sudden tightening of line over my fingers. It is an electric shock that brings me instantly to full readiness. This time I knew what to expect. That initial pluck was the early warning of more serious attention. Sure enough, seconds later, an irresistible drawing of line galvanized me into action. Once more I was locked in memorable conflict with a big Ouse chub, a chub that I knew was something special as soon as I hooked it. The fight was entirely in keeping with the fish's status. For several minutes it hugged the river bed, coming up only grudgingly, and the longer the fight went on the more the adrenalin flowed. The pain from my back was but a memory.

There is something about battling with a big fish in the dark, and that alone makes it so much more primordial and exhilarating. Two or three times the clutch unwillingly yielded line, as the chub sullenly refused to be bullied. Soon, however, the battle was won, and my net sagged to the weight of a prize indeed. Even before the fish was weighed, I knew that I had caught my biggest chub ever from the Upper Ouse. The confirmed weight of 5lb 10oz also meant that for the seventh time in my angling career I had taken two 5lb chub in a session.

At that moment I really did decide to pack up, and after spending a few minutes organizing photographs of a truly memorable catch, I reverently lowered the superb quartet back into their home under the willow. It was almost as if the weather had been holding its breath for me, for no sooner had I commenced the long walk back to the van than the rain returned with a vengeance, a freezing rain that stung my face and chilled me to the very core. I was cold, wet and my back ached. The thought of a warm fire, a welcoming smile and a steaming mug of hot tea created a pleasant vision as I hobbled across the fields. It therefore made little sense when I stopped abruptly by one of the swims I had baited earlier, but had not yet fished. Despite myself, I had to have a cast alongside that little clump of rushes. They were drawing me like a magnet, and as I baited the hook in the blackness I was overwhelmed by an overpowering sense of anticipation. At that moment I knew that I was only moments away from another big chub. I cannot explain it. You will have to believe me when I say it is so.

The bite I expected came quickly, no more than five minutes after my crust had settled against those inviting rushes. It was a dramatic affair, the rod thumping round as another leviathan chub snarled away with the bait. A truly memorable tussle followed, before the broad, silvery flank of my adversary glided over the rim of the net, its large scales glinting brightly in the torch beam I was forced to use in order to relieve the Stygian blackness.

As I unhooked another gloriously conditioned chub, I knew that I had achieved a feat unique in my long angling career: three five-pounders in a day. The proof came with the weighing – 5lb 5oz, the final statistic of a fabulous quintet.

Only an angler can appreciate the feeling of absolute euphoria such an event brings. I would worry about the pain in my back tomorrow, but that night, as I walked at last back to the van, there was a spring in my step despite the aches.

Memories are Made of This
~
Roger Miller

There are a number of anglers, indeed I have met some, who have told me of their utter love of the Wensum. They have enthusiastically discussed with me the sheer loneliness of the deep bends on Carrick's Stretch, the strange and foreboding atmosphere that pervades whenever dusk settles over the old Saxon mill-pool, and the pulsating sense of impending drama whenever a lump of meat is cast to the Costessey barbel lies. Their knowledge of each uniquely individual stretch is admirable, and their ability to quote great captures of the past, from where and by whom, is truly remarkable. But what is even more remarkable is that they have never actually seen the river at all, let alone fished it.

One could argue that the river has received an inordinate amount of publicity over the years. Moreover, the quality of writing that has emanated from the sessions described by the likes of Bailey, Miles, West and Wilson has certainly elevated the river to almost celestial status for the likes of me, who once moved 50 miles just so I could fish it. In reality, one has to look beyond the classic angling tales and examine what actually inspired the great anglers and writers to be so moved. Certainly it could not only be what they had caught, there was always so much feeling attached to their writing. To me, this says a great deal for the river and I can honestly say that I have never fished the Wensum without enjoying, albeit to varying degrees, a unique edge to the session, a sense that just about anything is possible.

If I have learned anything from my time on the river then it is certainly to expect the unexpected. I recall dawns of great optimism as I trudged across humid, mist-shrouded floodplains in conditions so perfect for big roach that I simply knew I had to catch that day, only to trudge back across them again in darkness, per-plexed and without having had a bite. Conversely though, some memorable sessions have begun with me tossing a coin to see whether I even go, and then tossing it again to actually get out of the car and into a wind that makes your eyes water. On these occasions I have been buffeted and windswept for hour upon hour, but have landed fish after fish to my utter astonishment.

I know of no other river quite so unpredictable as the Wensun, so contrary and yet so capable of greatness. To its credit, the river rewards its most loyal subjects handsomely, if eventually, but perversely it can also play strange tricks like awarding an 11lb barbel to an angler who has never before caught one in his life.

For some years now the river has been in decline, and whilst excellent con-servation work is practised along part of its course, the choking abstraction that occurs daily is bleeding its clear waters dry. But even with all the evils at work against it, and in spite of those long odds, the river still manages to spring its sublime surprises. On the occasion I wish to describe, the event was so astonishing that I, one of the river's most dedicated patrons at that time, could scarcely believe it . . .

Perhaps it is appropriate to begin the tale during a period that Bailey and I had looked forward to for months, namely the Christmas pike week at Lyng. With Norwich a snarling mass of traffic, happy shoppers and sickening commercialism, he and I would be virtually alone by the pontoons, with just old man Leary live-baiting on the point, Bill and Reg 'twixt our two camps, and dear old 'Witless' and 'Wanless' spinning everywhere else. As ever, it would be a week of great intensity and hopefulness.

With just one solitary eleven-pounder for five weeks of Yuletide effort, it was not unusual for me to take a walk around the lake and along the river that ran not 10yd from the north bank for much of the way. Bailey would often tell of a session that took place years before when 200 roach fell on a single sitting to him and a friend. The bend still looked enticing, and I would always stop and study it.

On one icy, blank and God-forsaken day he and I listened intently to a tale, solemnly delivered, that concerned a chub of no less than 7lb having trapped itself in the cage that covered the end of the lake's inflow pipe from the adjacent river. It seems that whilst casting a nymph for trout during the summer, our friend's attention had been attracted by a great commotion that resulted in him discover-

ing this massive fish. It was duly weighed and returned, though sadly to the lake. Ordinarily the stretch was chubless, but we reasoned that perhaps other odd chub of the calibre so eloquently described to us may also exist, and immediately hatched plans to find out if this were so.

Returning in the New Year suitably equipped with chubbing gear, I can vividly recall that first session on the bend as I write. It was an evening so moist and yet so mild that to don a wax jacket would have caused one to be uncomfortably hot. I began by flicking a bait to the tail of the bend, with Bailey happy to let his lump of flake fish the middle ground. I never felt happy with my position and, what with the river carrying an extra couple of feet, I was always struggling with the additional water as it constantly pulled the bait out of position. I have never worried about moving early in a session and this occasion was to be no exception. I simply had to put a lump of flake into the head of the big slack. The current was racing through a bit, but the far bank held a lot of slower water and I really fancied fishing on the crease where it met the streamier, mid-river water. This swim did not really inspire me chub-wise, but it screamed fish and I was quite happy simply to try for whatever was there.

The flow pulled and plucked at the line, with the quivertip taking on a healthier arc than was usual. It was one of those rather strange, midwinter days when darkness takes forever to come, and when the dusk is obscured by a gradual bleeding of drizzle and low cloud into light values already so low that you barely notice darkness has arrived at all. Eventually, nightfall was confirmed as the green glow of the Betalight on the end of the quivertip remained the only thing readily visible.

A bite! Surely not, for it was too slow by half – almost gradual in fact. But there it was, the tip extended to the full; clearly a clump of something borne on the semi-flood had been sent to annoy and irritate me. A token flick on the rod was my vexed excuse for a strike, when suddenly, as if to compound my frustration, I caught the bottom to boot! 'Damn and blast it John, I'm snagged,' I bleated.

'Yes, a swimful of old boughs as I recall,' was a good way to appease me, but I was forced to respond.

'Well, I'm giving line to a weird sort of bough,' I replied, as a sack of sand appeared to fall on to the tip of the rod. Something with a circumference of awesome dimensions turned against the lively flow and I was suddenly in all sorts of trouble. The 4lb line twanged and stretched, and it didn't help that I couldn't see where the fish was half the time as the darkness was almost total.

For an eternity, the fish seemed happy to plough upstream, turn, then let the pacey flow push it back downstream again. The fish strained my tackle to the limit and I hung on, praying for fate to be uncharacteristically kind. Suddenly, the game was being played in mid-water, this doing nothing to improve my chances of landing this hugely exciting fish, the species of which I was still unsure. My cynical side suggested that it was a scrappy bream of perhaps 8lb, but the optimist in me glung to the slight hope that it was a contemporary of the chub that had so fired our imagination. More time passed before a swirl appeared, so heavy that I became convinced I had foul-hooked one of the many double-figure pike in the stretch. But then again, the strange gyrations that were transmitted to the rod tip as the fish dived also hinted at a big, old barbel.

Then suddenly it was all over. There it lay, or at least that's what we assumed, as the big landing net was guided to the spot where, by the faintest of perceptions, we discerned the fish to be. I could tell Bailey was taken by surprise at the sheer bulk of the creature he had just enmeshed beneath us. A bream it certainly was, and I shall never forget his words: 'How big is your best bream old boy?' I didn't have to reply as Bailey already knew, of course, but I felt it was a nice way to announce a new personal best.

A sheer 11lb 5oz of the most exquisite looking slime-free bream beams out from the illustration. Although I was not actually bream fishing I shall always cherish that lovely moment as one to savour, especially now that maturity and family responsibilities have gradually diluted my longing and single-minded pursuit of Norfolk's most difficult and challenging fish. Memories, as they say, are made of this.

Close Encounters
~
Bob Morris

There really wasn't much doubt that the swim I was fishing was a total waste of time during the day. I sat on my bed-chair under the brolly in the midday heat and pondered over the situation. The carp were here, at least, but as was their normal routine, they would not make any real move until well after dark and, even then, would probably refuse to pick up a bait before midnight. I was set up in one of my favourite spots, and would be on the water for three days and, more to the point, three nights. I had done pretty well here in the past, taking some good fish and only ever blankling once.

Being a fairly impatient angler, however, I always felt that I should be trying somewhere else during the day, even though I was very confident of at least one chance every night. I would frequently reel in all the baits and take rod and net for a walk, looking for bubbles and any other signs that might lead to the chance of a bonus carp. So far this activity had failed to produce anything positive, apart from a 6lb bream on a bunch of brandlings and a couple of horrendous experiences with some large carp under a particularly snaggy tree. The latter had very quickly either smashed my line or straightened my hooks, and had left me in fear of either damaging the hooks in the branches or suffering a severe heart attack in the process.

My chosen swim was also unusual in that it seemed to give results even when the rest of the lake was fishing at its worst, as was the case at that moment. It was the classic midsummer carp situation: a prolonged clear spell, hot days and cool nights, with mist forming over the water at dawn. The prevailing breeze that sprang up on most afternoons usually pushed a thick belt of scum and algae into the corner I was fishing. Frequently, a number of carp that had been cruising up and down the main lake during the morning would end up under this murky blanket, that on occasion might be anything up to 25yd wide and covering the entire end of the bay. This was also the deepest part of the lake, with at least 16–17ft of water only a rod's length out all the way around the bay.

The marginal shelf was no more than 4ft at the deepest, and a good bit shallower at certain points under the thick branches of the trees and bushes on the opposite bank. I was able to cast my baits (after some practice) into three gaps in the foliage on this bank, and on to clean gravel patches. My normal drill for this spot was to walk round and bait up under the trees during the late afternoon with particles and small boilies. This baiting covered a stretch of some 20yd, with most of the boilies positioned on the three clear patches.

As the positioning of the hookbaits was rather difficult, needing extreme accuracy in direction, height and distance, I tried to restrict the number of casts as much as possible, one a day per rod being the ideal. All three gaps were tight, and if the cast was short you would miss the shelf and end up in the deep water. On the other hand, a deviance in height or direction meant that you would get hung up in the trees. The three casts were also of different lengths: 10yd, 20yd and 30yd as the bay widened to my left.

As you might imagine, on most evenings I would put aside the last couple of hours of daylight to position my baits before settling down for the night. I did manage to recast the middle bait on one occasion when the moon was bright, but generally if I had to retrieve a rod during the night it would not go back under the trees until morning.

I had tried the deep water in the middle of the bay, but had never had any action. The margin on my side of the bay was interesting as it was the same depth as that under the trees. It also had a gravelly feel, but there was no cover except for a low bank of reeds that started just to my right and stretched underneath my rods and up the bank for some 40yd or more. I had never paid any attention to this near side as fish could usually be seen in the afternoon under the trees opposite. I had never seen a thing move along this reedy bank, night or day, or at least not until the previous night . . .

So here I was, sitting down and recalling the events of the previous night. After baiting up with the usual mixture, I had managed to position the three baits in their respective gaps by 8 p.m. Carp were moving under the trees shortly after I

arrived, and I had settled down confidently for the night. After a brew up, I dozed off whilst lying on top of my sleeping bag as I was really tired, but then I woke up to a series of short bleeps on my right-hand rod at around 11 p.m. This was not unusual as the carp often gave line bites when they started to get active. However, it was only just after dark and very early for movement in the swim. A minute or so later, the bleeping started again as the monkey-climber moved up the needle in short jerks. In no time at all I was out of my chair and striking into a fish. I had a well-honed procedure for handling carp in this situation – I bent hard into them and then walked steadily backwards so that I could move them away from the branches before they knew what was going on.

This time, however, I fell over on my back as a 4lb bream succumbed to the pressure, skated out towards me and then sank in the deep water as I lay there trying to assess the situation. This was obviously a disaster, as I was down to two rods on the baited area with the whole night ahead and a possible shoal of slabs moving in. I decided to drop the bait just over the reeds to the left and leave it there for the night. After scattering a few boilies along the near margin, I climbed back on to my bed-chair, this time with the sleeping bag and cover pulled over me as it was a clear, cold night with mist already forming.

It is uncommon to get belting takes in this swim. The fish feed confidently as they feel safe in the area, and this allows for a quick strike that usually takes the fish by surprise before it can bolt into the snags. To assist in this process, I always use free-running leads and bite indicators to cut resistance to the fish. The only weight comes from the indicator which balances the sag of line across the deep water. This night, however, at the worst possible time and for whatever reason, I was wrenched from the arms of Morpheus by an absolute scream on my middle rod. Rolling on to the ground, I struggled to free myself from the tangle of my sleeping-bag cover and a whole host of other items that suddenly seemed to be in the way. After what seemed like hours, I got to the rod and attempted the normal routine. However, on closing the pick up, the rod was almost pulled out of my grip and the clutch screamed as an almighty thrashing started in the thick branches about 10yd from where the bait had been. All I could do was hang on and wait for the fish to stop moving.

It was a pretty hopeless situation; the carp had managed to put a number of sunken trees and bushes between me and it, and no matter how I tried, I could not gain line. After about ten minutes of competing in a grim tug of war, the see-sawing action of the line on the snags caused it to break and, with a final thrash from the fish, we parted company. I hate losing fish under these circumstances, for although I use barbless hooks even in swims like these I worry about the fish being left tethered. Walking round to the far bank, I sat for a while straining my eyes and ears for any sign that this might have happened, but all was silent and I returned to my swim satisfied that the fish had gone.

Why had the carp bolted? Perhaps the lead had tangled or maybe two fish were competing to get the same bait? Who knows? Whatever the reason, I needed a brew up to calm my nerves. I had fished this swim many times in the past and had a good track record. In fact, this was only the second fish I had lost. As I sat drinking tea at 2 a.m. looking at the cool mist hanging over the water, I wondered if I had just been fortunate thus far.

I dozed off in a half-sitting position while trying to decide whether to set up my third rod again, then woke with a jump. There I was, ready to do battle again, but this time nothing was happening – my indicators were stationary. Everything was quiet as I shivered and realized that I was damp and cold. I had a strange feeling that something had woken me, but I didn't have the advantage of latching Optonics at this stage and so I was not sure if I had heard a bleep or not.

My watch showed a time of 3.40 a.m. and I decided to put the kettle on again. Half-way through my cuppa, a bleep on my near-margin rod made me jump. I stared at it, willing it to go. It bleeped again and I stepped down to turn the Optonic off; in the early morning silence, the sound somehow seemed out of place.

I stood by the rod just knowing that a take would come, and sure enough it did, the indicator with its isotope inching up the needle, stopping once, then moving steadily to the top. I clamped my hand over the reel and raised the rod, expecting fireworks, but no, I seemed to be attached to something less lively than a carp. The fish moved to the left and then back again. I tried to exert some pressure, but the fish just changed direction again and swam to the right, passing under the rod. As I tried to wind down, the hook pulled free. I was not sure what to make of this, but after some consideration I came to the conclusion that a reasonable tench had been responsible. Nothing else occurred and I slept soundly until 9 a.m. when I woke to another clear, sunny day.

I spent the morning exploring the near margin, plumbing and dragging a lead along to find a mainly gravelly bottom with 3ft of water in front of me. I baited under the rod tip with a few handfuls of chopped baits and decided to do a bit of float fishing. After setting up an 11ft soft-action rod that I normally use for tench, I was soon pulling out roach and rudd like they were going out of fashion, some of them a reasonable size. It was noticeable, however, that they could only be caught on the shelf.

By 2 p.m. the activity on the float had ceased. It was hot and clear, with a gentle breeze blowing into the corner of the lake. Things were looking good again for that night, and I decided to fish the margin properly in the evening using the light rod as the area appeared virtually snag-free. There was no sign of carp during the afternoon, not even under trees, and I was a bit disappointed at this as they usually showed themselves under these conditions.

Nevertheless, I baited up my two favourite gaps with my normal particle/boilie mixture at 5 p.m. and then set about cooking dinner. While the pots were boiling and the pan frying, I scattered some of the same bait mixture along the near margin in both directions for some 5yd or more. I even managed to position both of my hookbaits perfectly under the trees opposite, a fact which pleased me greatly and which put me in a hopeful frame of mind for the night.

Poking the rod out over the reeds just to the left of the swim, I decided to freeline a small boilie no more than 10ft from the rod, which was inclined towards the margin. In order to keep the line fairly slack and not tight to the bait, I planned to use a roll of silver paper hanging in front of the spool. This is classic margin fishing, in fact, but is only possible during calm conditions. It was a pity I didn't have my old Mk IV and straw hat with me, but such is life.

I lowered the bait into the margin, opened the pick up and attached the silver-paper cylinder to the line. I then checked the Optonic, thinking to myself that it should have been a penny on the spool with a metal plate underneath to catch it. Those were the days . . .

It was a perfect evening. The breeze had died away completely, leaving the surface as calm as a mill-pool, while an evening hatch had attracted an armada of swifts, swallows and martins. The birds took advantage of this bounty, competing for supremacy as they zoomed in and out of the trees, at times skimming the water's surface. With everything in place, I returned to my bed-chair to consume my evening meal. It was true that I had seen no signs of carp that day, but on the other hand it was a very productive swim under these conditions and so overall I was still in a confident mood.

After the meal I put on the kettle and reclined on the bed-chair, feeling drowsy. It was a very mild evening and nearly dark. The isotopes on the two rods cast across the bay stood out like beacons as the whistle of the kettle brought me to my senses. Bats were replacing the birds as I sipped my tea, and while I thought of straw hats and tin plates I listened to their twittering as they circled in and out of my vision.

At exactly 3.40 a.m. I woke up. It was still very mild, in spite of being clear, and I stared at the silver paper on the margin rod, strongly suspecting that it would move. The beacons were hanging motionless, as if glued to the sticks, but I had no interest in them as I waited and watched the margin rod. 'Bleep'. The cylinder twitched up. I was off the chair and over to it in two steps, almost tripping over my tea mug. Turning off the Optonic, I stood by the rod. It twitched a few times and then rose steadily towards the butt ring. With my hand round the spool, I struck and connected with a fish 10ft from the rod tip. The rod hooped over and the fish moved to the right. I tried to apply some pressure and the fish turned again. I seemed unable to get a good bend in the rod as the fish was intent on darting up and down this short section of the margin. This situation seemed to go on for ages but probably only lasted a couple of minutes, during which time I couldn't tell what manner of beast I had on the end. On the one hand it refused to take any line, but on the other I failed to bring it to the surface in only 3ft of water. Suddenly, there was a lurch and the poor rod was bent round to the butt as the clutch screamed.

Still the fish didn't seem to be going anywhere – and then I realized that it had simply gone over the edge and towards the deep water. At this point I guessed that I was into a carp, and a decent one at that, although had catfish been present I might have thought twice.

I can honestly say that I have never experienced a fight like the one that followed over the next thirty minutes. The fish bored around in front of me, at no time taking more than a few yards of line. All the carp I had previously landed in this spot had fought it out near the surface after being prevented from reaching the branches, and most were brought to the net within ten minutes or so. Eventually the carp tired, and I netted it on my first try at 4.15 a.m.

I couldn't wait to see what it was. It turned out to be a beautiful chestnut-coloured leather carp that was both long and deep, and in the light of the torch it looked absolutely enormous. I was convinced that this was my personal best as I'd caught 30lb-plus fish from the water before, but when I lifted it on to the Avons the fish would go no more than 29lb 14oz. It didn't really bother me, but the fish looked so large that I vowed to weigh it again later on someone else's scales. With this in mind I put the beast in a sack for a few hours and, as it was starting to get light, decided to retire to my bed-chair for a couple of hours until someone arrived.

By 8 a.m., miraculously, no one had turned up, so I decided to photograph the carp myself and weigh it again, which I did with the same result. After setting the camera up, I took several shots of myself holding the fish, but sod's law intervened and none came out particularly well. However, I will never forget the excitement of landing that particular fish on what turned out to be my last ever visit to this water. Every time I think of the fish slipping back into the reedy margin, I still find it incredible to believe that it did not reach 30lb.

Lady of the River
~
Bob Mousley

Winter fishing on my local rivers is usually a complex affair, albeit completely self-imposed as I bear no loyalty to one particular fish. Deciding which of about half a dozen species to try for, where to go and when to go can be confusing, so I usually leave planning a session until the last minute if I want to have anything like good results. Weather and water conditions, as always, are the ever-changing variables that must be considered.

This particular day's pursuit, however, was an easy choice. There had been no rain since the floods of Christmas, the result being that the rivers had already gone through a really productive period for roach and pike, both species going off the boil as the water became clear and dropped fast. For some reason the chub were not going that well and temperatures were too low to stand much chance with barbel.

During the preceding couple of weeks I had spent three half-day sessions grayling fishing, each successive trip giving better results with the improving water conditions. I decided that it was high time I spent a whole day at it, hopefully capitalizing on circumstances that may not recur for months or even years if low rainfall trends continue. So, it was no accident or mere whimsical fancy that had me driving urgently through the dawning countryside, that feeling of boyish antici-pation growing with every passing minute.

After the noisy, enclosed environment of the car it was a good feeling when I finally arrived at the water, my heart pounding in my eardrums as I stood there quickly weighing things up. Only the distant mewing of a buzzard and the turbu-lence of water tumbling over itself could be heard in the chilly air. The water-level had dropped an inch or so since my last trip, and I could just make out the bottom in depths of around 2ft.

Close to where I stood, on the outside of a bend where the river necks in, was a small spot that had produced a couple of fish on previous trips. At this point there was a confusion of currents which, when crystal clear in the autumn, could be peered through to reveal fish holding position on the bottom at an angle of forty-five degrees to the surface flow. It is very awkward to present a bait on the float here in low water-levels, and pretty well impossible in these conditions. Only by completely abandoning traditional grayling methods would there be any likely response . . .

A tiny block feeder holding a couple of dozen maggots and loaded with an extra half-ounce was carefully lowered down into the 4ft-deep boil from my seated position, this concealed by sedges a little way back from the water's edge. The power of the current created enough vertical bow in the line to act as an upstream rig and so register takes as a sharp rattle.

A few minutes after the second cast, the rod reacted violently, tingling my arm into an instinctive strike. I stayed seated for a few seconds, enjoying the first action of the day and marvelling at the fact that I was actually back-winding upstream as the fish burrowed into the flow in a good impersonation of a salmon. There are no short lulls or gentle rod-nodding during a fight with these characters; every second from hooking to netting is spent desperately struggling with every ounce of their quite considerable strength. And without fail, every grayling caught needs to be nursed carefully back to life – I have never known one to swim straight off when released. A good strategy with big grayling in these fast swims is to walk the fish downstream to steadier water, thus not tiring them too much or spooking others.

Sliding off my seat and pulling in a downstream direction soon had the fish fol-lowing, albeit begrudgingly. After moving some 10yd, I collected the pre-positioned landing net and carried on down, eyes straining to get that first glimpse. A gorgeous salmon-red-edged dorsal appeared some 18in down, but this quickly transformed into a gyrating silver shape, the fish obviously not keen on being that close to the surface so soon. After further back-winding upstream for a few more minutes, the fish was mine, not beaten but, like most grayling, still indignantly splashing and wallowing as it was guided into the net.

All those will-o'-the-wisp colours were there. Kneeling alone, holding the fish at differing angles to the light against a background of bleached sedges, had me thinking that this must be one of the prettiest sights of winter. I guessed it at 2lb

and a bit; with the fish in the tissuelene bag and on the brass Salters it came to 2lb 4½oz. Superb. What a start, with my actual fishing time amounting to no more than ten minutes.

I slid back on to my feet and fished on for another twenty minutes, but to no avail. Either my grayling was the only one in residence or, more likely, the others had temporarily taken fright. It was time to move on so that the swim could be rested before I returned later. I tried a couple more spots on the way upstream, one of which fishes well when the river is higher, the other when it is lower. Nothing happened in either, despite the fact that I searched through every inch with the float and fed liberally with maggots and small worms. I suspect they were devoid of fish, but they were worth trying none the less.

So I moved on to a swim that was almost certain to produce: a gully some 4ft deep and 30ft long under the near bank, and surrounded by shallows. Four small worms were tossed in above the head of the swim, followed by one under the float, a 4 AAA Crystal Avon set 3–4in overdepth. Holding back hard for a few feet and then easing off allowed the bait to drop naturally into the start of the gully. After it had dropped a few more feet under slight thumb restraint on the centre-pin's rim, the float stabbed under on the first trot. The fish accelerated fast out of the gully on to the shallows in mid-river and then headed off upstream, a carbon copy of the first encounter.

Trying to bring a grayling directly across river when its dorsal is working the current is no easy task. But by dropping the rod tip to touch the surface and applying pressure from downstream, I eventually eased the fish back across into deeper water, where it instantly shot off downstream in a blur of whirling reel handles. Tucking the net under my arm, I set off in pursuit, and after another relentless struggle scooped the fish out 'on the hoof' while keeping pace with the current. At 2lb 5oz this grayling was the twin of the first and just as pretty.

After trying a few more worm-baited trots with no bites, I changed to maggots and had another positive bite in the same spot – this time from a smaller fish of about a pound that was doing its best to feel larger.

During the trudge upstream I was bubbling, the anticipation having been well justified thus far. I felt that the way things were going, fish could pop up anywhere. Approaching the 'S' bends with this in mind, I stopped at the lower bend. Under normal circumstances this was not a swim as such, just a clean patch of gravel slightly deeper than the surrounding rippling shallows. That day, however, the bottom was not visible because of the extra water and a crease had appeared, running out from a slight protrusion of the bank and carrying on for about 20ft downstream. It seemed worth a try before going on to the upper bend – the real swim. Careful plumbing at the head of the crease revealed a depth of 3ft, but I knew that it shallowed up rapidly downstream. I fed in a dozen maggots while I adjusted the tackle, the float set to fish 3in off the bottom with the lowest shot 9in above the hook. This would allow the whole swim to be covered by holding back over the lower section.

On the third trot the float shot down and bumped off something. It was too quick to be a fish for certain, and was possibly just the bottom. After a few more trots I was sure that it had been a fish as the float was going through perfectly every time. I'd convinced myself that whatever it was had been spooked, when the float shot under again in the same place, a fish definitely being responsible this time. Because of the shallow nature of the area the grayling was instantly visible as it powered off downstream into the ripples. It looked enormous as it charged about, its proud dorsal slicing through the surface.

After a nail-biting tussle over runs of submerged ranunculus, I eventually won the fight some 30yd down from the starting point. This one was not quite such a perfect fish, with a couple of replacement scale patches, but it was extremely pleasing none the less, and bigger than the first two, at 2lb 7½oz. A tiddler of about 8in followed a while later, then nothing further. It was time to fish the upstream bend, this change of scene coinciding conveniently with lunchtime.

The upstream bend is a relaxing swim, consisting of a small, whirling eddy with a dead spot in the middle, ideal for fishing a static bottom bait, rod-in-rest style. Having positioned a small blockfeeder on the crease between the main current and eddy, I sat back to reflect on the day over a welcome cup of coffee and some sandwiches. Three fish over 2lb before lunch and half the day still to go. The grayling were obviously feeding confidently, and I tried to imagine what the afternoon and evening might bring.

With my lunch finished, I was still day-dreaming when the quivertip tapped once and then lurched over. Reacting quickly, my strike saw a large grayling tail-walking across the pool. The fish then tore off downstream and leapt a second time as I back-wound furiously and struggled to my feet to keep up.

The fight of a big grayling is so spectacular and varied that each capture stays etched in the memory for a long time, a different case altogether from other small species such as roach, where only the actual fish are remembered rather than the accounts they made of themselves. This grayling leapt a third time and then ploughed off unstoppably back upstream to deeper water. It took a full five minutes to win the encounter, almost unbelievable for a fish of such small size.

As I lifted the net I knew instantly that it was even bigger than the others. The hook was so firmly embedded in the fish's top lip that the disgorger was required for its removal. Any grayling angler will know how awkward this can be, for these fish simply refuse to keep still. I remember cursing as I tried to remove that hook, not through anger but over the sheer tenacity of this beautiful fish with the wiry strength of an eel, enough to damage itself despite my efforts to the contrary. However, after weighing it quickly and taking a couple of photos, the fish was nursed back to fitness in the rapids and all was well. It came to 2lb 12oz. Wonderful.

The afternoon passed enjoyably, several normally unlikely spots being tried just in case the floods had spread the fish around a bit. This tactic resulted in two more grayling of about a pound each, plus another good fish foul-hooked in the dorsal but coming adrift after an arm-aching ten minutes as it shot the rapids.

As evening approached, I arrived back at 'the boil' for a second try. After a short wait, an eager mouth took an instant liking to blockfed maggots, another two at 2lb 2oz. This really was too much to keep in perspective; after all, a whole winter's grayling fishing often fails to amount to as much as this day's catch in terms of size. I would have packed up quite happily there and then had it been dark. However, there was at least half an hour of daylight left . . .

One swim had been untouched all day, a swim from which I had never caught or seen a fish but which always looked a dream. I felt that if I was ever going to get one out from there, it would be on this day. This swim is on the outside of a slight bend in a gap between the second and last of a line of willows. Under these trees is a depression in the gravel, a foot deeper than the surrounding area, and an undercut bank. The flow was even quicker than I had expected, and some branches of the last willow were trailing in the water. This meant that the swim was no more than a 15ft trot, so catapulting loose feed upstream would be too haphazard. A filled blockfeeder with an unbaited hook was lowered down to within 6in of the bottom at the head of the swim and in the line of trot. I sat down for a few minutes to sip the last of my coffee.

The day had been marvellous in every respect, not just with the grayling. I had not tangled, lost a hook or snagged up once. The sun had tried to break through while I ate lunch, and slight breezes, favourable in direction, had sprung up seemingly from nowhere just when required to help with difficult trots.

With my coffee finished and the empty blockfeeder retrieved, I adjusted the float tackle to allow the bait to trip along the bottom while holding back slightly, the current speed in the depression being less than that at the surface. I kept well back, my 14ft rod allowing for an easy trot from the rod top to some 6ft out from the edge. After about a dozen trots the float vanished right on the point of retrieve. The fish maintained position and stayed deep for a few moments, then started to back off downstream under the trailing branches. It suddenly occurred to me that there was no way I could play out and net a good fish in this current, because bringing it back upstream would be impossible.

By this time I had the rod tip submerged to prevent the line fouling, while all the time the fish was taking more. I could just make out a huge silver shape gyrating beneath the surface downstream of the branches. There was no argument, I had to get below the tree.

I threw the landing net along the bank behind the trunk and slithered precariously between tree and river, my fingernails biting into the bark as I kept the rod tip submerged and in contact with the grayling. Somehow I managed it without falling in, and with a tremendous feeling of relief I found myself in friendlier surroundings playing what was obviously yet another big fish.

As the grayling wallowed and thrashed over and into the net, I realized that my final fish of the day was also the largest. Not only this, it was also the most beautiful as well, absolutely scale and colour perfect. I knew that this fish would be close on 3lb. In fact, it came to 2lb 15oz and was 18in long from snout to tail fork. What a way to end a perfect day – definitely the cherry on top of an unbelievable bag which had included six over the magical 2lb mark.

Ambling back to the car, thoughts of how this unique and relatively rare fish is sadly maligned by both coarse and game angler passed through my mind; not really accepted as a coarse fish, the grayling is either exterminated or treated patronizingly as some kind of second-class trout by game anglers. But all I knew was that I had not enjoyed a day's fishing so much in a long time.

Winter Perfection
~
Andy Orme

The rod top thumped over and I found myself attached to a fish more powerful than anything I had experienced before. At 1½lb that barbel left me wide-eyed, shaking and very, very proud. Another of 1¾lb half an hour later left me so excited that I was almost incapable of speech. My reactions weren't too surprising when you realize that the event happened in 1965 when I was only twelve years old. Ever since that day on the Kennet it has been my privilege to be a barbel addict. Tench, chub, roach and other fish I also love, but I'm crazy about barbel. I also happen to adore the Hampshire Avon, which is pretty convenient because it's the best barbel river in the country.

As a teenager living in Watford with no transport of my own, barbel fishing was never readily available. However, I managed to persuade my parents that Hampshire and Dorset were perfect counties for holidays. So began a long association with Throop Fishery and the adorable Mrs Sainsbury's Rosalie Guest House. I caught loads of barbel on those summer holidays and met many fantastic people, some of whom are now my best friends. During those marvellous days on the Dorset Stour, my personal-best barbel rose steadily from those early Kennet tiddlers to almost 9lb. But of more importance was that these experiences taught me about baits, tackle, feeding behaviour, playing, location and other essential facets of the barbel fisher's armoury.

What I failed to achieve on these holidays, however, was the penultimate aim of all keen barbel men – the capture of a double-figure fish. That was my ambition in my early and mid-twenties, but then I moved to Exeter in Devon – about as good a place to go barbel fishing as the Sahara Desert is to go skiing! I regard these as my wilderness years. Then a move to Reading in Berkshire landed me in the heart of barbel country. Although I was within walking distance of the Kennet and Thames, after two years fishing those lovely rivers I still hadn't caught a double. And always there to rub salt into the wound were reports in the angling press: 'Boy's first ever barbel weighs 11lb', and other such ego-destroying stuff.

It was the writings of great anglers like Richard Walker and Peter Wheat that turned my gaze to the middle Avon. Here, it was said, were barbel not just of double figures but leviathans of 15lb or more. This was the sort of stuff I wanted to read about, and so I resolved to forget all other venues and instead concentrate on four or five middle-Avon fisheries. That decision was made in February 1981.

As my home was still in Reading, each journey to Hampshire involved a 150-mile round trip and at least £10 in expenses on petrol and bait. As this constituted one hell of a lot of money and effort, I had to shift the odds for success in my direction as far as possible. My tackle, baits, planning and approach were as near perfect as I could make them, but most important were my careful records of the weather – I regularly monitored wind direction, rainfall and temperature. Before any trip was undertaken I would phone for weather forecasts for the Hampshire and Dorset area, and if the elements were not favourable I would postpone the session.

From February 1981 to 14 March 1982 I made thirty trips to the glorious Avon Valley, caught seventy-three middle-Avon barbel and had had a great time in the process. Thirteen fish were over 9lb and two were over the magical 10lb mark at 10lb 1oz and 10lb 6oz. The latter fish was my first-ever double, and I well remember whooping with joy when I caught it. However, I was lucky not to be killed on the night of its capture as gale-force winds had torn across Hampshire, causing a large tree to crash to earth not 10ft from where I was sitting. If I had held my Mk IV Avon out sideways the tip would have been smashed off. The next day the headline in the *Daily Mail* read: 'The Gales of Death' – apparently others had not been so lucky.

My aim for the 1982–3 season was clear. I wanted a big Avon fish, preferably over the 12lb mark. I knew where such fish existed, and I believed that with my approach and application, it would only be a matter of time before I caught one. The value of being eternally optimistic is reflected in the tenacity with which one fishes. Every trip I made, I expected to land something big.

Between 16 June and 31 December 1982 I managed only fifteen trips because of pressure of work. Twenty-four barbel were landed, five of which were nine-pounders to 9lb 14oz, but still the monster had eluded me. That made a total of eighteen fish of 9lb plus, with just two ten-pounders. Other fishermen had taken elevens and Tony Hart of the Barbel Catchers had even landed a fabulous twelve-pounder. Was my approach wrong, I asked myself. No, I decided, and reckoned that it was just 'the run of play' that had produced biggish fish for me and bigger fish for others.

The arrival of 1983 saw perfect winter barbelling weather: warm westerly winds and masses of lovely rain. Even at night air temperatures were 50 °F, incredibly warm for January.

A two-day trip was planned for 4 and 5 January. After loading my gear into the car on the morning of the 4th, I then discovered that the battery was flat. By the time I had removed, recharged and replaced it the time was 2 p.m., so I didn't make it to the Avon until 3.30 p.m.

The river was brown and flooding over its banks, and with the water tempera-ture at 49 °F my confidence soared sky-high. After two hours' fishing while shelter-ing under my brolly from the gales and torrential rain, the rod top pulled round. Five minutes later, following a spirited fight, a good fish graced the landing net. One glance was enough to see that it was another nine – 9lb 3oz to be exact, and in perfect deep-bodied winter condition. 'Great stuff,' I thought, 'they're feeding.'

I caught no more fish that night, but nearly managed to contract double pneu-monia. Soaking wet, I sploshed my way back to the car, vowing to get a full day's fishing in the next day. I drove to my usual snoozing spot in the New Forest, reclined the car seats, crawled into the sleeping bag and tried to doze off. Some hope! The rain was falling in buckets and hit the car roof like lead bullets dropping on to a metal baking tray.

Dawn saw me back in the fishery car-park absolutely shattered from lack of sleep. Somehow I dragged myself out of my car, loaded the gear on my back and trudged off on the long walk to the barbel hole. Boy, did I feel like a zombie, just like one of those creatures from that great film *Night of the Living Dead*. I bowed my head and plodded on.

On arrival at the selected swim, the normal gear was assembled: glass Mk IV Avon, Mitchell Match, 6lb line and a size 4 hook presenting a large lump of ledgered chopped ham with pork. About twenty pieces of bait were scattered care-fully in the hole, and then I settled down to touch ledgering. It was still blowing a tremendous gale, but the rain had ceased and I was quite snug under my brolly.

After an hour I began to get plucks and very fast, unhittable (so I found) pulls. I endured these bites for about half an hour before reluctantly scaling down the tackle. On went a quivertip, 3lb line, 12 hook and a small bit of meat. This is light gear for barbel, but then I was not certain that barbel were responsible for the takes.

It was about 11 a.m. when I flicked the modified gear out into the swim. With my rod in the rests, I sat back not knowing what to expect. Almost immediately the quiver dipped a couple of inches and a strike connected me with something solid and alarmingly unyielding. How big the fish was I hadn't a clue. Three weeks before I had landed a barbel of 8lb 13oz on roach gear. That one had taken me 100yd downstream and almost ten minutes to land, but the size of it had not been apparent until it was actually on the bank.

The fish I was attached to this time swam slowly and irresistibly out into the main current and sat there. Slight pressure from me produced no result, so I piled on as much as I dared on the 3lb line. Very slowly, I gained a couple of yards, but then the rod was wrenched down and I had no option but to back-wind furiously. Again I retrieved some line by straining the tackle to the limit, and again the response was an awesome retaliatory surge of power. This give-and-take situation lasted for about ten minutes and then, slowly but surely, I gained line.

Rather rashly I bent the Mk IV right over and, with the line singing in the wind, tried to get the fish to the surface so that I could get a look at it. A huge tail emerged and then, following a massive boil, the fish lunged back to the sanctuary of the river bed.

'That could be a double', I said to myself, and regretted the strain I'd put on the flimsy tackle. Suddenly, the fish decided to swim up and down the hole in midwater; 'I'm winning!' I thought. At last the barbel lay on the surface and confirmed its size. Very gingerly, I teased it towards my large net and, with a gasping sigh of relief, engulfed my prize in the deep mesh.

Grabbing the net below the frame, I lifted and was amazed at the weight of the thing. Retreating to the safety of the bank I pulled back the dark mesh and focused my eager eyes on a truly massive fish. It was perfect in every detail and was as thick-set as any barbel I've ever seen. Without more ado I slipped the fish into the weigh-bag and did a rough weigh-in without zeroing the Avon scales. My heart missed a beat when I looked at the dial. Almost panic-stricken, I rushed down the bank to ask two other barbel fishers to witness an accurate weighing. The pointer went past the 10lb mark, past the 11lb and 12lb marks, and on past the 13lb mark to rest at 13lb 12oz. The bag was weighed at 4–5oz and so I called the fish 13lb 7oz.

After a photo session and an attempt to contact Bob Mousley of Ringwood, I realized that the long fight and stress of handling had taken its toll. There was no way I was going to let that magical fish be harmed. For fifteen minutes I gently nursed the barbel in the shallow water, willing it to regain the will and stamina to survive the flooded river. Slowly but surely the fish's feeble struggles turned into strong lashes of its tail, and finally I released it, savouring the magnificent sight of it swimming powerfully off into the river's depths.

'Thirteen pounds seven ounces.' If I said that once to myself that afternoon I said it a thousand times – in between bouts of singing and such like! I even gave the nuisance swans some bread instead of the usual verbal aggro. After almost two years, forty-six trips and ninety-eight other middle-Avon barbel, I had at last climbed the barbel fisher's Everest.

However, one nagging doubt remained in my mind: were the scales accurate? They were about fourteen years old and had not been tested for some time. The next day I took them to the Department of Trading Standards to either confirm or deny my fears. I was told that scales of this age usually go soft and result in over-estimates. That was definitely not what I wanted to hear and I had to wait two agonizing hours for the results of the test.

'Remarkably accurate,' was the decision. 'Accurate to within half a division which is equivalent to half an ounce.' I could have kissed him.

Ships in the Night
~
Alan Rawden

On a personal level I have often found that real red letter days are very often something of a one-off experience. They can, to some degree, emerge from a series of well-planned events, and they can, perhaps, be a hopeful possibility when things are going really well. However, I do feel that only the most arrogant amongst us could ever say that they actually *expected* to catch a particular fish on any particular occasion.

Although red letter days can be predicted on a rather limited level, I feel that much of the actual substance of the prediction is often little more than a gut feeling. Indeed, these were the very circumstances that prevailed one early August weekend in 1987, during the heyday of rudd fishing at The Reservoir.

The build-up to the glorious occasion actually began on the Friday night when Bryan and I decided to fish for the umpteenth time that memorable season. As I rounded the corner from the dam and drove slowly up the bumpy track towards the top gate, I could see clearly that a car was already there. I parked behind it and took in the evening air, but I wasn't impressed. For early August it was cold, dull and windy, and the weather forecast had talked of rain. I quickly unloaded the car and made off down the track. Passing the Point, I continued briskly towards the pine trees, when the unmistakable figure of Bryan loomed towards me in the dying light. We exchanged pleasantries and discussed our mutual aversion to the conditions. A suggestion was made that we both fish the Double swim, as it would be about the only place out of the wind. This seemed fine with me, and so off we trudged together.

The Double swim was basically a small gap in the trees on the east bank of the water and was always a secluded spot in summer, with the two pitches set in a mass of green rushes and yellow irises, and surrounded by a canopy of overhanging trees. Bryan had already made camp on the left-hand side, so I had to make do on his right. Although the strong wind blew off our backs and the trees offered a little protection, the vast expanse of water in front of us was more akin to a wild and windswept ocean. I wasn't too confident as I prepared my swim.

A light groundbait of crumb, corn and maggots was catapulted well to my right, some 30yd out, and a first rod baited with flake was cast out to the baited area in what was by then total darkness. I was in the process of baiting the second rod some yards up the bank, when my Optonic burst into life and the bobbin flew to the rod. I dived forwards but was too far away and the fish was gone. (There were no back-winders with these rudd.) Bryan came crashing through the rushes with a 'Was that a bite?' 'Yes,' I replied somewhat bitterly, rather taken aback by the suddenness of the action. I hadn't expected a bite at all, let alone that quickly. I recast to the same spot and soon had the second rod positioned alongside it. Before finally settling down for the long night ahead, I decided to answer the call of nature. As I reflected on the missed bite and what might have been, it happened again! The Optonic screeched, with the bobbin smacking against the rod. There was another futile lunge on my part, but I was too late. I couldn't believe it. Two bites and both of them missed; most anglers never had two bites on this water in a lifetime.

I sat on my bed-chair licking my wounds and cursing my sheer stupidity. Having missed the first bite, I should have *known* that fish were in the swim. The torment went on . . .

Several short lifts on my bobbins kept me on my toes for the next hour or so, but eventually the activity subsided and I began to doze. A short while later I was jolted back to life when I heard Bryan's Optonic sound, followed by a rather meaningful 'I'm in'. I was quickly on my feet. Little was said as we both watched the windswept surface for signs of an approaching fish; eventually, a pale shape appeared at the waiting net and was duly lifted ashore. We knew instantly that it wasn't a monster and, having weighed it at 2lb 11oz, we quickly returned it to its watery domain. Obviously the fish had moved in front of Bryan, but although he sat eagerly by his rods for an hour or so, no further action followed.

It was approaching 2 a.m. and, with all quiet, I once again began to doze,

believing that any hope of further activity had long since gone. Then I began to get the occasional bleep on the buzzers. Initially I thought that the wind was responsible, but somehow there was a certain feel to the activity that suggested the rudd might be back . . .

I'd been listening and watching intently for some time when, sure enough, the bobbin on the right-hand rod began to creep upwards ever so slowly. After what seemed like an age it reached the rod, and not really knowing what to expect I struck and, rather surprisingly, connected with a fish. It didn't feel like a rudd, with its slow and heavy movements increasingly tench-like. But eventually, when the culprit was within netting range, a huge golden shape appeared on the surface and I realized that it was indeed a rudd – a very big rudd.

When it was almost in the net, the fish rolled and found a new lease of life. It kited powerfully to my right and it was then that I committed the cardinal sin of easing off. The very next instant the rod straightened and the fish was gone. I was devastated. How could so much go so wrong? I cast out once again, totally bewildered by the whole shooting match, and flopped on my bed-chair. It began to rain. This was the final straw. I really had had enough. At that moment Bryan came brushing through the rushes and suggested that we pack up. I didn't need much persuading.

After a good night's sleep and somewhat restored in faith, I returned the following evening. On this occasion I decided to arrive well before dark in order to prepare the swim and generally settle in. It was actually around 6 p.m. when I entered the estate and walked down the track to the water. Although I had a good look around I knew exactly where I wanted to fish: the Double swim, where Bryan had been the previous evening. I tackled up at a rather leisurely pace, drinking in the somewhat intoxicating surroundings – the luxuriant foliage, the wildlife and the almost overpowering aura of being in a secret place, away from the worries of the world.

Eventually everything was prepared and checked several times over, the groundbait having been introduced to an area some 30yd out in line with the pylons on the far bank, these serving as a marker once darkness fell. Although there was a relaxed atmosphere to the general proceedings, I distinctly remember feeling a twinge of nervousness brought about by the all-pervading air of anticipation and expectancy. After one last look around I settled down for the night, casting two breadflake-baited hooks out to the hotspot. With bobbins clipped on and buzzers tested, I was ready. It was all in the lap of the gods. Pouring a coffee from the flask, I began to relax. Night was approaching rapidly, the light ebbing away like floodwater through a sluice, giving the surroundings a different profile. I thought of Bryan, working at the chip shop and unable to fish – but we all have to earn a crust.

By this time it was totally dark and the adrenalin was beginning to flow. Experience had taught me that the most productive time was between 10 p.m. and midnight, and as ten o'clock approached I recast and sat back in anticipation, my concentration intense. In the undergrowth the 'furry folk' went about their nightly routines, while the constant cacophony of thousands of roosting gulls in the centre of the reservoir momentarily distracted me from the job at hand. The wind had dropped, and although there was still a ripple on the water any rolling fish would be seen easily. The minutes ticked by as I scanned the surface near and far. Eventually a fish splashed, way out to the left, while later another surfaced out to the right. My eyes constantly flashed between the water and my bobbins.

Sometime around 11.30 p.m. I began to get single bleeps on my Optonics, accompanied by short lifts on my bobbins and several short pulls. I hovered over the rods in an atmosphere best described as electric. Eventually, the left-hand buzzer sounded continuously as the bobbin drilled up to the rod. In an instant I was playing a fish 30yd out in the darkness, feeling the satisfying 'thump, thump' of a big rudd.

After some initial resistance the fish was soon in the net, and it looked huge. I guessed a weight of 4lb, but the scales said 3lb 10oz. Although I was momentarily disappointed at this, I soon felt pleasantly overwhelmed with my success.

I quickly rebaited both rods and cast again to the same spot. During the next half-hour or so I experienced several short lifts and two good bites, both missed. The first was a butt-ringer which was hit perfectly, but there was nothing there;

the second was an up-and-downer – one of those bites that goes up a bit, then drops back, then goes up a bit more, and so on – and I hit it when it looked like it was going, but alas it wasn't.

A little later I had a very positive drop-back bite and I was in action again. Once more, a big rudd was brought to the net and, although smaller than the first, it was clearly well over 3lb. As the scales confirmed it at 3lb 4oz, I had succeeded in catching the first brace of threes from the water. Sadly, there was no more activity – like ships in the night the fish had gone. I decided to wind the rods in and go back to the car for a couple of hours' sleep. Eventually I was woken by another angler as he parked his car near by shortly after daybreak.

Returning to my swim, I decided to change my end rig and fish for tench until it was light enough to take some photographs. Several tench to just over 6lb fell to my rods over the next hour or so, as they fed avidly. I could have done better but my heart wasn't in it and I was, by this stage, very tired.

Despite the tench activity, it was a cold, grey morning and didn't really look like brightening up at all. I waited until around 7.30 a.m. for better light, but it obviously wasn't going to improve, so I began to set up the cameras. With everything finally ready, I was carrying the net containing the two rudd up the bank when a figure suddenly appeared from behind the bushes. (It's always quite embarrassing when a complete stranger turns up just when you're in the process of taking some photographs.) The character introduced himself as Keith Salter and asked if he could help. After a short chat it became apparent that Keith was no slouch with a camera, so, with the formalities over, I let him take the pictures.

With the fish safely returned it was time to relax and reflect. For Keith it was time to start fishing, but all I wanted at that moment was to go home to my bed and dream of those huge, golden rudd of The Reservoir.

Persistence with Confidence
~
Pete Reading

I t was a typical early autumn afternoon. The Hampshire Avon was low, clear and warm, gliding placidly – almost tiredly – beneath an oppressive grey sky. The ranunculus was at its peak, and in this particular stretch it was coated in a blanket weed which trailed downstream in long, slimy strands.

I was slumped in a swampy swim, annoyed by the sticky closeness of the weather, the inquisitive bullocks, the flies and the lack of fish. It was a difficult length of river – wide, featureless, full of weed and with few obvious barbel swims. For four years I had walked it, baited it and fished it dozens of times in the hope of contacting the big barbel I knew had to be there.

With few apparent holding areas, it seemed that the barbel were prone to roaming through the thick streamer weed, enjoying brief feeding spells every now and then. I often imagined them lying comfortably under the weed, never needing to work hard for their food, surrounded as they were by an abundance of shrimps, snails and caddis. A simple barbel whim could send them a hundred yards up or downstream to a new hidey-hole.

I had been baiting such a spot, I hoped, all season now, and had been encouraged by the occasional six- or seven-pounder every half-dozen trips. To encounter small, solitary barbel is unusual, but I suppose it is to be expected on a sparsely populated stretch. The occasional chub would come along and break the fishless monotony. I had often wished that a barbel would demonstrate the greed that those chub did — I have no doubt that a four-pounder can eat a tin of corn in a matter of minutes, and still come back for more.

Chub or maybe dace were tugging and twitching at the bait. I reeled in to find my three grains of corn on a size 6 mashed out of all recognition. It was definitely a chub; they can slurp in a bait, crunch it up in their throat teeth, then spit out the bare hook. I selected three big grains of corn and slipped them on to the hook. There was no need for hair rigs and braided links for a big, hungry barbel that hadn't been caught before, I mused optimistically. I dropped the bait carefully into the run between the rushes and thick streamer, and followed this by a few more handfuls of corn and hemp to feed the ravenous chub.

The rod tip stayed stock still, flexing only very slightly in the flow. Blue damsel-flies perched on the tip, a little spider ran up and down the rod and a bumble-bee collided with it drunkenly, all in the space of a few seconds. It was clear that the chub had gone. Then it was dragged savagely downwards with a sudden boldness that jolted me out of my torpor more surely than a poke in the eye with a rod rest. It certainly was no chub that thumped and bored under the streamer weed, and the fish soon began to show a stubborn power as only the bigger barbel do. I squelched a little further downstream, and put on a bit of pressure. There was little response from the barbel, apart from more solid thumps and a cloud of silt and silkweed.

Some big barbel run and rush about, some swim sedately upstream, and some go head down into a 'tail-up-and-thump-in-one-spot' performance. This fish was a 'thumper' and I knew it was only a matter of time before it tired. Slowly and steadily, the old glass rod creaking (or was it the line in the rings?), I persuaded a great slab of a barbel out from under the weed. The first time it showed tiredness it turned almost upside-down and flashed deep, bronze flanks and a great white belly, before diving into the rushes one final time. They know when to give up though, and soon my long-sought-after double from this stretch was drifting, gulping and beaten, into my trusty 24in round-framed net.

At 11lb 15oz but with the length of an eight-pounder, the fish was almost carp-shaped, like a big, brassy bullhead. I wished that it had been a twelve, but as I watched it swim tiredly back under the streamer I felt more than satisfied.

The next morning I returned to find a keen angler in my swim. Let him have it I thought, and trudged down to swim B. I was confident and almost carefree as I felt I could fish the rest of the season and still be content with that first big barbel.

Swim B was more open, deeper and faster flowing than swim A. I'd been

dumping bait into it all summer, and was happy to turn up and plonk a hemp-feeder in, adding sprinklings of corn. I soon found a clear spot, and lined up my casts with the reflection of a tree on the opposite bank. I'd had a few fish to 9lb from here before, and again the odd single fish in a day was the norm. It was impossible to spot fish here, and you could only imagine them meandering through the weed until they came upon the little patch of hemp and corn and hopefully tucked in.

I'd been plopping the feeder in for several hours, and the ever-hungry chub were bumping and nuzzling it continually. I lengthened the tail to try to avoid hooking one, cast to the tree reflection, waited until the feeder hit bottom and gently tightened up. Avoiding the bits of drifting weed, I sank the line and rested the rod. The tip was close to the water in a little bay among the rushes to avoid clumps of troublesome loose weed – there must have been some weed-cutting recently, or maybe someone was clearing a hatch upstream.

The rod top dipped once, then curved round confidently. I thought it was a carp, for it zoomed upstream really fast, then moved in under my own bank, raced off downstream and came up to the surface. There was a crash of spray as a barbel, not a carp, came to the top and, with a slap of its tail, dived back into the hole. It

then steadied down a bit and eventually lay gasping on the surface, jammed up against a raft of cut weed in mid-river. I had to slacken off and let it recover enough strength so that it could swim off into the flow again. By lowering the rod and pulling gently from upstream, I managed to persuade it into clearer water, and soon my second double in two days was hoisted clear of the water. It was huge – long and deep, but a little hollow in the belly. I would have believed it if it had been a thirteen, but I was more than happy with 12lb 10oz, a personal-best Avon fish at that time.

Something made me return early the next day – the river just looked right and the barbel were feeding. I more or less skipped down to the swim, my second choice the previous day but looking first rate that morning. The weedbeds downstream were obviously thick with barbel, and these homed in on my baited patch, eagerly hoovering the gravel and grubbing around the weed roots in search of my hookbait.

I'd calmed down a bit by mid-afternoon. The usual 'cast-and-bait-and-wait' routine returned, with long, thoughtful glances up and downstream. Where were the barbel? What were they doing? Would they eat my bait or just ignore it? Having failed in the past to catch barbel I could see, why was I trying to catch barbel I couldn't see?

Such contemplation is part of the therapeutic value of fishing – I should be grateful for the success of the previous two days, I thought. I was content to rest on my laurels when another bold, rod-wrenching bite resulted in the capture of a lean, powerful 10½-pounder. After three doubles in three consecutive days I'd really cracked it – I would never fish this stretch again with the dull, agonizing worry that I was doing it all wrong.

Persistence and confidence are needed when fishing blind for barbel, but it can be even more frustrating when you can actually see fish that are refusing to feed, let alone take a hookbait.

A few years before, I'd fished really hard for a couple of barbel that were often visible in the summer, yet rarely did they show any interest in doing anything other than just sitting under a weedbed with their tails sticking out. I sneaked up to them many times, loose fed the freshest, most fragrant hemp and watched them ignore it. It seemed that they spent most of their time in a sort of comatose, non-feeding trance, thinking deep, whiskery thoughts and holding station with the merest waft of a tail fin or slight twist of the pectorals.

Then one day they turned on. I arrived at barbel fishers' dawn, which is about half past ten, and was more than gladdened to see one of the fish cruising about in the middle of the river. There was a glowing yellow patch of clean gravel at the top of the hole where they lived, and on to this I carefully baitdropped three measures of hemp and six of maggots. I sat back and waited.

Almost skittishly, the two big barbel moved out of the weed and were soon pigging themselves on the baited patch. I couldn't believe it – after watching them demonstrate ultimate uncatchability for a couple of seasons, they looked like absolute suckers. These fish had been caught before though, and the most delicate cast of a tiny bomb and long tail that drifted a small hookbait just upstream of them rattled them considerably. They shot off under the weed and took half an hour to return.

I soon learned to recast only when they were out of the swim, casting well across river, and letting the bomb swing round and sink gently on a tight line on to a small patch of bottom weed. The hooklength of nearly 4ft allowed the bait to sink slowly on to the clean area of gravel created by their grubbing.

Fork-in-the-Tail was the first to make a mistake. As I dozed in the hot, late-afternoon August sun, the rod tip I was trying to concentrate on through half-closed eyes shivered, then shot round violently. I was pulled to my feet by a long, powerful rush downstream, and after some vicious head-shaking the fish swam back upstream, burying itself in the weed under my rod top. The markedly deformed tail that gave this fish its name was clearly visible as it burrowed into the thick streamer weed, but steady, firm pressure and much grating and squeaking of line brought the fish to the surface. Weighing 12lb 6oz, it was – apart from the scruffy tail – a lovely deep, clean, big-scaled barbel.

While I allowed this fish to recover in a gravelly slack upstream, I returned to the swim to find the remaining big barbel still feeding, by then with a much smaller partner that had appeared on the scene. I spent several more agonizing hours watching this giant of a fish move in and out of the swim, feeding greedily at times, its head obscured by clouds of silt as it discovered another little patch of gravel on which to concentrate. By late evening the eels had moved in, and after I had hooked five or six little wrigglers I moved out. Tomorrow was another day, and I was back early – this time at a tench fishers' dawn!

I loose fed hemp and maggots little and often, as the morning mists drifted downstream and evaporated in the rising sun. Soon I would be able to look into the swim, and I prayed that the fish would still be in a feeding mood.

The big barbel let me know that it definitely was still feeding in the best possible way. At a little after 10 a.m., the rod curved round in one slow, firm movement and the butt was lifted off the ground before I could grab it. Down in the hole I saw a flash of white. For one awful moment I thought I'd hooked the little 'un, then a great golden lump of a barbel rose to the surface, shaking its head like a pike, it vast pectorals spread out like wings. Time and again I pumped it to the surface, and time and again it boiled on the top and thumped down into the hole. I'd never felt so terrified of losing a fish and never so elated when it finally drifted exhausted into the net. I hardly dared weigh it – its sheer bulk defied belief – but weigh it and reweigh it I did. It went to 14lb 2oz – a queen among barbel that I shall never forget.

Looking Back, Looking Forward
~
Barrie Rickards

On a rather quiet day in March, at the end of last season, Tim Cole and I sat back in our chairs, staring at motionless floats, and reminisced on the season that had been. We'd just had a really good run of results, with nine twenty-pounders over a ten-day period, quite a few big doubles, and a bag of 185lb in one morning. The smallest fish we'd had for a few weeks was one of 15¾lb – except for a small jack that grabbed my buzzer lure as I demonstrated its action under the rod tip while sitting on my chair! After running through the results, the baits, the feeding times and all the other matters that so occupy keen anglers' minds, we realized quite suddenly just how much effort we'd put in to get those results.

The good spell began with a trip north in the snow, this ending with Tim landing a fish of 21lb on half a mackerel. On a day of glorious sunshine and gentle breeze, the snow disappeared as if by magic, and we spent much of the day in shirt sleeves. And yet the round-journey had been hundreds of miles, and on both days we'd arrived before dawn on a new water. We are now experts at finding somewhere to stay, wherever we go; meals and real ales are easy to find these days if you carry the appropriate guides. Even the hotel owner halved his charges because we were the only people staying there; he also provided endless cups of coffee until late into the night whilst we and an AA official laboured to break into Tim's car, inside which the keys had been left. (Note that a Ford Sierra 2.8, 4 × 4 is one of the hardest cars to break into, much to the despair of the AA roadsman!)

Another trip followed our mini-freeze last winter. As the last ice melted we arrived before dawn after a hairy drive. The wind was about force 5, south-westerly and mild. The barometer was rising sharply and we anticipated, rightly as it turned out, that as this was a shallow water they'd still feed on our deadbaits, for that is all we had with us. Dawn came, and we'd sat there for perhaps half an hour when, at 6.55 a.m., my half-mackerel rod was away on a steady run. A somewhat spirited fight saw a fish of exactly 20lb in the big net. There's nothing like an early 20lb fish to help you face the day ahead.

At 7.15 and again at 7.25 Tim had half-mackerel runs giving fish of 10lb-plus and 17lb; both had been savaged by other pike. At 8.10 I was jiggling a buzzer up and down the rod tip, watching its action, when it disappeared in a toothy maw, and a little 2½-pounder was landed in a flurry of spray. At 8.25 I had a dropped run – unusual on this water – and at 8.30 a repeat run in the same spot resulted in a snapped trace. Over a long period we have snapped traces three times on this water, and always in exactly the same spot, never anywhere else. But we have never seen a fish with our hooks in it, although the rapid strike could only have jaw-hooked the fish, as is almost always the case here.

There was little let-up that morning for, at 8.40, off went Tim's half-mackerel again, this time to a fish of 15½lb. My next turn came at 9.05, once again on half-mackerel, and this time the pike went to 22lb! Only ten minutes later I had one of 10½lb on half a sardine, and twenty minutes after that I took a fish of 5lb on a whole herring that I'd used to replace the sardine. At 10 a.m. I had a violent run on half-mackerel again, this one weighing 4lb. Then at 11.55 – note the two-hour lull – I missed a take on a whole herring (which was pinched by the pike!). Minutes later its replacement, a very small herring, trundled off across the water and I had a fine, fat fish of 22¾lb. What a morning it had been! We were fishing together, incidentally, but it happened that the twenties were picking up my baits, even though, at times, the baits were very close together.

Tim had a little bout of spinning and pulled out three jacks, then forgot that big ones take lures and pulled out of a good twenty-pounder! It wasn't his day for the biggest fish. At 2.15 – note the two-hour lull again – I had yet another herring run and a fish of 10¾lb, and then at 3.15 another splendid fish of 22lb 6oz on a herring head (the bait was running low). Finally, Tim took one of 16lb on a half-mackerel. It had been quite a session, and was the first time that I had caught four twenty-pounders in a day.

JOHN SEARL.

Then I thought of all the effort, in reality, that had given us that day. Although we are only able to make infrequent visits, we had kept the baits going in, trying to encourage the pike to be catholic rather than selective in their choices. And we had put out wire parcels of chopped baits, to attract but not feed. (If you do this, incidentally, try to change the attractants once a week, something we were unable to do.) Also, in the summer we'd taken spades to try to cut something resembling a seat on the difficult banks. We'd also taken the trouble to make certain arrangements with the farmer so that our access route could be eased a little. In short, we'd put in days of groundwork, and it had paid off in one glorious morning and a pretty good afternoon. Normally, the water here is slow, and that, I think, is the message that comes through when Tim and I objectively examine our past results. It is easy to get carried away with the euphoria of a good catch, but time and time again it has been preceded by considerable effort on our part. However, I must say that we enjoy the effort too, and we always have at least half a dozen hair-brained schemes on the go – even though most of them fail!

I had another good spell over a couple of days or so last season, on two quite different waters. We were at the water very early on the first day, on this occasion with a guest. Indeed, we were away so early that morning that I was cooking bacon and eggs on the bank even before my usual breakfast time. It was an odd sort of day. At 6.55 a.m. I had run on half a herring which resulted in a fish of 15¾lb, and at 9.10 I had another run in exactly the same place and to the very same half-mangled bait, this time from a fish of 18¼lb. And that was it; even though we had two rods apiece, both runs came to the one rod. However, the interesting day was the next one.

On the first day we'd tried another water as well, just to try to get our guest a fish, and he did have a follow on a lure from a lovely pale-coloured double. We decided on the same two-pronged approach the next day, even though it involved the disruption of having to move venues. The plan paid off. At 7.20 a.m. Tim's half-mackerel went off at a run, resulting in a fish at 17lb; at 8.10 my smelt was away, and my own run of luck continued with a fish of 21¼lb. The smelt had had wool soaked in added smelt juice stuffed down its throat, a trick taught me by Colin Dyson. Tim then took a half-herring fish of 19½lb (just his luck at that time) at 9.20 a.m.

Then the water died. Later, when it was obvious that it really had died, we moved lock, stock and barrel. We had one take, which fell to my rod, to a 6in Kilty Lure. Yes, you've guessed it, it was our guest's pale-coloured double, and it weighed 20lb 2oz!

What had paid off for us on those trips was not so much the preparation, though there had been some of that, but the planning and the sensible decision not to stay rooted to the same spot or water. On a subsequent visit, you'll be pleased to learn, the roles were reversed and Tim got not only yet another 19½lb fish, but a twenty-pounder too.

One for the Books
~
Phil Smith

W riting about a red letter day allows you to choose from a range of possibilities – first fish, big fish or even overcoming a particular difficulty in order to catch a very ordinary-sized fish. However, the one single aspect that seems to hold true for any red letter day is that the memory of the event stands out from the normal catches of a fishing season.

My red letter days are many and varied, but for this particular piece I have taken the liberty of making it a red letter weekend rather than a day. It will come as no surprise that I spent this weekend, like so many others over the last few years, at Queenford Lagoon in the pursuit of the monster bream that swim there.

A normal weekend session at Queenford is usually like a quiet holiday, with no fish or bites to disturb the syndicate members passing yet more hopeful hours at their Mecca. But arriving on the bank that weekend in early August 1989, I found Jeff Mills in a jolly mood as he related the capture of his personal-best bream at 14lb 4oz, taken in the early hours of the Friday morning. The fish had been caught about one-third of the way along the north bank from the Caravan Corner. The problem with big bream in general, and Queenford bream in particular, is that current events offer no guide as to their future actions, but at least Jeff's fish indicated that the bream were feeding on anglers' baits.

After much deliberation I decided to split my options and fish two different bars which were positioned off the east bank. One of the two bars had produced a 15lb 6oz fish to me earlier in the season, whilst the second bar had not even resulted in a bite after several sessions. This night was one for the books in Queenford's history in that there were anglers on all four banks for the first time. I was on the east bank, Tony Miles was on the west bank, Derek Quirk and his guest Andy Mundy were on the north and lastly, Pete Coates was on the south side.

Using an Eagle echo-sounder, I quickly placed my marker on the bar that had produced the fifteen-pounder and moved over to the other bar, sweeping back and forth to find the nearest point to my fishing position. This proved to be a near-vertical drop-off that fell from 5½ft to 12ft, creating a truly remarkable feature which just screamed to be fished. Having checked the layout of the second bar, I positioned my marker about 10ft back from the drop-off and baited up with two cans of sweetcorn mixed with brown breadcrumb. Following my practice at this time, I flavoured the crumb lightly with strawberry in order to make it different from other groundbait beds that the fish may have browsed on. A pint of casters was scattered about and I felt that all was ready – all I needed was for the fish to move in.

My rods were 12ft through-action, with a 1½lb test curve, and with 6lb line going down to a double-hook rig. The top hook, a size 14 Drennan Crystal, carried a caster/sweetcorn cocktail, and the bottom hook, a size 6 Drennan Specialist, was loaded with my first-choice bream bait of lobworm/sweetcorn cocktail. The latter was achieved by threading four large grains of sweetcorn over the hook and up the line, then hooking the lobworm through the end and again threading up and over the hook. Once the lobworm was on, the corn could be slid down the line to rest on top of it.

I positioned the baits very carefully, and after my quite active spell of preparation I sat back and relaxed – an aspect of our sport that most non-anglers seem oblivious to. At peace with the world, I lay back and looked above to see satellites tracking their way across the starry sky. Very soon though, my star-gazing was interrupted when the rod on the far bar developed an indication. The strike proved good as the rod bent over into an unseen fish, but the fight was short and very poor, quickly resulting in a tench on the bank. A good number of tench get caught at Queenford but this fish, at 7lb 12oz, was a new best for the syndicate. Any joy at this, however, was balanced against its quite unnatural shape – it was so fat that it was almost certainly spawnbound.

The next indication came at 1.30 a.m. to the same rod, and I played the fish by walking along the bank to make netting easier. The only problem was that I forgot the torch and hence had to net the fish where the splash or swirl showed. At the

JOHN SEARL

time I thought it was another tench, but when I looked into the landing net at a nice bream I thanked the angling gods for their help; I had been very casual with its netting and could easily have lost it. Any bream from Queenford is an event, and at 10lb 12oz this fish was most welcome. No more indications occurred during the night and as day-break came I was very pleased with my two fish from this new swim.

On Saturday I inspected the bar that had produced the fish and was quite surprised to find that it was enormous, extending some 80yd away from the point I was fishing. With a width of between 10ft and 30ft it dwarfed any other such feature known on the water and was soon named the 'M1'. Indeed, in seasons to come this was to prove the most productive spot on the lake.

Moving to my left, I positioned myself opposite the productive area and also baited up a second swim on the same bar about 30yd further left. Having had my success the previous night, I prepared both rods in identical fashion. I could only wait to see if the bream would return.

Within half an hour of darkness I was getting the odd twitch and lift of the indicators – this could have been caused by tench, but my hopes soared as I thought that the bream might be back. At 11 p.m. the indicator fell back to the floor. After a good, hard sweep of the rod, the 'thump, thump' of a hooked fish could be felt as I played something that fought far better than either of the previous day's specimens. Some five minutes later I slipped the net under a bream that was obviously bigger than the 10lb 12oz fish still fresh in my mind. Having zeroed the Avons against the weigh-sling, a weight of 14lb 7oz was the heart-warming result that met my gaze.

My next priority was to get the baited rod back out into the swim and, that done, I again sat back, anticipating no further action. However, the twitches continued and I wondered whether I would have another chance. By 3.15 a.m. my nerves were nearly gone as I kept expecting one of the lifts to carry on up to the rod. Then, at long last, one did, and in very quick order I was weighing a 13lb 12oz bream. Brilliant!

The baited rod was soon out again, and although twitches and lifts indicated fish were still in the swim, dawn came without another bite. I reflected on a very satisfying night, with two excellent bream and many more heart-stopping moments. Just as I was dozing off, a loud animal scream woke me. A quick look around revealed two mink working their way along the bank in my direction. As it had been a fine night I had not bothered with a shelter or umbrella, and very soon one of the mink had disappeared under my bed-chair. Thoughts of rabid mink and their large teeth came to mind as I jumped up, scaring the pair of them back from whence they had come. As I said earlier, non-anglers think we only fish!

At 6.30 a.m. the indicator fell back to the floor yet again, and looking out to the marker I could see a tufted duck leaving the swim. These birds can be a downright pest as they dive to take your bait, and thinking I had hooked its mate, I picked up the rod and pulled into a solid resistance. As I pumped and reeled, I wondered how long a duck could stay under water as it still hadn't surfaced. By this stage there was quite a resistance, but still I thought, it was only a duck. Surprise, then, is not the word that fully described my condition when, some little time later, a very large bream obviously attached to my tackle rolled in front of me. What had I done? Did I still have a hookhold? The questions tumbled through my mind as I gingerly played this fish as though on gossamer line, when only moments before I had treated this same line as if it was a tow-rope capable of pulling a 10cwt car.

Angling memories are mostly of moments; high in my store of such moments is the net slipping under this obvious giant and the realization that I was breathing again, for I think I stopped using air completely over the last 20yd of the bream's trip to the waiting net!

At 15lb 14oz the bream set a new personal best which still stands today, perhaps never to be bettered, although I always live in hope.

Mirror Image

~

Peter Springate

During the closed season of 1991 I fed Chum Mixer to a large carp that I had never seen before at Wraysbury, and that I estimated to weigh in the order of 45lb. There and then I resolved to catch that fish if I possibly could, even if it took a whole season. On 4 July the fish was mine, taken by stalking and using a Richworth birdfood boilie. It weighed 45lb 6oz.

I continued to fish at Wraysbury for the rest of the season in the hope that I might catch one of the known 30lb-plus commons in the water, also suspecting that my big fish would eventually be landed at an even greater weight. In June 1992 my first five-day session at the lake was a complete blank, with not a sign of a carp moving. By July I had arranged to take the first Thursday and Friday of the month as holiday, planning to set off on the Wednesday evening. Unfortunately, I didn't finish work until late on the Wednesday and as I went to bed with the rain teeming down and a strong northerly wind blowing, I hoped that the fish would be pushed down to a swim I had made on the Point the previous autumn.

The early morning call at 5 a.m. was a complete waste of time. I was so exhausted from my long day's work and readying all my tackle that I just went back to sleep. Eventually I woke up at 8.30, but by the time I arrived at the lake it had gone midday. I chatted with a couple of lads, only to find that they thought the prospects looked grim as nothing much had been caught recently. Still feeling confident though, I made my way to the swim where I had started my campaign at the beginning of the season.

I set up my 12ft 2¾lb test rods with baitrunner reels carrying 20lb Abu line to combat the heavy weed growth and gravel bars. The first rod was baited with two 14mm Richworth condensed-milk boilies on a small hair to the hooklink, a couple of inches above the hook. From the back of the hook itself I used a pop-up made from a cork ball and held down by the weight of the two boilies. This was then cast about 20yd in front of me to a clear spot some 12ft deep and around which I scattered about a hundred free offerings. My second rod had a simple pop-up rig set at 2in off the bottom and cast to a bar running between two islands about 100yd to my right.

I sat up until 11 p.m. watching the water for any signs of moving fish, but as I saw nothing, not even a tench, I turned in for the night. At 5 a.m. I was woken by two sharp bleeps on my buzzer and immediately jumped up. The bobbin on the first rod had dropped back a couple of inches. After another bleep I struck, the rod arching over into what I knew was a big carp. The fish started to move into deep water, so I flicked off the anti-reverse and began to back-wind, slowly at first, then faster and faster – so fast in fact that I had a job keeping up with it. By this stage my rod was bent right round and I was sure it would break. With the reel groaning in protest, I prayed the handle wouldn't snap off in my hand.

After taking about 80yd of line the fish tried to get into a weedbed, but steady pressure brought it back. Then off it went again; there was nothing I could do about it. Eventually I managed to get the fish to a position where I could wade along a gravel bar running from the bank and try to net it. Without doubt, this was the hardest fight I'd ever had from a fish, and at first I wondered whether I might have hooked one of the uncaught commons. Finally, I saw the fish roll in front of me – it was a huge mirror carp. But what a job I had trying to get it over the net! It was like trying to pull a dead weight inch by inch, until eventually the carp went in.

Dropping the rod and grabbing the landing-net arms, I tried to lift the fish out, but it was so heavy that I had to get a better grip, and even then I only just managed to struggle up the bank. I laid the carp on the unhooking mat and couldn't believe my eyes. It was colossal! I was glad the arms of my landing net were made of solid glass, otherwise I'm sure they would have broken under the strain. I quickly unhooked and weighed the mirror at just over 47lb, settling for 47lb exactly as my scales only weigh in half-pound divisions. Then I put the fish into a keepsack.

I sat down and put the kettle on in a daze. Was this the big fish I had caught

during the previous season or another? I thought it looked much deeper. Should I bring in the other rod and telephone Bob Baker and Richard Skidmore? Then I realized it was only 5.15 a.m. – a bit early, I thought. I'd wait until 8 a.m. I might as well get the rod back out. Rebaiting, I cast to the same spot and sat back thinking over the events of the morning and drinking lots of coffee. The time seemed to take forever to pass.

I was just finishing yet another cup when the second buzzer sounded. I was on it like lightning. Another bleep made me look out through the gap to see if any coots were responsible, but there were none to be seen. As I watched the line where it entered the water, it started to lift and, grabbing the rod, I struck. With the fish on, and remembering that the far side of the bar was very sharp, I held it on a tight line until it boiled on the surface. Pumping it back, the fish kited at a forty-five degree angle to my left and I had a job to keep up. I knew from the general direction of the move that the carp was heading for the gap behind the small island on my left, and I had to turn it or it would be lost. Only just managing to keep the fish on my side, it then headed for some overhanging bushes on the island, finally going through a gap on the shallow side of the gravel bar.

I waded out into the bay behind me, confident now that the carp would be mine. Holding the landing net, I played the fish towards me but it wasn't quite ready and nearly got tangled up with the other carp in the margin. I could see that this was another big mirror and eventually managed to get it into the net. I laid the fish on the unhooking mat and had to use forceps to remove the hook. After I had hoisted the scales for the second time that morning, this one pulled the needle round to just over 37lb 8oz. I sacked the fish quickly alongside the other mirror and finally reeled in my second rod, still unable to believe my luck.

The date was 3 July and, but for the fact that it was a leap year, it would have been exactly one year to the day since I last caught the forty.

Success or Failure?

~

Dave Steuart

M y friends are lying! I most certainly have not told this tale more than a thousand times. I would admit to having mentioned it casually when reference is made to the photograph in the living room, and I have written the tale before for the lovely old *Angling* magazine, but the chance to rewrite the story cannot be missed.

All narratives should have a beginning, a sequence of events, and I suppose a good start to this one would be when my good friend, Brian Harris, Editor of *Angling* at the time, asked me to share a salmon beat with him on the River Avon in Hampshire. The beat was to be on the Severals Fishery at Ringwood, and although it was not a particularly prolific beat for salmon, I jumped at the chance as quite a few very big salmon had come from the Severals over the years. As a keen salmon angler, the chance of catching a really large salmon particularly appealed to me.

What is a very big salmon? When I was a youngster most seasons produced a

40lb salmon from southern rivers such as the Frome, the Stour and the Avon. The Wye also gave forth some of these monster fish, as did a few of the famous Scottish rivers, notably the Tay. All of these rivers, and others, also produced a good crop of thirty-pounders. Alas, this is no longer the case. Some may accept the decline of very big salmon as being in the order of things, merely part of a natural cycle, but I do not. The greed of man in overcropping the salmon at sea once the feeding grounds and migration routes were discovered is a prime reason for the disappearance of these very big fish, and Britain's southern rivers have suffered so badly from abuse that salmon of all sizes are declining in numbers. The few fish that do return are not spawning very successfully due to the filthy condition of these once gin-clear rivers. Intensive farming, land drainage and increasing sewage have contributed greatly to the decline, but in my opinion the final straw came when fish farms were allowed to proliferate and spew forth their untreated effluent into the rivers.

So, to ask again, what is a very big salmon? I think that now I would have to say 30lb. However, I must not give the reader the impression that I thought a 30lb salmon was a *very* big fish at the time I joined Brian Harris to fish the Avon. I wanted to catch a 40lb salmon!

Back in 1977, the year of this reminiscence, my friend, the late Malcolm Wink-worth, used to spend a lot of time in my fishing-tackle shop. He would spend hours confusing me with chat on amino acids, proteins, high-value carp baits, low-value carp baits and so on, and for me, who used to carp fish with little else but bread, potato or worms, it all seemed a bit much. Equally, I doubtless confused him with chat of salmon fishing, the why's and wherefore's, and tales of the majestic and huge silver fish that had come from the Avon. I do remember a discussion that our native fish, the salmon, grew a lot bigger than those immigrant carp. The Avon record salmon was a fifty-pounder (actually 49¾lb), and many fifty-pounders had come from several British rivers, the biggest of all weighing over 60lb! I was prejudiced of course, but until the 1960s salmon did grow a lot bigger than carp, and were the thing to go for if one was after big fish.

Whether or not my enthusiasm for salmon had rubbed off on Malcolm, or, more likely, it was the closed season for coarse fishing, he asked me to take him salmon fishing. Perhaps I tried to put him off, as I explained to him all the problems associated with Avon salmon fishing on a mediocre beat. I told him what a bore it can be, working a long length of river for cast after cast without a touch, or any indication that there is anything in the river at all. And when at last the rod hammers over it turns out to be some damn great coarse fish that you would give your eye teeth for if it was in season – a 7lb chub perhaps – but it's the closed season so it don't count, mate! Or even worse, it is a fine spring salmon that makes your adrenalin pump as it leaps high in the air and shows itself to be a fresh beauty, only to fall off!

Salmon are notorious for coming unstuck, and both my wife, Kay, and myself have had seven salmon come unhooked consecutively before one stayed the

course. Bernard Aldrich, a well-known head gillie of the famous Broadlands Salmon Fishery on the River Test, told me he once lost thirteen salmon before he managed to land one. He was in such a state that he was almost too frightened to hook another one in case it fell off. After such traumas things get back to normal, and only about one in four throws the hook.

As I recall, there had not been a salmon caught from the Severals Fishery beat so far that season, and so I was far from optimistic. However, there had been plenty of water, and although the river was still full and carrying some colour it had dropped back a bit, was fining down and was well fishable. After the high water there would be a very good chance that a fish or two had come up and was thinking of settling into a lie in the more comfortable conditions. I should really have been a more optimistic cove when salmon fishing the Avon, as I had caught a lot of salmon over the years after heavy water conditions on the Dorset Stour, this river having far fewer salmon running its waters than its sister, the Avon.

We were on the river bank fairly early, only to be confronted with a thick, white frost. But as frost often means a warm, sunny day later on, I accepted it happily – but I do hate the cold!

It is difficult to know what lure to fish in heavy and slightly coloured water. Devons are a good choice for heavy water conditions as they will get well down in the increased water pressure when compared to other lures such as bar spoons. There are plenty of other spoons and lures that will get down in heavy water, but on the Avon there is not a great choice of lure as Water Authority bye-laws restrict one to revolving baits. Wobbling baits are forbidden until 15 May, as is the use of prawns, shrimps and worms, and as our day was the last day of March we were a bit early for those! In clear water I prefer dull colours like brown and gold, and in dirty water, the Avon favourite, the yellow-belly Devon has little to equal it. In this still coloured water it seemed a good idea to hedge our bets, and so I suggested that Malcolm use a yellow belly, while I tried one of my special brown and gold Devons in the hope that it would get close enough to a fish for it to be seen.

Although Mal had not fished for salmon before, he took to the work like a veteran, with me leading the way and he following some 30yd behind. Basically, one casts at about forty-five degrees downstream, lets the bait swing across to one's own bank, retrieves, moves two or three paces downstream, and then repeats the process, trying not to miss any possible holding water. It can become somewhat automatic, but it shouldn't. There should be a certain feel for the water and the pace; an instinct that knows the bait is fishing right. And if the bait *is* fishing right, one knows that a fresh fish will take, or at least knock the bait and show an interest.

We worked down the top stretch very carefully, this being one of the more productive bits of the fishery, until we reached the bridge and its adjacent pub at about lunchtime. The early frost had not been a forerunner of expected sunshine and heavy rain was falling in the distance, so neither of us needed to persuade the other which direction our feet should take.

With food in our bellies and having partaken in a small amount of alcoholic beverage, we felt warmed and more hopeful as we returned to the task of trying to catch salmon. Still leading the assault (although we would soon change so that Malcolm fished through first), I fished on downstream of the pub through the fast, broken run. Although of no great depth, I thought that this stretch might well hold a fish, what with the extra 18in of water. Cast followed cast until suddenly the rod was well bent as a fish thrashed the surface to foam, shaking its head again and again in an effort to throw the hook, until it went a good 20yd downstream of where it was first hooked. The line had gone through a bramble bush growing on the river's edge, but that was easily cleared as I scrambled below the bush, following the line's entry into the water as it poured from the spool. As I came level with the fish, and with the line running vertically down into the water, it was obvious that unless the fish was digging its way to Australia, the line must be caught around a snag. I had to feel my way carefully out over a lower mud bank (usually dry but covered in water on this day). Although I sank in the stuff somewhat, I got far enough to push out the line and free it.

I had expected the fish to be well downstream after all this – perhaps through the old railway bridge that was covered with debris from the flood – but (thank you Lord!) it was way upstream. I would guess that it was at least 60yd upstream, and as I leaned into it to bring it back down it moved to the other side of the river. Before the fish came level with me, I managed to swing it over to my side and brought it under the rod by applying side-strain and with the help of the current. After applying more pressure the fish rolled to show a solid flank, and I told Malcolm – to whom I never stopped chatting, giving a running commentary while playing the fish – that it was certainly over 20lb and probably 24lb or so. However, the fish didn't like the pressure and charged off upstream again, taking an unbelievable amount of line with it.

Altogether the fish went off on five of these long runs; each time I pressured it back it came down on the opposite bank and, using the same technique each time, I finally manoeuvred it so that it was under the rod top. The number of long runs should have indicated to me that this fish was a bit special, but I had had some very hard fights with salmon in the past, so did not give it a thought.

Eventually, with the fish making only little surges into the current, I thought I could end the battle, but it was not to be. All the pressure that could safely be applied did little to move the fish, and it withstood the bend of the rod, simply treading water for over a quarter-hour. The way to move a fish is to get downstream of it and turn its head into the current. The fish then has to move or at least fight to regain a head-upstream position. I was fearful of using this tactic as a salmon will often make a hard, unstoppable run downstream as a consequence – and downstream was the damn bridge, its iron girders hosting a mass of branches and logs. But we could not go on like this forever – my arm was aching!

I loosened and freed my feet from the clinging mud, did a soft shoe-shuffle downstream a couple of yards or so, and with the changed angle of rod pressure brought the fish straight to the surface. I then swung the fish into the bank and over the shallow mud bank on which I was standing. 'Gaff the ******* thing!' Mal did so, and then really struggled up to the high bank. I couldn't understand why this took so much effort for the fish was covered in mud and did not look much over 20lb. But as I washed off the mud, like Topsy it grew . . . and grew . . . and grew . . . until, looking at this great silver springer, I thought I had caught my 40lb salmon. Malcolm had timed me as I played the fish, and although I had not thought it to be much more than twenty minutes, I was surprised to learn that I had played it for twice that time – forty minutes, in fact.

Malcolm and I fished through the rest of the beat without further incident, this time with me following him. I would have loved it if he had caught a fish as it may have given him a yen to do some salmon fishing, but he didn't, and he didn't.

A bigger fish has not come from the Avon since I caught this fish, although a couple were almost as large. It is a pity that it is unlikely that bigger fish will ever be caught in future unless there is a drastic rethink of how to conserve the world's salmon resource and how to return rivers to their former ecological purity – something very different from the chemical purity parameters used by scientists.

We anglers are a funny lot. We tend to classify our bigger species in 10lb weight blocks – ten-pounders, twenty-pounders, thirty-pounders, forty-pounders and so on – and so my fish, which weighed 39lb, would fall into the thirty-pound block. I was over the moon when I caught this fish; but as I considered at the time that a salmon had to be 40lb to be a really big fish, I guess it wasn't a successful capture but a failure! What do you think?

Bitter-Sweet

~

Peter Stone

The sun was beating down from a hot, cloudless sky as I arrived at the pit. It was July, and the previous day I had spotted some large tench rolling in an area along a line of overhanging willows. To my frustration, work prevented any fishing until early evening. I knew the water well, and many, many hours spent in search of its tench had shown that the middle of the day, no matter how hot, was the time to be abroad. In ponds and lakes dawn and dusk are usually the most productive times. One of the older writers, whose name escapes me, had this description of the best times for tench: 'When the mist rises from the water foretelling the hot presently.' He was, in his defence, referring to lakes and ponds, but tench in gravel pits, in my experience, are different animals. In this particular pit few tench had graced my net during the evening, but they had moved into the area and I was feeling fairly confident.

Loading my rucksack and rods on my back, I started the quarter-mile walk to the swim. Ten minutes later, drenched in sweat, I put my gear down, and as I did so a tench rolled.

A puzzling feature concerning the tench in this particular pit was their apparent reluctance to roll. My experiences of fishing the water over twenty years had shown that the tench behaved differently to their counterparts in other waters. Although on most days I saw one, possibly two, roll, to see several do so was rare. On the occasions when consistent rolling did take place, a bite was almost assured. On this particular evening, seeing a tench – and a very big one – roll immediately on arrival was exciting, for the chances were that others would follow; even more exciting was the confirmation that tench were still in the area. I quickly assembled the rod and threaded the line through the rings, my fingers trembling as I did so.

The area I intended fishing, some 20yd from the bank, was 10ft deep and fairly clear of weed, but the overhanging willows made casting difficult. Breaking off three small branches – reluctantly, I should add – I waded out several feet so that I could get my rod far enough back to cast. With the water almost to the top of my gumboots, my stool would be redundant; it would be a standing-up job. But the last thing successful anglers think about, or should do, is comfort. If the situation demands that you are uncomfortable, then so be it. The fish don't care.

Securing two rod rests in the hard gravel proved difficult. A mallet would have made life easier, but such an item is never part of my kit. My indicator was a cork bobbin attached to the front rest by a length of cord; nothing fancy, but effective. Bait consisted of two grains of corn on a size 12 hook attached to 6lb bs Drennan line, and the rod was my trusty fibreglass Legerlite.

After introducing two pouchfuls of corn to a gravel bar 20yd from the bank, I cast, tightened to the ½oz bomb and nipped the line into the ladies' hair-grip in the bobbin. I then pulled this down so it hung some 15in from the rod.

Further along the bank a friend, Colin Tyler, was fishing. Colin had noticed my arrival and we had already chatted. Nothing had come his way, so he moved his gear close to me so we could have a natter. Although I don't mind fishing alone, even at night, I much prefer the company of a friend. For me it adds to the occasion, and if one or other catches a biggie the pleasure is shared.

Tench rolled at intervals – most times well away from my baited area, but occasionally right over it. The adrenalin was already flowing, for some of the tench were very big indeed. I prayed that the bobbin would rise.

The pit was a hard one, and although my tally of 7lb and 8lb tench was growing steadily, the water gave up its fish reluctantly. My best was 8lb 14oz, but every fish had been hard earned with many hours – most of them fishless – spent in their capture. The few anglers who fished there fished for bites and nobody expected a bag, although on one occasion I did take four. If and when a bite occurred, it was imperative that contact was made, for second chances were rare. Complete concentration was vital: no sleeping over rods in a bivvie on this water, this was proper fishing!

For two hours my eyes rarely left the bobbin. Just a twitch suggesting that fish were close to the sweetcorn would have been enough encouragement, but it

remained motionless. Was this to be yet another blank session? Surely not, with fish so close to my offering. These and other thoughts passed through my mind when suddenly, without warning, the bobbin started to rise and, at the same time, my heart gave several leaps. Standing over the rod, hands at the ready, I did not make a mistake. With two inches remaining before the bobbin touched the rod, I pulled it back and the clutch on my trusty Mitchell 410 started screaming.

I have spent a great many years catching tench, but on no other water have I known tench run and fight like these particular fish. To have 30yd of line stripped from the spool within seconds was the norm and this tench was no exception. Applying maximum pressure, I turned the fish and regained a few yards of line, then the clutch screamed again. What a lovely sound! Back-winding is not in my repertoire, although my mind was far removed from lovely sounds as the tench battled for its freedom. I knew it was big – hopefully the long-awaited 'double' that had figured in my dreams so many times. The adrenalin was now flowing strongly.

Some three minutes elapsed before I saw the fish, albeit briefly, and I could see it was a big one. But the fight was far from over – one roll, then it set off in another fast, 15yd run. Slowly I regained line then, when the fish was less than two rod lengths out, it surfaced. 'A good eight!' I said to Colin who was at my side by this time, the net in his hand. Following another much shorter but equally determined run, I pulled the tench over the net and Colin lifted it on to the bank.

I could see that it was much bigger than I had first thought. 'How big is that then?' I said.

'It's as heavy as my baby daughter,' Colin replied.

'How heavy is she?' I asked.

'10lb 4oz,' came the answer.

After extracting the hook, I placed the fish in a plastic bag and asked Colin to weigh it. He studied the needle closely, then looked up with a large grin on his face. '10lb 4oz,' he said.

After taking some shots of the fish, I placed it into the water and watched it swim away. Now then, when returning an exceptional fish I always watch it *very* closely as this gives me a very clear picture in my mind of how large a particular fish looks in the water. This fish looked no bigger than an eight; the reason I mention this will become clear in a minute.

Although I fished on, no further bites occurred, but I did not mind – my dream of a 10lb tench had been realized. Unfortunately, my work permitted evening visits only, which was frustrating for I am convinced that had I been able to fish for several days around midday I might have caught another.

I returned to the swim several evenings later. Again I was forced to stand up in the water, but with a tree to rest my back against it was no hardship. Putting my gear down, I pondered whether I should fish a float in the margin instead of ledgering. Most of my seven-pounders and one of the eights had come to this method, and the temptation was very strong. While I was debating, a tench rolled some 20yd out. A ledger it would be, although this was a decision I was to regret later.

I had been fishing for an hour when a movement to my right caught my eye. Turning my head, my eyes focused on a fish a rod's length out from the bank coming towards me. At first I thought it was a good carp, but as it got closer I realized it was a tench. I stood quite still and watched the fish carefully. Seconds later, I was spellbound as the tench stopped at my feet, turned slightly towards me, up-ended and picked up several grains of sweetcorn which had fallen from my catapult. The tench was less than 10ft from me in 3ft of gin-clear water. It was like looking into an aquarium, for every one of its minute scales was clearly visible. As it picked up the last grain it regained position and slowly swam off out of sight.

I described earlier how, when returning a big fish, I watch it closely as it swims off so I have an idea of how big it looks in the water. The comparison between my 'ten' and the fish I have just described was considerable. If my life depended on it I would have no hesitation in saying that this tench was not an ounce under *15lb*. My decision to ledger rather than fish a float in the margin probably cost me a tench that would have made history.

The following season a dramatic change came over the pit: two massive pumps appeared, one at each end. Within weeks the water-level was lowered by 10ft. Where the ten-pounder had picked up my bait on hard, clean gravel, rushes now grow over thick mud, and the bottom where the massive tench picked up my loose corn is now covered with grass 3ft high. Today the margins are gone; no longer do big tench swim just past my rod. Man, with his infernal machines, has robbed me of possibly more great fish. Only my memories remain, but these no one can steal.

All Your Birthdays
~
Fred Sykes

T he wonderful catches of big perch taken in the last few years have prompted me to recall a red letter day in 1977. Today's big perch are really monstrous fish, and I can only stand in awe and envy before the stamp of fish Peter Garvan and his contemporaries are now taking. It seems only a matter of time before a perch in the 6lb class is recorded, and we might all then have to reappraise our specimen standards for this species in the same way that tench fishermen have had to readjust their sights.

Big perch are something special. I've always wanted to catch a whopper since I first gazed at the splendid 1lb 2oz fish I caught accidentally whilst carp fishing in an Epping Forest lake in 1956. Unlike other species that respond to intensive study and effort, it always seems to me that a big perch is like a birthday present rather than a prize. The number of top-class anglers who have yet to capture a 3lb perch seems to bear this out.

When I first moved to Cumbria in 1965 I had not fished seriously since my schooldays. I was 'between hobbies', and at that time I neither owned a car nor had the ability to drive one. A Friday night treat was a bus ride to a famous coaching inn on the shores of Lake Bassenthwaite in the Lake District. Inside that posh pub there were two stuffed fish – a 24lb pike and a perch of 2lb 11oz, the latter caught by a Mr Groves in 1921. As much as I looked forward to my Friday night pint at The Pheasant, I was never in so much of a hurry that I couldn't stop on my way in and admire those fish. The pike was a fine fish, but it was the perch that captured my imagination. It brought back memories of the most impressive fish of my schooldays and I was soon between hobbies no more – I'd rediscovered angling!

During the following twelve years I did a lot of perch fishing. It was not the out-and-out single-species addiction that we associate with other species, but thoughts of catching a big perch were never far away. I suppose that 2lb 11oz perch in The Pheasant became a target of sorts. I didn't set out specifically to catch a 2lb 11oz perch, or a three-pounder, but I would dearly have loved to get one of that sort of size. Plenty of nice perch came my way: lots of fish up to 1½lb, brilliantly coloured and well-proportioned; and sometimes nets of them, 20–30lb at a time. I did my share of club match fishing and explored lots of waters with my friends in the Carlisle Specimen Group.

At that time our group was ultra-keen. We were fishing far afield in pursuit of all species, anything up to 150 miles each way being a possibility for a day-trip! We did a lot of perch hunting without much success in the early days. Bearing in mind that nearly every lake and loch within a hundred miles held perch, it seemed an endless task to find a 2lb perch, let alone one big enough to fire my imagination. Slim Baxter and Chris Bowman eventually came up with some two-pounders on a local gravel pit. They fished hard and well for them, and earned every ounce. The best went to about 2lb 3oz. Strangely, I couldn't get worked up about them; I knew they were good perch, but I wanted a fish just a few ounces better. I remember chatting to Kevin Clifford about specimen perch in 1976. At that time it seemed that big perch in the 2–2¼lb range were attainable with time and effort, but fish in the 3lb class were rare beasts indeed. The perch disease, of course, didn't help. Slim and Chris's gravel pit succumbed the year after they caught their two-pounders, and before those fish had had the chance to get bigger.

Throughout that whole period of perch hunting, one water really puzzled me. It was large enough to support a head of big fish of any species, and although I've no idea how many acres it covered, I would guess that its banks measured in miles rather than yards. I'm no biologist, but I was sure it was pretty fertile – much above the average of other waters we explored. However, you could cast out the ubiquitous worm on three rods all day in summer and not have a single bite! I don't know how many blanks the Carlisle Specimen Group shared on that water over the years, but we kept on going back for an odd session when we had nothing else 'on the boil'. Surely one day a fish of some species would pick up a worm!

The autumn of 1977 was an eye-opener. It was during a very wet spell of

weather when all the rivers within a 50-mile radius were in flood, and big floods too. Lots of local gravel pits and lakes were also bank-high. Out of the blue, Chris Bowman decided on a trip to try to drown three more worms rather than sit indoors and cry about the weather. That evening I received a phone call: 'Fred, you won't believe this. I've caught eight perch from the Lake of Many Blanks, four of them over 2lb, with the best 2lb 15oz!' I don't know which of us was more excited – a breakthrough at last!

The high excitement and anticipation of the next trip was hard to describe. We were talking about the probability, not the possibility, of a 3lb perch. We were there by first light the very next day. Six rods were cast about 80yd into 15ft of water and we waited. The previous day all Chris's fish had come between 12 p.m. and 3.30 p.m., so we sat confidently. The first bite came at around 12.30 p.m., a perch of 1lb 6oz to Chris. My first bite came shortly afterwards, another 'small' perch of 1lb 4oz. The second bite never came.

I couldn't wait for the next weekend to arrive, and kept hoping that the weather would be kind. I could think of no explanation for our disappointment of the previous week. Perhaps the perch were just roaming around, and if there were only a few of them they might not pass this swim again for weeks. I didn't think we were likely to better Chris's bag, but I hoped that I'd get one to equal that fish in The Pheasant. That's all I wanted.

Sunday 20 November 1977 was very cold and clear. The weather had held and we were back at first light, eagerly awaiting the first lift of the bobbin at midday. Sure enough, it came on time, to Chris's rods on my left. I did the honours with the net. It was a tremendous perch and one that I never thought I'd see. It was quite breath-taking and every bit as beautiful and bold as I'd imagined. Chris, of course, had seen one before, but he started jumping up and down when I confirmed its weight at 3lb 1oz. Twenty minutes later Chris caught another at 3lb 1½oz, and it was still before 12.30 p.m. I hardly had time to be disappointed when I was in. At last, a *real* perch of 2lb 13½oz. I was over the moon. Then Chris lost one, leaving a few yards of nylon in the fish – a snag had frayed his line some 40yd out. By this time it was about 1.30 p.m. and I would happily have gone home without another bite.

Once in an angling lifetime you hope the gods will smile on you. The next two hours were simply out of this world. I can offer no explanation as to why the next six fish came to my rods, except that it was all down to luck! The whole session was euphoric, and we both marvelled at the succession of perch that found their way into my net. The order of capture is long forgotten, but those next six fish weighed 2lb 15oz, 3lb, two of 3lb 2oz, 3lb 4oz and 3lb 4½oz! Such was the excitement that we dared not leave our rods until the feeding session ended at 4 p.m., and by then it was too late to do these fish justice with the camera. But the photographs didn't matter; I don't think either of us will ever forget the sight of those ten perch laid out on a wet sack for the final photo. They totalled over 30lb and were quite the most beautiful deep-bodied perch you could ever wish to see. All those years of hoping for a perch of 2lb 11oz to equal that of Mr Groves in 1921, and then I catch seven in excess of that weight in a single session. What more can I say?

Although we went on to catch many more perch in the next few years from that water, only one more three-pounder came our way, to Slim Baxter in 1978. The last big fish came out in 1980 and perhaps they are no more.

In the passing of time that heady day in 1977 may have to take its place way down the order in the list of big perch. But by golly, it was exciting – like having all your birthdays in one year.

A Priceless Jewel
~
Chris Turnbull

W here most specialist anglers are concerned, crucian carp rate somewhere near bottom in the list of popular species. My old, battered
copy of Crabtree went missing years ago, but as far as I can recall
even Crabtree didn't consider them worthy of his attention.

So much has changed since those long-ago days of the 1950s. Then, a large
proportion of Crabtree's time would probably have been spent beside atmospheric, intimate pools; a far cry from the expansive pits and reservoirs that have
become predominant in modern angling. Whilst the challenge of big waters can
be hugely exciting, all too often the fishing itself merely tests one's boredom
threshold. Fishing for crucians in small waters, however, provides the perfect
antidote, reawakening the charm of intimacy in our surroundings and returning
us to the application of more traditional skills usually associated with Crabtree's
time.

Despite volumes being written on most species, crucians have received precious little attention and catching them requires the angler to work out every problem for himself; it is far removed from the lottery that modern angling has become. Big crucians, in particular are far from easy, and in order to catch them consistently the approach must be very finely tuned. Even then, when everything is right, they still prove utterly bewildering.

The first specimen fish I ever caught was a priceless jewel of burnished copper and gold weighing 2lb 3oz. It came one damp, muggy morning when I was fourteen years old and very much an apprentice of Mr Crabtree. The memory of it has not faded to this day. Since then, I've often dabbled with crucians and got to know a little about catching them, but it took me a long time to find a water that inspired real commitment to the species. Rumours of monsters in one water or another had me launching campaigns in their pursuit, but always the odds were stacked against me and my efforts were abandoned after endless fishless sessions with no clues to follow.

In September 1991 all that began to change when I discovered a small pit only 7 miles from my home that held a good head of fish to over 3lb. Ever the opportunist, I decided that it would be easy to slip in the odd mid-week evening session and, with the nights drawing in, I'd have over four hours of darkness in which to fish and still be back in time for last orders.

On each trip I had the water to myself and found the fishing so absorbing that I couldn't wait to get back. Unfortunately, before I could get to grips with the place the first cold snaps of autumn began to chill the water, making it increasingly difficult to tempt a bite. All told, I made only four visits, but two were productive and provided a stack of fine crucians, including two new personal bests of 2lb 7oz and 2lb 4oz.

By this time I was so absorbed in the challenge of crucians that I resolved to set aside the following August in an attempt to catch a three-pounder. Though not impossible, the chance of locating a fish of this size in my pit was very slim, but remembering a press report mentioning a brace of three-pounders from an undisclosed local water, I set about making enquiries through the grape-vine. Eventually, I identified the location of a small gravel pit of around 3 acres.

Although I'd seen the water before, that had been ten years ago when it had been something of a raw working. Subsequent closed-season observations, however, revealed it to be gin clear and rich in aquatic plants, with milfoil and stonewort cladding the shallow areas, and a wide fringe of miniature and yellow water-lily pads spreading from its reeded banks. Obviously some keen aquatic gardener had been at work here.

Eventually I established that the lake held a large head of medium-sized tench, along with the inevitable over-zealous number of small carp. All in all, it was a specimen hunter's nightmare. Of crucians I saw nothing, and toyed with the idea that perhaps these reported fish were hybrids or little commons. In June, however, I came across the club bailiff who confirmed that crucians were present. 'Not many,' he said, 'but once or twice a year one was caught. Usually they were big,

invariably over 3lb, and always they came from that swim there!' He pointed towards a spot in the corner of the far end of the lake. It was exactly the swim I had fancied to start my campaign. The odds, it seemed, were against me still. One or two captures a year made it all something of a long shot, but then crucians have a habit of evading capture unless the approach is aimed specifically at them. I had no proof that I wasn't dealing with hybrids, so the only option was to catch one and see for myself.

I started the campaign on Friday 31 July, intending to fish throughout the first weekend of August. Luck was with me as I had the lake to myself and quickly secured my chosen swim, reserving the next pitch for my companion, Jim Bigden, who would be along later. First, I carefully plumbed the marginal drop-off. It seemed that the lilies grew out to around 4ft down the slope, and beyond them an 8ft-deep channel ran parallel with the bank. At a distance of 8yd to my left and surrounded on three sides by lilies, the channel dropped into a distinct hole of nearly 12ft. On the far side of the channel, around 10yd away, the bottom shallowed steadily to form a plateau covered in dense milfoil. According to a friend who knows far more about these things than I, deep holes with plenty of cover are the hallmarks of a good crucian swim. What I had before me matched that description perfectly.

I decided to focus around two rod lengths out, where the channel began to deepen into the hole. Before going further, however, I trimmed a small gap in the pads, through which I might play a fish to the net. Tackle was then put together – a 12ft 6in float rod, coupled with a fixed-spool reel and 4lb bs Trilene XL line. At the terminal end, I set a 2AA crystal waggler, very slightly over-shotted and over-depth, so that when the tell-tale AA shot lay on the bottom, I could tighten up gently to the float and the tip would stand proud of the surface. Two inches from the shot I tied a size 12 Drennan spade-end chub hook.

Baiting the swim would be kept simple: little and often, as bites dictated, with mashed bread laced with a few grains of corn and hemp. Hookbaits would be alternated: sometimes corn, but mostly breadflake – the crucian bait *par excellence*. Unfortunately, both of these baits are also a smash hit with tench – and so it proved, as fish after fish churned up my swim on their way to the net. After dark the tench frenzy subsided, but unfortunately only into a period of total inactivity. Eventually, long after midnight, I reeled in and retired for a few hours' sleep.

Dawn came cold and still, followed by more tench madness. By 8 a.m. I seriously doubted that these crucians could ever be a practical proposition. Then, suddenly, the unmistakable form of a huge specimen crashed excitedly in the swim. I was stunned, and instantly all doubt was cast aside. My quest began in deadly earnest and as serious as any I have ever undertaken previously.

By 9 a.m. the full heat of the day was upon the water and I thought my chance was over. Turning away to put the kettle on, I heard the sound of carbon scraping gravel. Something had dragged my rod off the front rest – so much for delicate float rigs! Grabbing the handle as it slipped towards the water, I lifted the rod into its fighting curve and held on as all went solid. My adversary had found sanctuary in lily stems, but steady pressure told and the fish was soon wallowing on the surface, its scales brassy and flashing in the sunlight. Not ready yet, the biggest crucian I had ever seen dived down again into the pads, and by the time I'd pulled it back to the surface Jim was at hand to shuffle it, weed and all, into the net.

On the bank the necessary checks were made, confirming the fish to be a true crucian weighing in at 3lb 6½oz. I was ecstatic; my wish had been granted – and

JOHN SEARL

at the first time of asking.

Again that night and the following morning I ploughed my way through the tench, but no crucians showed. We packed up before noon and I drove, still on cloud nine, to the pub for Sunday lunch and to toast my fish.

I returned on Tuesday at tea time and stayed until midnight. Three crucians rolled over the hole, but only tench took my bait.

I hadn't intended to fish on Wednesday, but all day long visions of rolling crucians had haunted me. By late afternoon I could take no more and dumped my tackle in the car. I fished into the small hours, but took only two skimmer bream and the inevitable tench.

For Thursday 6 August, plans had already been made to fish as a guest of a friend, Steve Allen, on a small private estate lake stuffed full of big carp. At least six of these carp were over 30lb, with the biggest nudging 40lb. Crucian fever, however, gripped me, and obviously it must have been infectious as Steve ended up joining me at the pit. We both shared my swim as I had seen no evidence of crucians in any other. As usual it was tench-infested and there seldom seemed a peaceful moment when one or other of us was not bent into one of these fish.

As the sun descended behind the tree tops, the crucians once again started rolling. Steve's eyes, like mine, bulged wildly at the sight. By 10 p.m. the tench activity had slowed down but – for the first time – the crucians carried on showing into the dark.

The air was electric with anticipation. At 10.30 Steve's float lifted and fell flat, only for the bite to be missed. As 11 p.m. approached, he began to pack away hesitantly, despite the fact that crucians were showing right over the baited area. At a time like this (for me anyway) work and family responsibilities definitely take second place, and I couldn't believe his commitment to reality in choosing to leave. My float lifted an inch and, as I struck gently, the rod bent into a token resistance. The fight was short-lived and lacked the aggression of tench, and soon a large crucian rolled on the surface and was hustled into the net.

I remember Steve's excited comment on how impressive a 'big specimen' looks, no matter how small the species. As I admired my prize in the torchlight, I knew exactly what he meant. The scales trembled uncontrollably in my hand, but with Steve's help we eventually settled for 3lb 8oz.

Twenty minutes later I sat dazed and in rapture watching the lights of Steve's car turn away up the track. Unsure whether I should stay or not, I was startled out of my pondering by another crucian that rolled quietly but unmistakably over the baited area. Picking up the rod from where it lay, I rebaited the hook with flake and cast in. Midnight came and a thin, ethereal mist steamed off the water. The little green Starlite glowing atop my float was fading slowly, when suddenly it began rocking from side to side in the ripples as another crucian splashed noisily beside it.

Minutes passed like an eternity before the float trembled almost imperceptibly. I hesitated, tensing my grip on the rod butt, and as the float suddenly lifted I set the hook. This time the fight was far more characteristic of crucian carp. The fish bolted off, down into deep water, yielded, chugged around, boiled on the surface, then dived back to the bottom. I felt confident, almost nonchalant, and let the rod do the work until, before too long, another huge fish rolled into the net.

At 3lb 3oz this beautiful creature completed a remarkable brace. Unfortunately, it also turned out to be the last of the season, despite several more sessions there. But next year I shall return in the hope of achieving the ultimate crucian challenge: a four-pounder.

Once Upon a Time
~
Eddie Turner

I t started like any other trip really. Hopes were high; at least we were on to a water where there was a realistic chance of a biggie. Keith's 35lb pike caught a month previously hadn't shown again and the 27-pounder I'd taken recently had left us on a bit of a high after we had blanked on other waters in classic style.

This morning, like most others, I was to pick up Bill. I was round at his house by 5.30 a.m., and had on my cap and gloves ready to chauffeur him down to the lake. Nobody stirred. Leaving the engine running, I looked for his gear – normally left outside the house – but it wasn't there. Then I noticed the hastily scribbled note stuck to the door: 'Had a curry last night. Feeling Tom and Dick. Give you a call.' Bill never was one for the Queen's English.

As I arrived at the lake the security guards started to approach, but on recognizing the car they just waved and returned to the warmth of their hut. After I had unpacked my tackle I waited a few minutes for Keith to arrive, but it seemed he also had other plans. I headed for the hotspot, where a large gravel bar which ran the entire length of the lake had been exposed by water pumping.

Still Keith hadn't arrived, so I set about putting up my tackle. With the fourth rod finally in place, I sat back for a customary cup of hot blackcurrant. By this time it was fully light and, as I looked towards the site office, a familiar car rolled up. As it happened, Keith wasn't going to fish but just wanted to see whether I'd caught anything.

I reeled in the drifter float and made ready a smaller but livelier bait. Up until that time the wind had been coming off my back but, typically, as I cast out it died away completely. The float settled some 40yd distant, and in the mirror-like water discernible rings emanated as the livebait began to work. Suddenly it was gone. Holding the rod in one hand I jerked the line and, turning, said something about another Jack. Then, winding down almost half-heartedly, I felt a slight resistance and struck into what was obviously a small fish. Keith looked on. Before long, however, the 'small fish' I was attached to grew considerably in stature and started pulling back *very* hard indeed. At my request to get the net, Keith grinned, only relenting when panic set in.

From the size of the pike's tail as it was eased into the landing net, we knew it was big, but not until we were peering anxiously into the mesh did we realize that here might be another thirty-pounder. Taking the net and fish up to the unhooking mat, I gently laid the fish down and removed the hooks from its great jaws. Once in the weigh-sling and on the Salter scales, it registered 34lb 8oz. I was ecstatic, to say the least, and put my arms around Keith – in a manly sort of way! We decided to sack the fish whilst Keith phoned Bill and picked up some film for his video camera. I just sat there in a contented stupor.

It must have been an hour or so later, as I gazed at the flat-calm surface towards the furthest rod – baited with a pilchard-injected sardine – that I saw the oily patch appear. Within seconds the buzzer screeched into life, and I leapt to my feet and ran, landing net in hand, the 20yd or so to the swim. I'd cast the bait into about 8ft of water to the left of a large exposed pipe which dissected the gravel bar. With line steadily pulling from the spool, I picked up the rod, pointed it in the direction of the fish and tightened. The rod took on a frightening curve as the pike fought hard all the way to the net, at times getting too close to the pipe for comfort, but grudgingly submitting to the irresistible force placed upon it. Then I saw the fish, equal in size to the first, and as it rolled into the outstretched net I shouted out loud with delight.

Back at the unhooking mat I found that the hooks were only just in place and easily taken out. And when the fish was placed on the scales the needle finally settled at 32lb 8oz. I was gobsmacked. Fumbling in the bottom of my rucksack, I produced another sack and gently positioned the pike next to the first in the deeper water immediately behind me. Without really thinking, I rebaited the rod with another sardine and sent it out into the Pipe swim again. I then slumped back into my chair for a much-needed drink as I pondered the quite unbelievable

events of the morning.

Some thirty minutes later, as I glanced out at the Pipe swim, a flat patch suddenly appeared in the slight ripple that had just sprung up. I started to walk towards the rod. When I was still 20yd away it came to life and I quickened my pace. By this time line was rattling off the spool. I lay the net in the margin and picked up the rod for the third time that morning, wondering what on earth I was going to make contact with. Pulling the hooks home, what felt like a very powerful fish kited to the right and directly under the exposed pipe. I leaned into it, gaining a bit of line and bringing it to the surface where it showed me an impressive sized tail. Then it happened. The fish came up in the water and proceeded to swim over the pipe. Now I was in trouble! On the tight line the pike started to thrash about, so I released the bale arm to let it move away. I was sure the pipe had a large cap on the end, so the only thing to do was to inch slowly along on my stomach, and sink the rod and reel under the obstruction. Fortunately, it worked and, with the fish free again, I gingerly backed along the pipe to terra firma.

After that performance the fish soon came in without much trouble and, as it lay in the net, I had visions of another thirty-pounder. Carrying the pike back to my swim I could see that it was shorter than the other two, but at 26lb 1oz I was more than chuffed. Until then it had always been my ambition to catch three twenty-pounders in a day, but I never expected to do so in this manner. With both my sacks in use, I only had a pike tube left and, opening one end, slipped the fish in and staked it with the others.

Two hours slipped by before my comatose state was reawakened by the sound of a van door slamming. Bill had arrived. As he approached, his eyes fixed on the sacks.

'So you've cracked it then?'

'Yep.'

'How big is the thirty?'

'*Which one?*' I replied.

His jaw locked open. 'You're joking,' he said.

'Nope . . . and a twenty-six.'

For the first time in his life Bill was speechless! Then Keith arrived and an identical conversation took place.

We set up an area for the picture-taking session, using the matting from the boot of my car which was the same material that we use for making unhooking mats. The fish were quickly removed from the water, but try as I might I couldn't hold them all together and ended up sitting down with just the two thirty-pounders straddled across my legs. The 26lb fish was put back into the tube to be photographed after the others had been released. When the time came to collect this fish, Keith burst out laughing. It seems he had forgotten to do up the end of the tube again. What a silly chap. I wasn't really bothered though, for I'd had my moment.

Since that day I've been fortunate enough to enjoy other memorable catches, including realizing my ambition of landing a pike over 35lb. It hasn't changed my life, but it certainly felt good!

Cold Water and Frosty Air
~
Bruce Vaughan

Although the water was preserved for trout fishing with 'dry fly or upstream nymph only', season rods were granted on the occasional day during the winter months for those after grayling. At these times either fly or bait could be used. I had had a rod on the estate for three seasons, hugely enjoying the trouting – particularly at mayfly time – but equally revelling in the grayling fishing on short winter days. I loved to watch a buoyant Avon or Loafer float hurry down a gravelly glide on one of the fishery's narrow carrier streams, or swirl round and round one of the myriad little hatch pools that were built years ago at regular intervals along the carrier streams to hold back the flow.

On all my grayling jaunts I had never caught a coarse fish, nor even seen one – not even in summer when wearing polarizing sunglasses to spot nymphing trout. However, there was one carrier or, to be exact, just a part of it, that looked as though it might hold some coarse fish. About 100yd above the spot where my carrier flowed into the main river, the Kennet, it was joined by another. This second stream flowed right across it, and in so doing it held back the water of the first. This damming effect caused the first carrier to slow down and run more steadily for about 50yd before the confluence.

I had really only looked at this stream properly the previous winter, and then only just as the season was closing. So much water was available on the estate that even if you spent a full day roving after grayling, not every carrier would be visited. But one day I did wander down this carrier, catching the odd grayling and rainbow trout in the higher reaches. Eventually, I reached the steadier water and ran the float through for about half an hour. I caught yet more trout and grayling, but had a feeling that the float might dive under at any moment in response to a bite from a chub or roach, or something else without an adipose fin.

After the season ended I forgot all about the little carrier, and even during my trout forays that summer I failed to wander its course. Pressure of work kept me away from the fishery for much of the winter, and it was not until mid-February that I was back on its well-manicured banks.

I was a little later arriving than planned, due to the traffic, then spent an agreeable half-hour chatting to the keeper beside a roaring fire of trimmed branches. It wasn't until well after 10 a.m. that I actually began fishing. There had been a moderate overnight frost, with a forecast of the same for the coming evening, but such things never put off grayling. Indeed, nothing really seems to deter them from feeding – a truly obliging fish!

I began right at the top of the fishery and quickly got into a steady rhythm of casting, feeding and trotting, this helping to keep the cold at bay. Slowly the sun rose into a cloudless sky, and without a breath of wind to disturb the valley the day became quite warm, reminding me that spring was not that far off. Fish came steadily to trotted maggots as I gradually worked my way down the estate, criss-crossing from one chuckling carrier to another. The shoals of grayling tend to be small on this water, and after half a dozen or so have been caught it pays to move on. Anyway, there are so many mouth-watering pools and glides to fish that it's pointless remaining in one and flogging it for all that it's worth.

As the afternoon waned and a chill returned to the air, I arrived at the top of the little carrier from which I had thought I might catch something different the previous March. The upper, shallower reaches produced some good grayling and the inevitable trout, which more often than not would career all over the stream and frequently skyward, before eventually, but still grudgingly, allowing themselves to be brought to hand for unhooking – usually in a final cascade of water.

Working steadily down the carrier, I came at last to the slower water backing up from the confluence. A fat rainbow resulted from the first run through of the Loafer, followed by a trio of grayling to about 1lb, then a rake of a brownie still nowhere near recovered from the rigours of spawning. All the while I kept a small but steady trickle of maggots running down the smoothly flowing glide. The float was set at 3½ft, with the bait – double white maggot on a size 14 eyed hook – just tripping bottom.

The next bite came about half-way down the swim, close in to the near bank. It was nowhere near as positive as the bites given by the trout and grayling, and my resultant strike met with very little resistance. Believing it to be only a small grayling, I quickly brought it upstream towards the spot where I was kneeling on the edge of the grassy bank. Sliding it across the surface the last few feet towards the waiting net, I realized that it was a dace of about half a pound. I returned it immediately, feeling rather pleased that my suspicions about the carrier had been proved correct, and confident in the knowledge that dace don't normally live on their own.

The next few runs down the glide provoked no response at all. Then came a brief flurry of grayling and trout on half a dozen consecutive casts, one of the rainbows recognizable as the fish caught on the first trot through! (On several occasions I have caught the same trout as many as three times in one day, though this has been on the estate's short section of main River Kennet rather than on one of the carriers.)

By this time the light was failing rapidly, and there was a distinct feeling of imminent frost in the air. The last rays of the setting sun glowed away to the west and gave just enough illumination for me to see the float as I sent it back down the glide again. When about half-way down and again close in to the bank, the float slowed almost imperceptibly and at the same time appeared to begin bobbing as if a fish had taken hold of the bait but was too small to pull the float under. I struck with no result, curious as to what had caused such a strange bite. Half a dozen more maggots entered the head of the swim, closely followed by the float and two fresh maggots at the business end. At precisely the same spot, the float began to dimple in the surface film yet again, sending out tiny ripples – almost as if the hook was catching on the stream bed. In the near-darkness, it was difficult to make out exactly what was happening. I had a feeling that something wasn't right, so I struck.

This time my strike met with resistance, the weight on the line feeling like a modest grayling. But it fought differently, registering regular kicks on the rod top rather than the more frequent 'rat-a-tat-tat' of a grayling. The fish came to the surface just short of the outstretched net and was instantly recognizable as a big dace, its broad, silver flank standing out starkly against the black water.

I tensed up at the sight of my dace, but almost immediately relaxed as it slid over the net rim and down into the soft mesh. Resting the net on the grass well back from the edge, I pulled aside the mesh to look at my prize. I realized that I hadn't just landed a big dace – rather, I had caught an *enormous* dace! The fish was a big female with a plump stomach and was incredibly broad across the back. Fin perfect and without a single scale out of place, this fish was a magnificent example of the species and had, I felt certain, never been caught before.

After weighing the dace carefully and quickly taking a few photographs, I had a last lingering look before I slipped it gently back into the stream. My hands stung from the combination of cold river water and frosty air – a welcome, if painful reminder of what will undoubtedly be the biggest dace I shall ever see, let alone catch, in my lifetime.

Subsequent checking of the scales with a weights and measures test, and a scouring of the Kennet records confirmed the dace's weight at 1lb 3oz, equal in size to the best that had ever been recorded on the river. I returned to the estate a week later and, not surprisingly, made straight for the swim that had produced the big dace. In three consecutive casts with identical tactics to those used on the previous visit, I had three more specimen dace, two of which weighed 15oz, with the other at 1lb 1oz.

One sunny day the following summer, I had a good look at the glide through polarizing sunglasses. At first glance the whole of the stream bed appeared to be uniform in depth. Closer inspection, however, revealed a narrow, shallow gully tight in against the near bank. It extended for about 5yd and, however insignificant it looked to me, it was clearly the reason the dace had been lying in that part of the run. Although I remained in the trout-fishing syndicate for another two years, I never caught another dace from the water.

The Amber-Tinted Water
~
John Watson

T he little outboard engine struggled to push the heavy wooden boat and its two occupants along the ever-winding Meadow Dyke of Horsey Mere, just as it had on my first visit five years previously. A feeling of expectation was within me, for I was returning once more to fish the water which had until recently boasted the British Record pike. Since the capture of that fish by Peter Hancock in 1967, however, the mere's fish stocks had been completely obliterated; yet, twenty years on, it seemed that a full recovery was not too much to hope for. Pike anglers at this time were very infrequent visitors to the Broads, and consequently the true potential of these waters had yet to be realized. Fortunately, Horsey Mere held a strange spell over me, and although I'd spent many a pikeless day there, I always felt that one day I would be rewarded with something special. Little did I realize, as I guided the boat through the heavy early morning rain, that the day of my dreams had finally arrived . . .

I suppose it's fair to say that an element of good fortune had put me on the path to Horsey that morning, for my companion, David 'Pondo' Pond, had won the toss of a hastily flipped coin in the pre-dawn darkness over an hour earlier, and had chosen Martham Broad on which to focus our attentions. However, when we arrived there we found conditions anything but to our liking, and so a quick about-turn saw us leaving the headwaters of the River Thurne. Instead, we headed towards the venue I would have chosen had I called the toss correctly.

The mere was deserted save for an assortment of waterfowl, and after cutting the motor we paddled the boat Indian-style into a secluded bay fringed with tall, golden Norfolk reed. This bay had produced a pike or two for me over the years, and although these catches had been very few and far between it was a spot I always fished with confidence due to its proximity to the entrance of Meadow Dyke, along which pike traversed from the mere to the rest of the Thurne system. With sand weights quietly lowered and with the large deadbaits positioned at varying distances around the boat, we both settled down for a long wait and a most welcome cup of coffee. The rain fell incessantly, but as the weather was mild and not a breath of wind ruffled the mere's surface, conditions were far from uncomfortable, especially for such seasoned boat anglers.

The wait was nowhere near as long as anticipated, with a pike of 23lb in the boat within the hour, having succumbed to one of my mackerel-tail baits. With such a good fish under my belt – a fish only a few ounces less than my best ever from the venue – and so early in the day, anticipation was naturally high, though one run in a day was more than the norm. However, nothing breeds success like success, and Pondo, his interrupted breakfast hardly finished, pointed out that the float on my ledgered herring seemed to be on the move. Closer inspection revealed that it certainly was and, quickly winding down, I made contact. The culprit set off towards the boat, and I reeled back slack line until the pike veered off to the left. I soon had it under control, and at a rod's distance let the fish have its head as it powered slowly and deliberately the length of the boat and back. With the water well coloured, we were unable to get a clear view of the pike until it rolled, breaking the surface and revealing a very broad and deep expanse of flank. Immediately, the realization dawned on us that here was a very big pike, much bigger than we had at first thought, and consequently the sooner it was in the net the better.

Pondo made no mistake, and at the first attempt enveloped the huge fish in the spacious landing net and hoisted, not without considerable effort, all aboard. Clearing the folds of the net away, we were able to gain our first real look at our prize: here indeed was the fish of a lifetime! With the hooks out, we manoeuvred the pike's massive bulk into a weigh-sling, but the 32lb Avons would have nothing of it, bottoming out even though I wound them back as far as possible. With a minimum weight of 34lb, the fish was quickly photographed and then secured in a keep tube. I left everything in Pondo's care and set off back to Martham to get heavier scales.

The journey seemed endless, but eventually I pulled the boat up, dashed to the

car and sped off towards Barton, where I knew Jacko was fishing that morning. On my arrival I could hardly speak, such was my excitement, but I calmed down enough to recount my tale, and received a congratulatory bear-hug from my long-time pal. Soon we were on the road back to Martham and, some three hours after the capture, I was back at Horsey, where, much to my relief, everything was in order. Each of us gazed in awe as the massive fish was freed from its temporary home and laid on the grassy bank, taking turns to guess what its weight might be. This we soon ascertained, with the scales supported on an oar which bridged my shoulder and Pondo's, at an ounce in excess of 38lb – the biggest pike from Horsey for over two decades. For my part, I could hardly believe that such a tremendous fish was mine, even after fifteen years of concentrated pike fishing, yet there she lay in all her glory. After hearty congratulations and numerous photographs, I lowered her gently back into the amber-tinted water and wondered, as she swam away, whether one day she might even eclipse Hancock's great fish.

Over the Gate

~

Peter Wheat

I must be rising and I must be going
On the roads of magic that stretch afar,
By the random rivers so finely flowing
And under the restless star.

Neil Munro

The letter from my old friend brought tidings of great joy. At last, in his
seventy-seventh year, he had caught his first 2lb roach. And as he went
on to describe graphically how he had just sat there, and sat there, lost in
a world of his own as he stared down at this fish of his dreams, I, too, felt thrilled
with him. It had been a journey of a lifetime, and he had travelled it well.

Robert Louis Stevenson once said: 'to travel hopefully is better than to arrive'.
But in angling endeavour, surely, is it not better still to travel hopefully *and* arrive,
as my old friend had done? So let me share with you another roaching road, one I

travelled myself, more than a decade ago . . .

The river of my story is pure Dorset from beginning to end. It rises in the gentle Wessex landscape of Thomas Hardy as a chalk spring in the ridge of Evershead, and takes a mainly easterly course for 35 miles to mingle with the esturial shallows of Havenpool and the open sea beyond.

By Casterbridge it has grown with the influx of several tributaries along its highest reaches and is a wild brown trout stream of some significance. And below the town, flowing clear and rapid, it meanders to full river status through the lush alluvial pasturage of the Vale of Great Dairies, and on past the brooding manor of d'Urbervilles and the ruins of an ancient abbey to Georgian Anglebury, a mile and a half above the sea.

The river is primarily a trout and salmon preserve, with much of its length strictly controlled by game clubs and syndicates. But happily, in the serpentine twists and bends of its tidal lower section, where it runs deep and dark over a bed of gravel, sand and soft clay, there is coarse fishing available to satisfy the desires of the most discerning of specialist anglers. A pike in excess of 20lb, a 3lb grayling, or even that most elusive of all targets, a *genuine* pound-plus dace, is always on the cards. However, to my way of thinking, interesting and challenging as such specimen hunting is (and I've tried it often) it can never quite compare with the richest jewel in this river's crown: the nomadic shoals of giant roach that roam between the water meadows above Anglebury Bridge. It was these fish which first attracted my attention, the hum along the grape-vine speaking of catches that included not just one, but several two-pounders, and hints of fabulous beasts of 3lb and more.

I just *had* to go and indeed I did, but I did not find the fishing easy at all. True, I caught splendid bags of dace, some excellent sea trout and grayling, and had a memorable (if brief) tussle with a large salmon that grabbed a fingerling dace I was retrieving and broke me up in a scorching run for the sea. But I did not have one roach over 1½lb in over two years of hopeful travel. Was I downhearted? Not at all. Anticipation has always been the heartbeat of my fishing and patience the antidote to frustration or, worse still, depression. And so I waited, confident in the knowledge that big roach were in there, somewhere, and that it was just a matter of time.

The breakthrough came at the beginning of October in the third season. I discovered roach priming at Heron's Dip. They were rolling all across the river in front of a jungle of bushes and scrub trees, and by easing my way carefully through the tangle I was able to get right in close to the main area of activity. To say that my anticipation was fuelled by what I saw would be a total understatement; I was absolutely transfixed and shaking uncontrollably – these roach were not just big, they *all* looked like two-pounders! And from first sighting to day's end, they teased and tested my patience to its limit.

It rained heavily and continuously the whole time. I got soaked; I got in tangles; my tackle boxes flooded because I left them lying down the bank on a rising tide; I

lost a favourite float and broke two others, and there was more than an itch of frustration from the strong wind and tide that combined to turn the flow upstream. Float fishing was completely out of the question. I tried ledgering and had a fish a throw – all eels. And when I left the river in full darkness, the roach were still rolling.

Although I could not try again for several weeks, the vision of those roach never left my mind. By the time I next visited the river my anticipation had built up into a fever pitch.

The day followed a week or more of utterly mild, settled weather. I walked the causeway out from Anglebury in warm sunshine under a sky of clouds and blue, the golden salmon atop St Mary's tower pointing a strangely soft easterly wind. At the cottage I turned right and on to the track that leads straight across the meadows to the river. But this morning I was not alone. Ahead of me, already crossing over the gate, was the familiar figure of the school teacher, a local angler of repute, who was carrying rods and tackle. My heart sank. Had he too discovered the roach? And if not, would he still choose to fish at Heron's Dip?

I paused when I reached the gate and watched to see what fate had in store. The school teacher walked slowly on, reached the bank by the old willow tree, and – glory, glory, hallelujah! – turned off left and upstream. The swim with the big roach lay downstream. The gods were being kind, and already I sensed the promise of something special in the hours ahead.

Conditions were near perfect: the first day of neaps, a trifle bright, perhaps, but the water carried a nice depth of colour, and there was a light breeze coming from behind and at an angle upstream. No roach showed, but I had no doubt at all that they were still there, and that success or failure now rested entirely in my hands.

I will be brief about tackle, bait and tactics: a 12ft glass rod and Speedia centre-pin, 3lb line, an elderpith float and a size 14 hook tipped with two white maggots. A mix of maggots and hempseed had been prepared for baiting up – to be cata-pulted out, little but often, down a mid-river line and along the edge of the far bank.

I commenced fishing in the last half-hour of the run-off, with the first fish coming twenty minutes later – a reasonable dace. A few trots later and the fat orange tip stabbed under a second time, 20yd downstream, and I was into a roach. And what a roach it was, at 2lb 3oz! I was elated. On any other day but this, it would have been success enough. But to come so soon, with so many hours of fishing still ahead . . . well, it could only be seen as a start.

For the time being though, there would be no more bites. The run-off was fully extended and the river resembled a lake, with no flow at all. I took an early lunch, and for more than an hour sat on the bank slowly munching blue vinny cheese and Dorset knobs, staring out at the debris in the margins for signs of movement.

At midday, twiglets of broken reed stems began to float away. The current had returned, and after only a few casts I lost a heavy roach in the thick marginal weed and then netted one of 1lb 13oz. The next thirty minutes was an absolute nightmare: I managed to lose no less than three very big roach in succession, after playing each one to within inches of the net. I could blame nothing but my own incompetence for these failures.

You see, Heron's Dip is a particularly awkward swim, requiring you to wade out through a gap in the reeds as far as is possible in the soft mud, and then fish out over a wide belt of weed which reaches to the surface. 'Collecting' a hooked fish requires a telescopic landing-net handle extended to its full length, and even then the front rim of the net will reach only inches beyond the weed.

My classic mistake was in bringing these massive roach to the net too soon –

they still had strength left to dive into the weed, snag up and flip off the hook. The simple answer, which I should have realized much sooner, was to maintain light pressure on a hooked fish and let it tug away in midstream until it flanked up – and only then bring it quickly to the net. This ploy worked very well because the natural inclination of these fish, given their head, was to pull off for the weeds along the far bank where they were easier to control and wear down. As a result, I took three more roach in the next forty-five minutes: 1lb 10oz, 2lb 7oz and 2lb 5oz.

So far, all the roach had come from the mid-river line, but slowly the pattern was changing. I had to cast further and further across to get bites as the shoal worked up river and found the loose feed lying down the far bank. I changed to a Mitchell 300 and a fluted pith float rigged slider-style so that I could get across to within inches of the weeds opposite, with little risk of the 'tail' catching up.

The roach were in the edge right enough, but I hooked three in successive casts that all found the weed and slipped the hook. It was sickening to feel the line scrape through the stems and fall limp, and it did nothing at all for my emotions which by then had become a wreck of contradictions. It was a bitter-sweet enigma of gladness and sadness as I knew that although five roach averaging over 2lb were safe in the net, at least their number of equal size had got away. Success or failure? It was a hard thing to decide.

Into this witch's brew another impression began to form. From some primeval corner locked deep in my mind came the realization that the best was yet to come. I sensed the presence of roach far larger than any I had so far caught out in front of me, lipping up the hemp and maggots.

The feeling was strange and cannot be explained, but I had known it twice before: once during an evening's fishing on the Dorset Stour, when I sensed a massive barbel near my bait and caught it minutes later at 11lb 4oz; and again on the Stour in the company of Stef Horak, when we sat talking of 'Raggy Tail', the biggest known barbel in the stretch, and, at exactly the moment the vision of that fish went through our minds, I hooked it – 11lb 13oz. The feeling was back, clear and unmistakable . . .

At 2.30 p.m. I caught a 2lb 9oz roach, a new personal best. Then at 2.40 p.m. I landed an even bigger one of 2lb 13oz. At 3.15 p.m. exactly the black-and-white tip buried again, and the rod bent over to a roach which gripped the current like a vice. It fought for what seemed an eternity, and as soon as I saw it sliding over the net I realized that here indeed was a *very* special fish. It was fin and scale perfect, and, like all the roach of this river, short, deep and immensely thick across its width. I lifted it high in the weigh-bag, and watched the pointer of the pre-set scales flicker round and settle at just over the 3lb mark – absolute magic!

It was also – ideally so, in fact – the final fish of the session. I stopped to photograph the catch and turn the fish back in, but when next I cast it was too late – the tide was coming up and the river no longer moved. It was all over.

I stopped at the gate on my way home and looked back at the river for one last time. It had been the best day's fishing of my life: eight roach, six over 2lb, the best at 3lb, and average weight of 2lb 5½oz. I knew then, as I know now, that I will never again take a bag of roach as good as this one, and I gave silent thanks for that which I had received.

The wind had fallen to a whisper and there was a haunting stillness about the place. The western sky shone like a forge, flecking the ribbons of water in the ditches with glints of burnished gold, where the porcupine silhouettes of soft rush tussocks stood like guarding sentinels. In the half-darkness it was still warm, the mists rose ethereally all along the stream, and away in the distance the lights of Anglebury twinkled as stars.

That night brought the first frost of the waiting winter. By dawn the outside world was cold, white and alien. But it did not matter; I felt no urge at all to get up and go fishing. Instead, I pulled the duvet back up over my head and lay for a long time thinking of sunlit water meadows, a float dipping beneath ambered water, and blood-splashed silver beyond a waiting net . . .

> An' raïn-vill'd streams do brisker flow
> A-risèn higher to their brim
>
> William Barnes of Casterbridge

The Golden Season
~
Dave Williams

I was full of anticipation that Tuesday night as I drove towards the Medway; even the rain and heavy traffic on the M25 couldn't dampen my enthusiasm and only posed a minor distraction. Everything was right. Although it was late September it was extremely mild, and the extra water would mean the river would be slightly up and coloured. Coupled with that was the fact that I was also on a bit of a roll.

The Medway is a gruelling river, especially for barbel, with a whole season's effort producing only a few fish at best. Occasionally, though, small victories do come along, and at that time I was experiencing some success, having located a small group of fish in a particularly difficult area. The problem was that while I had landed two fish to 11lb 9oz, I had also lost two others. I also knew the river well enough to realize that by the time I arrived those same fish could be a mile away. Indeed, one of the biggest difficulties is the great distances these fish travel, let alone their small numbers. At times, fishing this river really is a lottery.

Within forty minutes of setting off I was at the river, and my hopes were raised still further when I found the fishery empty. Settling into my chosen swim, I baited a fast gravel run directly above the known snag with a few droppers of hemp, and introduced some loose offerings of the paste bait I was going to use on the hook. That done, and with everything organized, I took myself off for a walk to give the swim a chance to settle and myself the opportunity of having a look around.

It was a lovely evening: very still and warm with quite a lot of surface activity, mainly from small chub. Back at my swim I logged the details: air temperature at 58°F, and water rising and coloured – excellent conditions for the time of the year. At 8 p.m. a freelined bait was allowed to run as far as possible under the snag, in the same way that had previously proved so successful. Pouring myself a drink, I sat back to enjoy the session. In the distance a car pulled up and another two hopefuls made their way upstream. As the minutes ticked by it started to rain and, with the evening drawing in, I sat under my umbrella watching the increasing fish movement, sure that once or twice I heard the distinctive sound of a barbel rolling.

By this time the atmosphere was quite charged, and even though 10 p.m. was fast approaching and I still hadn't had a bite, my confidence remained high. With the worsening weather and the now frenzied fish activity, I had already sensed that the moment was reaching a climax when, suddenly, the rod slammed round with such savagery that the butt hit my chair. I knew from previous encounters that I had to take the initiative early and not give the fish an inch of line, but as the powerful rod took on a frightening curve everything went solid and my heart sank.

By my watch, ten minutes had vanished since I had first hooked the barbel, my arms aching from applying steady pressure from all angles in an effort to move it. Then, as if to add to the drama, the skies opened to release a deluge of rain and lightning crashed all around. Struggling to pull on my coat, I decided to haul on the fish in one final effort and, with the rod at creaking point, at last it suddenly kicked free. Thanking the stars that I'd brought along my large landing net, I decided to collect the barbel in a small slack near by. At this stage I still hadn't seen much of the fish, but as it finally slid into the waiting mesh it dawned on me that here, indeed, was something quite exceptional.

During the course of the struggle I had noticed the two other anglers return to their car, but I hadn't heard them leave . . . If I was quick I might still catch them. Sacking the huge fish, I dashed to the car-park just in time, and on hearing my garbled news they were more than pleased to help weigh the fish. Everything had been such a rush that even then I'd not had a proper look at the barbel, and it wasn't until we laid the fish on the wet grass that I could see it was a veritable monster. Oblivious to the driving rain, we shared estimates of the barbel's weight. A big thirteen was suggested, but I just knew it would be heavier. Still shaking, I let my new-found friends weigh the fish as I looked on excitedly. On two different sets of Avon scales it registered 14lb 7oz and 14lb 5oz, my scales giving the heavier weight. If mine were accurate, and I knew they wouldn't be far out as I had had them tested the previous year, I had just caught a new record barbel.

The lads were great and congratulated me enthusiastically. After taking plenty of photographs, and after allowing the fish a lengthy rest in the sack, I had a final look at it before it was returned – a magnificent sight. It was well past midnight by the time I got back to my car, thoroughly soaked, absolutely shattered but a *very* happy man. All I had to do was arrange for a weights and measures check on my scales. The next day they were sent first post.

I was elated all week, wanting to tell everybody the news, but I decided to say nothing at all of the capture until I was certain beyond all doubt of the barbel's true weight. Eventually, though, my thoughts drifted to my impending holiday on the Hampshire Avon that would start on Friday of that week. At least that would keep me sane, or so I thought . . .

At 6.45 p.m. on the Friday, I stood on the banks of that famous river in nothing short of perfect conditions. In fact, the weather forecast for several days to come was excellent. Despite rain all day the evening was very mild, with both air and water temperatures at 56°F. For some peculiar reason though, not a single fish showed, something that didn't inspire a great deal of confidence. By 10.45 p.m. I was beginning to think that a blank was on the cards.

It was the left-hand rod which signalled the start of an incredible sequence of events: over went the tip, and after a few minutes of solid resistance a good barbel slipped into the net. Barely had I time to remove the hook when, out of the corner of my eye, I noticed the other rod pull round. A few moments later this fish joined its companion in the net. What a performance! At 9lb 12oz and 11lb 10oz I was more than pleased. It was a remarkable start to my holiday.

At about 6 p.m. the following day, I strolled down to the river in glorious weather. Although conditions looked in much the same order as they had the previous day, I found the water up by a degree or so when I took the temperature. This was positively encouraging and I couldn't wait to get started. Before doing so, however, I had a quick walk downstream to see two friends who I knew would be fishing that night. Richard had fished the previous night and failed to catch, but in view of the weather conditions he had wisely decided to try again. After the usual banter we wished each other good luck, and within half an hour I was back at my swim.

For obvious reasons, I had elected to fish the same area as the previous night, and soon my two-rod set-up was ready with one bait placed into a gap in the weed downstream and the other in a similar spot just in front of me. I settled back to enjoy the lovely evening, the descending sun painting the sky various hues of red. The next day would be another lovely day. As I sat reflecting on the events of the previous few days, it wasn't long before I noticed Richard coming towards me announcing he'd just caught a 'fifteen'. Only when my chin hit the floor did he add that it was a pike. I daren't repeat what I called him. Within seconds, however, I got my own back when the left-hand rod sprung into life and, after an excellent fight, a cracking fish of 11lb 2oz was brought to the bank. Suitably inspired, and with his enthusiasm rekindled, he departed whence he had come.

After photographing and returning the fish, it was fast approaching midnight and I resolved only to stay for another hour or until the other lads appeared. In went a few loose offerings followed by my hookbaits, and no sooner had they settled than a bite, almost in slow motion, developed. However, this fish was quite different from the previous one; it was a heavy, dogged weight, tenacious and unspectacular, and typical of the very biggest barbel. Once the fish was in the net I hauled it on to the bank and, on unfolding the mesh, was stunned to see the enormous girth of the creature – it looked more like a carp than a barbel. I put the fish quickly into the weigh-sling and on the scales, and the pointer bounced between 14lb 6oz and 14lb 8oz. I couldn't believe what was happening. Popping the fish into a sack, I charged off in a blind panic to find Richard and Mark.

Fortunately, they hadn't left, and it wasn't long before we were all back at my swim armed with three sets of scales. Just as with the Medway fish I left the weighing to the others, and we each cross-checked the readings. Richard's showed 14lb 5½oz, Mark's 14lb 7oz and mine, on loan from a friend, 14lb 6½oz. Once again I'd have to wait for a weights and measures check. My head was still swimming as we walked back to our cars in the early hours of Sunday morning, not just because this was a huge specimen but also for the fact that it was an unknown fish. Rumour had it that only one giant inhabited this stretch, but now we knew differently.

I wasn't able to fish on the Sunday evening and hardly slept a wink that night as my mind constantly turned over the events of the past few days. Going out for a meal hadn't helped either. My mind remained a whirl and all I could think of was barbel, giant barbel, colossal barbel even.

By Monday the water temperature had risen still further to a remarkable 60 °F, and with it came six fish weighing 8lb 14oz, 9lb 12oz, 9lb 14oz, 10lb 6oz, 11lb 9oz and an incredible 12lb 15oz. This was too good to be true.

On Tuesday, quite surprisingly, not a single bite came my way despite innumerable fish rolling in the swim. Wednesday brought showers during the morning – and an angler firmly ensconced in my swim when I arrived. To my relief and delight, however, he only intended staying a short while, so I set up my tackle just downstream of him. In any case I wasn't in a rush to start, content for the moment to enjoy the evening and bask in the glories of the preceding days. How could I, how dare I, wish for more? But as I sat there pondering, I found my thoughts going back to the 14lb 4oz barbel I'd caught from this stretch last season. Surely that would be too much to hope for?

Biteless by 9.30 p.m., the angler packed his tackle and bade me farewell. I hastily moved into his swim, *the* swim. At last I was where I wanted to be. Nevertheless the barbel seemed wary, possibly because the colour was finally dropping out of the river and it was a particularly bright night. By 11.30 p.m. still no bites had materialized. Then, just as the allure of a nice supper and warm bed crossed my mind for the umpteenth time, it happened. The right-hand rod pulled slowly over and stayed bent.

At first the fish hugged the bottom with a sullen power, holding its position for some while as I unsuccessfully tried to move it. At one point I began to wonder whether the fish was still on. Moving downstream as far as I could, I applied as much side-strain as I dared. This had an effect, but not the one I desired, as the fish shot upstream against a screaming clutch, making my legs turn to jelly. In this instance, I concluded, patience would definitely be a virtue, but at least the fish was still there.

Working the fish back towards me, it gave the occasional kick, but after some minutes of steady pressure it was clear that it was weakening. On introducing the landing net the fish charged away, but grudgingly, inevitably, it succumbed and I managed to guide it over the rim. Quite exhausted, I half sat, half lay on the bank for perhaps several minutes. This really had been a breath-taking encounter, and even without looking I somehow knew that this was the same fish I had caught before and wanted again. Eventually, I found the courage to shine the torch into the folds of the net that still lay in the water, and to my immense satisfaction confirmed that here was, indeed, the other leviathan.

I was a nervous wreck as I sat there in the darkness, almost too scared to weigh the fish. Surely this couldn't be a third fourteen-pounder? With the aid of a nearby tree I supported the scales, and once again, amazingly, the needle settled at 14lb 7oz. How on earth could three different fish all weigh virtually the same? This was uncanny to say the least! Taking plenty of photographs on the self-timer, the barbel was ready to be released by about 1 a.m. Rather humbly, I cradled the fish's magnificent frame in the water, its thick, bronze back melting into golden flanks, and with pectorals the size of my hands. Then, with a thrust of its paddle-like tail, the fish was away into the darkness.

Although Thursday was the last day of my holiday, I couldn't have fished even if I had wanted to. It wouldn't have been right! But I had to have one last look at the river before leaving, the river that had given so much of itself and so much pleasure to me. I sat on the bank in the late afternoon sun reflecting on the heady events of those last eight days. Bathed in a warm glow, the placid river scene gave not the slightest hint of the wonderful secrets that had been unlocked, nor of the drama that had been played out. For me, it had been the time of my life.

If At First . . .
~
Nigel Williams

I can't honestly recall quite when I decided to fish for zander, but some years ago it occurred to me that in a lifetime of angling I'd never even seen the species, let alone caught one. So began my quest for this relatively rare fish, with my hopes and aspirations pinned on the drains of the Fens, where so many notable anglers had found success in the past. The one drawback to this plan – having to travel 160 miles to reach the fishing – was somewhat softened by the fact that I would be hunting zander in the company of Dave Phillips, an angler with an excellent knowledge of both the species and the drains of the district in which we would be concentrating our efforts. And what I lacked in personal expertise I would amply make up for in my enthusiasm, bordering almost on an obsession, to catch one of these enigmatic predators.

The arrival of October saw our initial foray, and how glad I was that Dave had come along. With so much apparently featureless water to explore, it was clearly going to be no easy task to locate our chosen quarry. A shared effort, at least in theory, should help narrow the odds in our favour. There was just one problem: the theory had not been explained to the resident pike, who proceeded to demolish our baits, one after the other, as soon as they hit water! Still, at least I'd gained a feel of the place, and I felt confident that given more time and effort, rewards would surely come.

On the long drive home my mind constantly turned over fresh ideas for the return trip, and zander-plans remained uppermost in my thoughts right through the week until, exactly seven days later, we were back. This time Dave suggested that we try a different and rather neglected drain, where previously he had made some respectable catches of pike, and where now, more to the point, he thought big zander might be present. Unfortunately, the session turned out to be a mirror of the first: innumerable pike (including a very pleasing 27lb 12oz specimen to my rod), but no sign of zander.

Over the next few weeks the weather took a dramatic turn for the worse, and it was not until early November that I saw the Fens again. To be honest, I'd been feeling rather disappointed that despite all the action Dave and I had enjoyed, not one zander of any size, let alone a big one, had put in an appearance. What more could I do? I felt certain I was fishing the right waters and with the right baits, and I reasoned there could only really be one factor that was not in my favour, and that was time. I resolved to create as many fishing hours as I could, until the zander did respond.

After driving down on the Friday evening of my next visit, I set about putting up my bivvy near a reputedly productive bridge swim at 10 p.m. and in the dark – an 'adventure' not to be recommended in exposed conditions, I can assure you. At first I was simply moderately uncomfortable, but as the night drew on, so the weather became nothing less than diabolical, testing my resolve to the limit through several very cold, wet and miserable hours. At 7 a.m., however, and much to my surprise, the weather eased at long last, and with the change I decided to move swims. So much for the productive spot!

After a twenty-minute slog I stopped off at an area that somehow took my fancy and decided to give it an hour or so, before 'leap-frogging' my rods back down the drain to the bridge and my car. I was hopeful that in doing so I would at least cover some zander during the day.

Putting out the first rod, the alarm sounded just moments after the bait had settled. Then it stopped sounding and the line hung limp and unmoving. I wound the bait in, checked that it was in order, and cast it back out. Less than thirty minutes later the alarm sounded again, and again nothing further developed, although a discernible twitching could be seen where the line entered the water. Perhaps these indications were line bites? I checked out the bait again, but like the first time there were no marks on it to suggest a fish had picked it up.

After recasting once more, I was toying with the idea of changing to a different terminal tackle when the alarm sounded for the third time – but now, excitingly, line was being drawn jerkily and slowly from the open spool. Up went the rod and

a fish, which felt like a reasonable pike, soon had the tip well over as it set off along the drain. Before long, however, steady pressure had it kiting into the edge, and for the first time I saw a tell-tale flash of golden pewter through the murky water. Clearly this was no pike, but rather my long-awaited first-ever zander – and a good one at that, to judge from the bend in the rod.

With more caution than was probably necessary, I carefully guided the fish into the waiting net and then threw my rod up the bank, scrambling up the steep incline after it, net and prize firmly in my grasp. Once on the scales, the fish pulled the needle round to a spine-tingling 11lb 1oz. I could not have been more thrilled.

After taking a few photographs on the self-timer, I gently returned the fish to water and sat back happy, if rather bemused, that my very first zander had weighed into double figures. Yes, perhaps there had been an element of good fortune in its capture, but then again, all things considered, I reckoned I'd earned every beautiful ounce of that fish.

I rebaited and cast back out to the hot-spot area to await further developments. I didn't have long to wait. Within minutes the line was again half-twitching and half-running to a take. Evidently I'd found a pocket of fish in a feeding mood. Winding down and striking hard brought a zander rolling to the surface, where it showed a flank every bit the equal, if not larger, than that of the first fish. And then it came off! In a few brief seconds elation had turned to despair in the gloomy thought of what might have been. But, as they say, hope springs eternal – and at least I knew for certain that feeding fish were in the vicinity. So, out went another bait in search of a second big zander to make a memorable brace.

However, to say that I was surprised when, forty minutes later, the alarm signalled a run, would be something of an understatement. I was totally stunned. This time I patiently allowed the fish to move steadily away with the bait before sweeping the rod back over my shoulder. At first nothing much happened, then a savage thrust of power had the reel's clutch buzzing angrily as the zander decided to put as much distance between me and it as it could. Slowly though, the pressure against it began to tell, sapping its resolve, until, just as with the earlier fish, it kited into the bank, rolling on the surface as it did so. The sight of that zander turned my legs immediately to jelly. It was absolutely *huge*. And as I gained more line and brought it safely over the net, I shook like a leaf – something I'd never experienced before in all my years of catching large pike.

Looking back at the photographs of that eventful day, I still marvel at the sheer magnificence of that wonderful creature. Its weight? 14lb 14oz exactly. Undoubtedly, the pinnacle of my angling career thus far.

Another February

~

John Wilson

During the 1970s, long before making programmes for television and running my own fisheries reduced dramatically my available leisure time, I spent an inordinate number of hours in pursuit of a lifelong ambition – to catch a really big chub. And 6lb was my target. I did, in fact, devote one entire fishing season to doing very little else other than wander the overgrown upper reaches of my local Norfolk rivers where such a possibility existed – the Waveney, Wensum, Bure, Yare and the Wissey. I saw a monstrous chub in the Waveney that was, in retrospect, closer to 8lb than 6lb, but failed miserably. Then, quite by accident, I took one at just a shade below 6lb from a heavily flooded stretch of my local River Wensum after a premonition about a certain swim. Another of exactly 5lb 15oz, also from the Wensum, came a few years later when I was stret-pegging for barbel one evening using a meat cube beneath a Betalight float, and there were several other big fives during following sessions. But it seemed my 6lb chub was not going to materialize from a river. So I switched my attentions to stillwaters.

Now, whilst most specialist fishermen would perhaps rate the capture of difficult fish from large stillwaters as the ultimate challenge, my own experiences have indicated that monsters inhabiting small, even tiny fisheries, can prove equally exasperating. And as far as gravel pit chub are concerned, this could not be more pertinent as they are nearly always the minority species.

It was with the knowledge of the way in which species change when grouped in just ones and twos that I gradually set about catching a particularly large chub from a small, overgrown gravel pit a couple of years later. On reflection, I just knew it would be an uphill challenge from the very start, although on the face of it just three chub in a little pit of barely half an acre would seem to be a doddle, especially one full of stunted rudd. But the trio was unbelievably wary. There were two big ones, whose weights had been put at somewhere between 5lb and 7lb, and one very much smaller fish. These three had, in fact, come from the Wensum nearly ten years before, and it was curious that while two had grown big on their diet of stunted rudd, one had fared really poorly. They could be seen clearly from a high bank during the winter when the water cleared after the first frosts, but they were only very occasionally spotted during the summer as the pit coloured up and became thick with weed.

The two monsters generally kept together, and I gave considerable thought to the problem of how to extract the biggest. A friend had, quite by accident, latched into one of them while ledgering at night for tench with breadpaste a few years previously. It had weighed 5½lb. So they were not invincible, although, so far as I could gather, it was the only record of one of these fish succumbing to an angler's bait. When I fished for them they were either conspicuous by their absence or seemingly oblivious to all the succulent baits I offered them.

My first attempts were short, impromptu sessions lasting an hour or so at the crack of dawn during the summer. I believed I could catch one of them off guard, just as you can with river chub, by plopping in a slug, lobworm or lump of flake. In theory it seemed fine, and when I managed to creep up and throw the biggest one a lobworm on my very first visit, I thought it really was going to be very easy. Having crept Indian-style into a casting position through thick marginal foliage, I could have sworn that the chub was unaware of my presence when I flipped out the worm. But something was wrong. The lob hit the water nicely, as though it had fallen from the overhanging branches, and started to sink – and then the chub swam off slowly in the opposite direction! There was not the slightest reaction from the fish, nor any indication that it was at all interested. Anyone who has fished for mullet will have been frustrated in the same way hundreds of times; it's as though the bait is invisible. And for the most part, as I was to find out on successive trips to the pit during the rest of that summer, this is how small numbers of stillwater chub are liable to react. They can be more obtuse and carp-like than carp themselves.

I tried surface plugs and divers, crayfish, twitched lobs, static lobs and air-injected lobs suspended at various levels off the bottom. And what a nuisance the tench were with the latter! I fished after dark with ledgered flake and cheesepaste,

both with and without prebaiting. I tried livebaiting and I tried deadbaiting, both static and wobbling, with little rudd from the pit. I fished mornings, evenings and occasionally after dark. For almost two years, on and off, summer and winter, I gave those chub my attention, but at the end of that time I was no nearer catching one than when I first started. Although I had become familiar with the area between a sunken bush and a thick bed of rushes where the chub always seemed to hang out, I had not had a single bite nor even a reaction from them.

The pit was a fairly long walk from the car, and while I was prepared for both this and the awkward fences I had to climb *en route* for just an hour's fishing or less, I did not like the rate at which a Dobermann pinscher bitch was growing up in one of the gardens through which I had to pass. Although I had obtained prior permission, this Dobermann, a puppy when I first tried for the chub, started to make the trips down to the pit a bit frightening. In fact, I had almost reached the stage of forgetting the whole idea.

Another February came, and just when I was thinking of calling a halt to expeditions for another season, we were treated to some unbelievably mild weather. I just had to have one last crack and decided to try something different. Carp can sometimes be encouraged to accept floating baits in the winter so, I thought, why not chub too? Floating crust seemed to be the obvious bait to try – although I have to say that so did all the other baits I had tried without success. Anyway, I put a plan of action together while the weather held, opting to risk the dog and visit the pit every morning and evening before and after work to introduce a few crusts so that the chub could get used to them. And on only the third morning I struck gold.

The crusts had slowly moved 50yd down the pit with the drift and had finally come to rest in the branches of the partly submerged bush. Just before the last crust entered the branches, up came a pair of lips and down went the crust with hardly a ripple. Was I seeing things after all this time? No, the crust had definitely gone and, when viewed through binoculars, those lips could not be mistaken for anything else.

Finally I was getting somewhere, and on the following morning, perched high up a tree, I was treated to the promising sight of the two big chub, one light and one (the larger) distinctly very dark in colour, circling slowly in midwater beneath the crusts I'd thrown in. However, they still looked incredibly wary. I considered my best chance of a take would be during the half-light immediately before darkness, and so waited until the following evening before putting a hook into a crust.

I arrived half an hour before total darkness, and as usual flipped out three crusts from my fishing position on a sandy spit about 20yd from the big sunken bush. One of the baits supported a well-honed size 4 hook tied direct to a greased 6lb line. Strangely, the two free crusts were ignored and disappeared into the bush with the drift, while the hookbait was slurped in within a foot of the branches. The line tightened and I struck hard and well back. The hook flew back to catch in the branches above my head; my first and only take from the chub in two years and I'd botched it! I was so choked I didn't even swear. Well, at least I hadn't spooked them, I told myself, suddenly realizing that if I had hooked or lost one, the chances of crust ever working again would have been remote.

The following evening saw me back at the swim with senses built up to absolute fever pitch. Although the light had only just started to fade, I crept into position and cast out just one crust – this time I really meant business. As I looked down to put a tube of foil over the line close to the reel, I heard a gentle suck on the surface. I looked up and peered at the spot where the crust should have been, but could see nothing. Then, three or four seconds later, the line started to snake slowly out across the surface. This time I made no mistake, and I allowed the rod tip to pull round before whacking the hook home. In the fading light I could vaguely make out a long shape well down in the clear water. The chub bored heavily and then ran to the right in an attempt to bury the hook in a bed of dead reed-mace stems. However, I managed to turn the fish, after which it came to the surface in a heavy boil before diving determinedly for the sunken bush. The Avon eleven-footer was fully bent and the 6lb line more than necessary as I applied full pressure to bully the fish out of the branches and up to the surface. The chub's huge head porpoised majestically on the oily surface and it flapped its tail as I eased it gingerly towards the net. My legs were shaking, for I instinctively knew that this was the bigger, dark-coloured fish I had been after for so long.

Suddenly though, it dived again and made one last-ditch heart-stopping lunge. It dived deep, then came up and in like a baby right over the middle of the net. I quickly heaved the net clear of the water and laid it down in the grass well back from the edge. The chub looked absolutely massive, completely spanning the 24in pan-net. And it was the big one all right.

After nine consecutive morning and evening stints in five days the monster was mine. And as if to show me what it had really been dining on, it coughed up the remains of a very large toad while being unhooked. Its weight? Exactly 6lb 7oz.

When Rivers Meet
~
Nigel Witham

T his is a story about how I caught my best ever fish, one which I expect never to better. It is about a quest that consumed the greater part of my fishing time for several seasons; it is about ambition realized and, in ways very real to me, it also reflects my own growth.

I will commence my recollections in the summer of 1978, when I was fifteen years of age and no more than a boy. All boys are enthusiasts and all anglers are boys at heart. Since I was also the keenest angler ever, I had an abundance of enthusiasm for which no man except a fisherman could have the capacity. I had been successful. My plans to catch carp, pike, perch and chub had all been fulfilled, and only one fish had eluded me: a 2lb roach. My need to catch such a fish had become the greatest urge of my life and little of my time was not spent in pursuit. When I could not be by the river; I sought surrogate consummation by conducting copious literary research when I should have been studying matters distinctly less piscatorial. This was revealing. I remember reading how Captain

Parker caught two-pounders in quantity. I recall reading from Carl-Forbes that Owen Wentworth and Gerry Swanton had each caught 200 such fish. Bailey was at his roach-catching peak, and I read from Frank Guttfield's *Big Fish Scene* (Ernest Benn, 1978) how he had outfoxed them with mass prebaiting campaigns. And I read from Walker about Wilf Cutting and Bill Penny, both former record-holders.

I thought I knew so much about roach that my brain might burst with all the information it had gorged. I fished whenever I could but, notwithstanding my zealous addiction, I was always unsuccessful. Nevertheless, I loved the river and persevered blindly, even through steamy summer afternoons, autumn thunderstorms and long into frozen January nights, from which I returned home, near frost-bitten, to my disbelieving parents, their sympathy with my ordeal long since extinguished. In my futile endeavour I employed all methods known to man. I ledgered bread, worms and corn; I trotted maggots and spent hours developing secret groundbaits, special floats and cunning bite-detection systems. But not once did I even scratch the snout of a roach over a pound.

My problem was that I couldn't fish the Avon, the Stour or the Wensum, but only the Kentish Beult, and that only where it flowed within cycling distance of my home. The Beult has something of a reputation for big fish, but I have learned that this is largely unfounded and due to inflated reports of the captures of a few big chub and pike from its lower reaches. Of course, I had heard about good roach, that is why I persisted, although I had yet to see any and no rumour could be corroborated by reliable witnesses or photographs. That was until the summer of 1980 when word concerning a three-pounder reached me. I followed, as did Steve Burke, who had just that season joined my struggle. In my presence, Steve promptly extracted a 2½-pounder from a spot just downstream from Hawkenbury road bridge near Staplehurst, at the time my home village.

Having located my quarry I redoubled my efforts. Success was still some time away but, as always, I was too proud to let myself be beaten. Consequently, during the following December, I landed my first big roach. It weighed 3lb 4oz. I didn't come back to earth for a month!

Looking through my records I see that I continued to fish the Beult frequently for the next three seasons, but other than occasional roach of 1½–2lb, I caught nothing substantial. I confess that my enthusiasm diminished as my boyhood faded, this being the source of deteriorating results.

My last year at university and hence the year of my final summer-long vacation came in 1983. I decided that before adult responsibilities finally consumed my whole life I would dedicate the entire summer to an attempt to beat my personal best. Like the prodigal I had been, I proceeded with uncommon vigour. My first step was swim selection, and this was followed by prebaiting with four loaves each night, for three weeks prior to the beginning of the season. Then I fished my chosen swim nearly every evening, each time until several hours after dark. I caught many roach weighing up to 1lb 15oz, but it was not until September that a truly big fish made a mistake. This time it weighed a remarkable 3lb 12oz.

Clearly, at the time, the Beult had the potential to produce a record fish but, by the end of that summer, I had been chasing big roach for more than five seasons. The autumn slipped by without a visit to the river, mainly because I had decided that my life was too short to permit continuance of my quest. And so I stayed away, encouraged by other less reliable temptresses. Christmas Day came and went, as did Boxing Day, but then, on the following day, I sensed an optimistic mood in the air and made my way to the river for a final farewell session.

It was late when I arrived, probably around midday, although my memory is somewhat jaded. The river was fining after a flood and appeared to be in perfect condition. Generally there was a friendly feeling about the world; it was warm, dry and overcast – just the sort of weather all anglers wish for. My usual swim was occupied, but as I was in an easy going mood I ambled upstream a little and found a large but gentle eddy rotating against the near bank. The bank itself pulled high above the water where it had been cut back by successive floods; overhead it was crowded by an ash wood which left me little room in which to manoeuvre my rod. Eventually, I chose a spot to sit and, as always, made do with a large, foam-rubber cushion. In my position I was well concealed, but because of the high bank I was still able to survey the entire area very clearly. Once again I had entered that secret world of anglers, and I like to believe that the river forgave my recent absence and welcomed my return.

I positioned my landing net and made up some loose groundbait, this consisting of half a mashed loaf and a few broken worms. This I distributed near to where I sat at the top of the eddy. I felt in no need to hurry; it would be an hour before the light began to lessen and I knew the fish would not be likely to feed before then. Without standing up, I assembled my rod and set up a light trotting tackle, before spending a few minutes watching the vagaries of the river's crinkly surface. Soon I became confident that it was time to cast, but five years of past results had taught me not to expect more than a few small fish. If I was lucky I might catch a 1lb-plus roach or one of the passable perch that had become common. With the latter in mind I baited with worm and lowered my tackle into the oily swirls at the head of the eddy, just where it formed a crease against the main current.

Gradually my float made its way hesitantly downstream, and when it had gone a little distance I held it back so that it entered the eddy and began to progress back towards me. Dip, dip and dip again. I struck and a greedy little perch was hoisted indignantly from the silty water. I held the fish up for an instant. Perch, even tiny ones, are blessed with a whole rainbow of colours and this one was no exception, striped like a miniature aquatic rugby footballer. I dropped the perch back to join its team-mates, but they didn't heed its lesson because I caught another of the players next cast.

I had no desire to fill my net with little fish, so I switched bait to breadflake in the hope that a good roach might emerge. Again my float set sail upon its voyage, a tiny sentinel making a brave expedition along the edge of the crease and then back towards me. It came closer and closer until it settled right under my rod tip, whereapon I gave up on the cast and ended its adventure. Another tactic was required, so I tore a small piece of crust from my loaf and set the lowest shot closer to my hook. Once more the float reached the bottom of the crease where it should have turned up into the eddy. But instead it dithered a little, as if the current had momentarily become distracted, bobbed twice, then disappeared altogether. It was a positive bite, clearly generated by a fish that had ventured hookwards with eager abandon. I struck, my rod clattering on the branches above, but the line stayed free and the fish was hooked.

I don't remember much about the ensuing fight, and moments later I couldn't think it through at all. The event must have been so intense that my mind couldn't contain it, and it lasted some while even though my tackle was stout. I recall my first sight of the fish as it rolled in midstream. At this my senses reeled, for I could see I had caught a two-pounder at last. Only I hadn't. When I weighed the fish I was forced to assume that my scales had become uncharacteristically optimistic. No roach could weigh 3lb 14oz. But the truth was before me and no one could deny it. I had caught the biggest river roach ever!*

After placing the fish in a loose sack, I called a friend from his armchair by the fire so that pictures could be taken. I had been fishing for less than an hour, so while I awaited his arrival I settled back to fish a little more and contemplate the situation. It was not long before two more fish of around a pound each slipped over the rim of my landing net. I released them back to the river, and as I did so I realized that there was also another river, one that existed only in my mind, a river of memories and of aspirations, a river of life that rose from a tiny spring at my birth and will flow into the bottomless ocean of my death.

Latterly, I have realized that on the day I have described the two rivers flowed together for a few hours, and because of this I made one of the easiest captures of my life. Their confluence has taught me to enjoy angling for true reasons, and since that day the rivers have become more and more entwined, and I have grown on from the mere boy who started out in the summer of 1978.

* The British roach record now stands at 4lb 3oz, taken by Ray Clarke from the Dorset Stour in October 1990.

Towards Paradise

~

Chris Yates

I t was the opening night of the 1970 season and, at midnight, Jasper, Dandy and I cast our baits into the inky blackness of the lake. That annual ritual of the first cast always has a magical air of expectation about it, as if you are the first angler in the world and the lake is full of idiot fish. However, on that particular night we certainly weren't the only anglers in the world. From all round the lake we heard continued swishings and splashings as dozens of other fishermen made their own initial offerings to the carp, offerings which, because of their simultaneous and abrupt arrival, would only persuade the well-educated fish to lie a little lower in the water. It wouldn't have been so bad if they'd all been using freelined flake, but this was the 'Great Potato Era' when everyone seemed to be using a two pound King Edward.

'Not exactly the classic opening,' muttered Jasper as he folded his silver-foil indicator over the line.

'And to think,' said Dandy, 'we had this place to ourselves last year.'

'It's like a bank holiday in Brighton,' I said.

'Except they don't throw potatoes in Brighton,' said Dandy.

Then it began to rain.

At about 3 a.m., over the faint hiss of the drizzle on the water's surface, I heard one sharper hiss of line running through the silver paper. It was a marvellous sound. I struck, and my old Mk IV went into an agreeable curve for about five or six seconds. Then it suddenly straightened again as the hook sprang free. It was the only chance we had all night.

After breakfast in our tent, we trudged a mile to a tiny and immensely deep quarry pool where a small colony of carp could nearly always be seen patrolling through the crystal-clear water. It wasn't a serious alternative for our opening-day venue as it was rather like fishing a crater on the moon, but being virtually unknown it provided a brief and welcome refuge from the populous lake.

We climbed the precipitous slope above the water so that we could look down, as if peering into an aquarium, and discovered the whereabouts of the carp. They were in the weedy, shallow end, where the depth was a mere 15ft or so: we could see the dark purple shapes slowly drifting over the bottom, oblivious to the smattering of breadcrusts above their heads. But then, as we watched, one of the largest fish – a mirror carp of around 17lb – rose up and casually engulfed our free offerings.

We came down the slope as cautiously as we could under the circumstances, but it still must have seemed like a major avalanche. Baiting our hooks, we spread along the bank and cast, keeping down and out of sight, though there was only sparse vegetation to hide behind. Gradually, all the dozen or so carp rose from the depths and began patrolling just beneath the surface, each one looking temptable. A fish swirled at Jasper's crust, but refused to take it. Then a carp nosed into Dandy's bait, only to sniff at it before sinking into invisibility. I was using floating flake rather than crust, and the first carp to inspect it took it confidently and without much hesitation.

My rod just pointed straight downwards as the fish made a crash dive into a seemingly bottomless hole. I'd never played a carp in such deep water before, and it was a fascinating and dramatic experience, even though the fish – a mirror – didn't quite reach 10lb.

After we'd released it, we were surprised to see the arrival of a lone angler, another refugee from the main lake, who, likewise, was surprised and a little disappointed to find us already at the sanctuary. He was a friendly sort though, and between casts we had an interesting conversation about fishing generally and how difficult it was nowadays to find any solitude in carp fishing.

'I suppose I shouldn't really tell you this,' said the newcomer, 'but there's a place only 15 miles from here where you can still find that solitude. It hasn't got any twenty-pounders in it, like the lake we've been fishing, but there are some lovely wildies, up to 12lb and more.'

We all had a special affection for wild carp, in fact we used to refer to them as

JOHN SEARL

real carp and speak of the others as 'artificials'. 'Tell us more!' we said, and within the hour we had left the angler in peace, walked back to our tent, upped sticks, piled everything into Jasper's car, waved farewell to the lake's encircling horde and driven off towards paradise.

It must have been mid-afternoon, after once getting hopelessly lost, when we finally arrived at our destination. The contrast to the place we'd just left couldn't have been greater – it was like the difference between a muddy ditch and a mountain stream, an urban car-park and a green wilderness, or a tin of creosote and a glass of wine.

'Lovely,' said Dandy.

'Exquisite,' said I.

'I think I'll stay all summer,' said Jasper.

The pool – an old monastery pool – covered about 2 acres, was stream fed and was almost perfectly circular in shape. Ancient crack willows leaned over their reflections, purple-flowering bistort clustered along the margins, the water was deep and clear, and it was beautifully tranquil, secluded and undisturbed. As we stood savouring the scene, a carp leapt out in the pool's centre, a great, high, exuberant leap that was obviously just for our delight.

'Quick,' said Jasper, 'get the strawberries!'

At last! We could now begin the season properly: strawberries and cream and a bottle of white wine, while the clouds slowly unfurled overhead and our optimism returned to the fore.

When the sun eventually appeared, low over the westward hills, we made a complete and cautious circuit of the pool, looking for signs and noting the most likely casting spots. There was a long-dead, half-submerged willow that looked like the wreck of an old galleon, and in amongst the rotting, drowned timber we saw the vague shapes of carp drifting slowly to an fro. Some of them were only of average wildie size, about 4–5lb, but there were also several much larger fish – great, long torpedoes that looked 15lb or more. We'd never seen such wild carp before. It was obviously a treacherous place to fish, suicidal even, but if we cast towards it from more open water there might be a chance.

At sunset we set up our rods in a little reedy bay to the east of the snags, casting our baits so that they landed about 10yd from the first visible branch. Our rods were Mk IVs, the lines were 10lb breaking strain and the bait was, as our informant had recommended, cheesepaste. We put the rods in rests, attached foil indicators and sat back on our groundsheets to wait.

It was a perfect evening – intensely still, clear and, as the last songbird flew to its roost, silent. Before the first star appeared, a full moon ballooned up behind the hills to the south-east. Nothing moved across the pool except for a thin finger of mist, slowly reaching out towards us.

'Cup of tea?' whispered Jasper after an hour. Dandy and I merely nodded, not wanting to intrude on the calm. But we didn't mind the inevitable sequence of noises that followed – the gurgle of water into a kettle, the clunk of the kettle on to the stove, the hiss of gas, the scrape and flare of a match, and the pop as the gas was lit. Then, apart from the whisper of the flame, the silence returned and we continued gazing vaguely at our rods, still fairly tense with anticipation, as we had been ever since seeing the big carp. They were down there, just 25yd from where we were sitting, and at any moment one of them was going to come upon one of our baits. At any moment . . .

There was a sudden hiss that made us readjust our focus, but none of the silver papers had moved. It was only the kettle boiling. Jasper made the tea and we gratefully sipped it, cupping the mugs with our chilled fingers as the night had become quite cool.

A black shape blinked across the moon, and a few moments later there came, from right above us, the fluid, haunting call of a curlew – 'twee-twee-tu-tu-tu-tu' – trailing away like a cry from the edge of the world. No one spoke. The place, already under several spells, was overlaid by another enchantment.

Now the carp will begin to feed, I thought, interpreting the curlew as a kind of signal. But of course the lines remained unmoved. The mist thickened and boiled up until it almost blocked out the low midsummer moon, then it gradually dissolved and even the moon's reflection reappeared on the surface. We all saw Jasper's silver foil jump abruptly to his rod butt, and almost before it began to hiss he'd reached down, clicked over the pick-up on his Mitchell and struck. The cane swept over and the reel made that lovely, slightly nasal screech, characteristic of the old 300, and nothing Jasper did could lessen its pitch until, suddenly, it stopped dead.

'Damn it!' he said, 'it broke me!'

We offered condolences and secretly vowed to ourselves that we would be much firmer if we got a similar chance. And then, even as Jasper was tying on a new hook, Dandy's line began to slither slowly and noisily through his indicator. He struck and took a step back, piling on the pressure. For a moment it seemed he'd stopped a big fish in its tracks, but then, as if he'd been kicked in the back, Dandy lurched forward and his reel squealed. Then there was another sound, a sharp splintering crack as his old carp rod broke cleanly at the butt. In all our years of fishing we'd never seen such a thing happen before. We were impressed. The fish hit the snags and was off.

Jasper cast again. Within minutes he'd hooked another carp, but within seconds he'd lost it. Then I had a chance, hooking a fish that ran straight out for about 20yd, before swinging round in a wide arc and rocketing unstoppably into the branches. Dandy set up another rod, and respooled with 12lb line, but it didn't do him any good. He lost another fish almost as spectacularly as before.

'More tea?' we said, and while it was brewing the curlew came back over the pool, making it echo magically with its call. Another one answered it, far off across the surrounding fields, then another even further away. And suddenly we noticed a glow in the north-east, the first touch of dawn that the curlews were obviously responding to.

We sipped our tea and watched the light gradually increase. Then Dandy spilt his drink as his line once more flew from his reel. After striking, he moved quickly to the left, away from the snags, and managed to steer his fish towards open water. I grabbed the net and crouched in the shallow margins as Dandy slowly worked the carp towards me. There was a sudden swirl, the first break in the surface we'd seen all night, and within another minute I'd reached out and, at last, we finally landed one of those amazing wildies. It was no monster, being just over 6lb, but it was a wonderful looking and incredibly muscular specimen, the sort of carp that makes a fat mirror seem terribly dull, even embarrassing.

Just before sunrise I hooked another fish, but didn't have to resort to anything particularly heavy-handed as it rushed off directly away from the snags. After a few moments I began to gain control, and even though it fought tenaciously it came in eventually without giving me a nervous breakdown. It was a five-pounder – small headed, golden and elegant, another beautiful specimen, like an animated bronze sculpture.

Then the sun came up over the distant hills and all the birds in the valley began to call. Jasper and Dandy curled up in their sleeping bags and fell asleep almost instantly. But I continued to watch the dawn, thinking that even though our season's opening might seem unremarkable when we told our friends about it, and even though it appeared that we'd been unsuccessful, we would never forget it.